HISTORY OF BEHAR

INDIGO FACTORIES

REMINISCENCES OF BEHAR

TIRHOOT AND ITS INHABITANTS OF THE PAST

HISTORY OF BEHAR LIGHT HORSE VOLUNTEERS

HISTORY OF BEHAR

INDIGO FACTORIES

REMINISCENCES OF BEHAR

TIRHOOT AND ITS INHABITANTS OF THE PAST

HISTORY OF BEHAR LIGHT HORSE VOLUNTEERS

MINDEN WILSON

GYAN

Published by

Gyan Publishing House
5, Ansari Road
Daryaganj, New Delhi-110002
Phone: 011-47034999, 9811692060
E-mail: books@gyanbooks.com

Distribution Network
gyanbooks.com
India, USA, Canada, UK, Australia

ISBN: 978-93-6780-444-5 (PB)

First Published, 1908

2nd Impression 2024

Printed at: Gyan Press, Delhi.

History of Behar Indigo Factories Reminiscences of Behar Tirhoot and its Inhabitants of the Past History of Behar light horse volunteers
Author: MINDEN WILSON

HISTORY OF BEHAR INDIGO FACTORIES

REMINISCENCES OF BEHAR

TIRHOOT AND ITS INHABITANTS OF THE PAST

HISTORY OF BEHAR LIGHT HORSE VOLUNTEERS

BY

MINDEN WILSON.

CALCUTTA:
THE CALCUTTA GENERAL PRINTING COMPANY.
1908.

PREFACE.

In writing this History of Indigo Factories in Tirhoot, Champarun and Sarun I have, I fear, set myself a difficult task. Under any circumstance it must be an imperfect one as to dates on which some factories were started and by whom. During the troublous times of 1857 many indigo concerns sent their title deeds for safe custody to Calcutta and a number of these are not now to be found. I am indebted to the courtesy of Mr. Levinge, our Collector, for the perusal of a lot of old records referring to indigo of the past. With these before me I hope I shall now be able to make this paper as interesting as such a record can be made. I propose giving names of proprietors and managers as far as I can go back, also the names of those buried at the different concerns where slabs still exist and any traditional history of those where tablets have been removed or were never put up *in memoriam* and any other interesting incidents connected therewith. Ancient Indian History (*see* Old Calcutta) tells us that Mr. Grand, whose widow afterwards married the famous Talleyrand, was the first European to introduce indigo in Tirhoot, while Claude Martin encouraged its growth in the North-West later on.

The records, which I have been allowed to take notes from, show that Mr. Grand was with Warren Hastings at Benares at the time of the tumult there when they escaped to Chunar.

This must have been a very hurried exit as the *Nautch* girls to this day, sing "Ghora per Howdah, Hatti per Zin, Baghey Chunar ko Warren *Hastin,*" which might be rendered: "Put on elephants saddle and howdahs on horses and let us skidaddle along with our forces cries Warren Hastings."

In 1782 Mr. Grand was sent to Tirhoot as Collector of Revenue, etc., etc., where he built three indigo factories—unfortunately he does not give their names. In these factories, he writes, he is conducting the manufacture of indigo after the manner of Europeans and he was evidently doing well and making money.

In 1787 we find Lord Cornwallis (who arrived in Calcutta in 1786), sent for Mr. Grand to Calcutta and according to that gentleman "praised him for his work and ability." But to Mr. Grand's surprise on the 29th August 1787, Mr. Bathurst was appointed Collector of Tirhoot and Mr. Grand ordered to go as Judge of Patna in 1788. He was shortly afterwards ordered to give up or dispose of his indigo factories in Tirhoot. He remonstrated against this "and finally proving contumacious and charges as to his conduct as a Judge at Patna having been laid he was removed from the service."

I find that in 17—(unfortunately the two last figures are torn away, but it must be about 1793) there is a memo. to the following effect—Names of gentlemen not in the Company's service noted as being in the district. Thus:—Dooria Factory, John Finch.

Year of arrival in the country	1778
Attur Factory, James Gentil	1773
Dholi and Dowdpore Factory, William Orby Hunter	1786
Kanti Factory, Alexander Noel	1783
Singia Factory, Thomas Park, a trader ...	1783
Shahpore Factory, Richardson Purvis ...	1783

There is a letter addressed to James Gentil, Indigo Planter, Attur Factory, from J. Neave, Judge of Tirhoot, dated 4th August 1793, telling him he must prosecute one *Chain* Chowdry in the Dewani Adawlut. But that previous to his filing his suit orders him to sign a penalty bond as prescribed by the 38th article of Revenue Regulation. He also requests him for the future to appear by Vakeel and not to address him personally on any subject when he is a party concerned "as your opponent may justly complain of my receiving extra judicial information when he has no opportunity of doing the same."

One Ounga Chowdry and some ryots of Kunouli petitioned against Mr. Hunter, proprietor of Doudpore Factory, for hoeing up land and oppression for the cultivation of indigo. There is a remark that Mr. Hunter seems to be a very troublesome man. The Judge wrote him referring him to a certain section which he could see daily from 9 A.M. to 4 P.M., Sunday excepted, at the Judge's Court and Mr. Hunter after some days, replies, asking, "In what Room!!?" In 1774, a Frenchman named Double or Donble, most likely Dombal, who was at *Serryiah* Factory, is asked if he has the sanction of the Governor-General to reside in Tirhoot: failing this he is ordered to at once go to Calcutta, giving due notice of date of departure when an officer of the Court will accompany him and place him in the hands of the Military Secretary. This is dated 2nd November 1793 and is from Mr. Neave, Judge of Tirhoot.

On the 17th February 1793 Mr. Neave writes to James Arnold of Dholi Factory, acknowledging his letter enclosing license to live in the country. He says:—Whenever the Brahmin you have beaten shall complain to the Criminal Court you will hear from me officially on the subject. In the meantime I caution you in the most serious manner against all ill usage of natives. There is also a letter to one Thomas Parke, a trader at Singia, to quit the district within a month and repair to Calcutta.

This punishment was for contempt of court. The Extradition Act under which the above orders were made was passed in 1784. All British subjects had to reside within 10 miles of some of the principal settlements unless they held a special license from the Governor-General, the East India Company or President and no one could reside beyond the time specified in the license.

The following is the extract from Allen's *Indian Mail*, Bengal, the Indigo Planter, Vol. XVI., No. 358, 2nd August 1858, p. 643. The first English planter in Bengal was one Mr. Robert Heaven who, in 1787, was permitted to proceed to Bengal to cultivate indigo for five years. Shortly after this the East India Company commenced to invest in the article, but finding the trade the reverse of profitable soon desisted. Private enterprise, however, continued to flourish. In 1802-03 Bengal had no rival in the trade throughout the world except Java. The produce then did not exceed 60,000 maunds. It has since that time reached 172,000 maunds. The production and manufacture of the article is a very precarious and delicate business like every other branch of enterprise in this country, it has to encounter native cunning and roguery at the very outset. The country dealers in the seed rubbed old seed with oil, to make it look like new, also mixed the seed with a peculiar kind of earth, which is impossible to be distinguished from it. The best soil for the plant is a mixed loam, the strong black loam being more nutritious, but less sure. Then the writer dilates on the difficulty of beating, the risks from rain, caterpillars, etc. The risk is so great that it is becoming usual to divide it with some other business. The largest indigo proprietors in Bengal possess extensive silk filatures. There are concerns all over the country which, for the last ten years, have season after season, been cultivated at a loss; capitalists have been ruined; and men who, ten years ago, were worth three or four lakhs, are not now possessed of a rupee, etc. We heard by last mail from a gentleman who having started without a farthing in the indigo business has returned to England with £50,000, etc., etc.

For a long time the British settler was not *allowed to possess in his own right, even the land on which he erected his house.*

He was liable to be deported at any moment upon the caprice of some Civil Servant of the Company who might treat him with insolence and misrepresent his conduct. The recent case of Mr. Chapman, C.S., in his relation with Mr. Deverill, the indigo planter, is one which shows that the animus or, as the *Times* justly terms it, the traditional policy towards the British settler, has not yet died away, etc., etc. Wherever the planters settled down, he was certain to be surrounded by a number of hostile zemindars, who just as much as the Company regarded him as an interloper, and an interferer with what they considered to be their feudal rights, etc., etc. Hence it was that the forces of the British settler and the zemindar were often seen drawn up in the face of the day and hence the establishment of *latyals* or bands of men armed with clubs, etc., etc. There is undoubtedly a good deal of roughness still prevailing, and it is this that induces the missionaries, without the least recognition of peculiar circumstances, and with the exaggeration characteristic of unrestrained zeal, to involve in one sweeping sentence of condemnation zemindars and planters as oppressors of the ryots. We may observe that this fierce antagonism of the missionaries to white employers of black labourers is not peculiar to India. Many of us can recollect the furious invective and monstrous exaggeration with which this class attacked the unfortunate West India proprietors; and no one who has read the life of the late wise and admirable Metcalfe, but will recall the frantic opposition with which he was encountered by the Jamaica missionaries, years after the slaves had been emancipated; an opposition originating in a desire possessing those gentlemen, analogous to what prevails among the same fraternity in India, to have the negroes submitted entirely and uncontrolledly to their influence and authority.—*From the Madras Athenoeum.*

I will now start the history of the different indigo factories in Tirhoot, taking them in alphabetical succession.

HISTORY OF BEHAR.

Agrail
H. & S.
A.

This factory is one of recent date. It was built in 1886-87 as a defence against interloping. The village was actually in the Dholi dehat, and as one Teg Ali, a native who had been interloping in different parts of the district, was trying to get this village, Mr. W. S. Mackenzie farmed the village with the intention of building a factory. This was carried out by Mr. C. H. Macpherson. On the sale of Jeetwarpore Concern Agrail was bought by Messrs. Hudson, Lamb, and others. It stands to the south-east of the District. Agrail Factory, as a matter of fact, stands in the village of Bela Sudun and not Agrail.

Anarh
L.
J. C.

This factory also is one of recent date; it was built by Mr. C. V. Argles in partnership with Mr. Prestwick (who was then a partner in Messrs. R. Thomas and Co.'s firm) in about 1861-62. It was eventually sold and passed through one or two hands, and now belongs to A. W. and C. B. Inglis. It is situated to the south-east of Durbhunga.

Benepore
W.
A., P in circle,
W. W.

The mokarrarie pottah of this factory is dated 1834 and stands in the name of Mr. Henderson, who was then manager of Hatte-Oustee Factory who manufactured indigo there during one season only. Mr. John Gale, of Pundoul, disputed (under the then Bye-laws) Mr. Henderson's right to build. As he claimed Benepore to be within his dehat the Pundoul Factory was eventually made over to Pundoul and became an outwork to that concern in 1844, and as far as can be made out from much defaced documents Mr. Roberts or Robertson became manager. The names of managers or sub-managers, for they were under Pundoul are, later on, Lamb, MacIvor, Wingrove, C. Gale, A. Wyatt, M. N. MacLeod, and others. Pundoul and consequently Benepore became the property of G. N. Wyatt, who sold Benepore to P Jones and others in 1890.

The only outwork, Hursingpore, was built when M. H. Gale managed Pundoul. One Nubbee Meah disputed the right to build and there was every chance of a serious row. So the Collector of Durbhunga went out specially to intervene. He unfortunately had a long beard and so had M. Gale, and the unfortunate Nubbee, taking the Collector for the planter, proceeded to assault him and badly wounded him. So it ended in the Meah eventually getting the worst of it, and where once lived the happy Nubbee family now stands the Hursingpore bungalow and Nubbee Meah repents taking the law into his own hands.

The only grave at Benepore is that of Charles C. Smith, who died in 1897.

Bhicanpore D. B. B.

Bhicanpore was built in 1818. The mokarrarie lease bears date 1225 Fasli. The lease was given by one Syud Meer Mahomed and stands in the village of Bhicanpore, Syud Salem.

The sanction to build this factory was given by the East India Company as per a letter, dated 19th March 1819, from the Board of Commissioners addressed to Mr. Cahil, in which they authorize him "to hold fifty bigahs of land required for the purpose stated in his letter." The letter is signed by L. Dunsmuir, Officiating Collector of Tirhoot. Bhicanpore was then an outwork of Contai or *Khanti* and belonged to Noel or Nowell and Company. It has outwork, Bochaha.

H. E. Hudson and Mrs. J. Begg—built in about 1872 by D. Begg—and Sahajpore in 1860 by T. Barclay. Bhicanpore now belongs to H. Hudson and G. Richardson.

Batowlia C. McK. B.

This factory was built by an interloper. Dr. Charles Mackinnon wrote me some years ago to the effect that a Mr. Meade, a shopkeeper in Mozufferpore, got a piece of land from one of the Patna Mirabdola family and started building. This he opposed and eventually he bought Mr. Meade out. I have no date as to when the factory was built. When purchased by Dr. C. Mackinnon it became an outwork of Shahpore Mircha Concern, and after passing through several hands eventually became the property of Mr. Rudstone Brown. He in 1892 built an outwork he called Rudstonegunge and also purchased Miachuppra. He also acquired Ramdaspore which was built in 1882. The machinery at this outwork was put up by Sir Salter Pyne, who afterwards became Engineer to the Amir of Cabul. In about 1858 Mahomed Baker Khan, one of the Mirabdola family, built an opposition factory in Inaitnuggur village. This factory worked for some years and Mahomed Baker having bought Batowlia sold the two places to Mr. R. C. Brown, Inaitnuggur as a factory has been abandoned.

Belsund Factory J. McK. & Co.

The mokarrarie document of this factory is dated 1794 and was given by Rajah Mustaffa Khan. It has outworks, Bagwanpore which was built some 60—70 years ago, mokarrarie pottah dated 1846: Belai, which was built in 1861 by C. Swaine, mokarrarie pottah dated 1856; Sukereah and Boijnathpore built in 1846 by David Brown mokarrarie pottahs dated 1846. These two are now abandoned also Luchmepore, and interloping factory built by B. Hickey in 1871. The furthest back I can get as to name of manager is one Mr. Paul, but there is no date. He and all his family, tradition says, were poisoned and are buried under a *pucca* slab on which there is no name or date. He was followed as manager by Mr. R. Robertson. Then by G. N. Wyatt and after him David Brown, then P. Macfarlane, who is buried at Mozufferpore (he was the elder brother of the late Sir Donald H. Macfarlane, M.P.). After him came C. Swaine, who died at Cawnpore in 1861 and he was succeeded by T. Lethbridge, then R. Lethbridge. The concern was sold to Mr. J. F. Mackenzie in 1873-74 and managed by his brother, W S. Mackenzie, followed by H. Manners, A. S. Tweedie, who died of cholera in Mozufferpore and is buried there. Then W. Mackenzie, followed by C. C. Smith, who died and is buried at Benepore. In about 1884 Belsund was sold and A. H. Rennie managed. He died at sea and is buried at Suez. After him came Carruthers in 1887, L. Crowdy in 1888, and H. E. Crowdy and then in 1899 G. R. Macdonald. D. J. Reid took over charge in 1903 and *now manages*.

Bhagwanpore M. M. Co.

This factory, though looked upon as in Tirhoot, is like Munjoul, actually in Monghyr. It was built in 1818. The mokarrarie lease, which is dated in that year, was given to John Christian of Bogchappra, a factory below Monghyr station or town where many years ago one Yankee Pratt, a fine big American, managed; he left three sons, all powerful and active men, namely, Charles, who died at Doomra, George, at Beerpore, and William, in Chumparun. John Christian built Bagwanpore, and old records show that a lease of some villages was given to Beebee Warren, or Warram, so probably her husband was before Christian. In 1822 John Christian sold the factory to P. Crump, and Crump and his wife lived at Bagwanpore for many years. He leased it in May, 1836, to W. Sloan, most likely Captain Sloane, of Dholi, but as Crump was back in November it is more than likely Crump never left the management. Before Crump acquired Bagwanpore he must have been an assistant on one of the neighbouring factories. As there is a letter from Mr. R. Morgan, of Dulsing Serai, dated October, 1822, addressed to him giving him advice and telling him he would come over and see him and introduce him to all old friends who formerly cultivated for him, so Morgan must have been at Bagwanpore between 1818 and 1822. He mentions John Brown as having been at Doulutpore. Messrs. Alexander and Company were Crump's agents though later on he did business with Bagshaw and Company. In 1845 Crump sold the factory to James Alexander Hoskins. Hoskins must have bought with the intention of making a sugar factory of the place. A cash book of 1845 shows that in that year sugar machinery was purchased and erected Potter and Company were the Calcutta agents then, though he got his outlay from H. R. Hoskins, of Liverpool, who was probably his father. The books show some sugar sold at Rs. 4 per maund, which shows that the sugar must have been very poor stuff. In those days they hoped to make sugar at As. 8 per maund and sell it at Rs. 8. Hoskins remained at Bagwanpore some four or five years, but as by that time sugar was a failure he left. In 1851 the factory belonged to Augustus Radecliffe for whom James Saunders managed. He sold in 1853 to Tom Martin for Rs. 12,000, Kenneth MacLeod being a partner, hence the mark M. M. and Company. In 1856 E. T. Harrington bought the place and it has been his since then. The managers since 1856 were: 1857 to 1861 Archibald Inglis, 1862 to 1863 L. Cooke, 1864 Tom Slade, 1865 J. C. Muir, 1866 Hooley, 1867 to 1871 Lawrence Crowdy, 1872 to 1882 W. S. Crowdy, 1882 to 1888 C. H. Crowdy and since then L. T. Harrington. Suroojporah, an outwork, was built by Crump about 1830 to 1835; it was in existence in 1837 as there was a pottah to Beebee Crump in that year. Agapore was built in 1856. There are no graves at Bagwanpore Factory.

The mokarrarie of this concern dates back to 1822. The factory belonged to R. Leverett in 1831. In 1838 W. H. Smoult sold to D. Hunter and H. Gouger and their trustees. In 1837 a deed of partnership was made between W. Smoult and Charles Mackinnon. This factory was eventually purchased by the Tirhoot Indigo Association of London and they again sold to the Tirhoot Indigo Company and they to G. D. Blake and others. One of the outworks, Shahpore, was taken over by Mr. J. V. Webb, a few years ago, Mr. Henry Gouger mentioned above was a brother of Alfred Gouger, who lived over his office in Tank Square in 1847. He (H. G.) if I mistake not was the man whom the Burmese locked up in a cage and who, after going through great hardships, managed to escape.

Chitwarrah
C.
C. McK.

There are buried at Chitwarrah Ed. Eph. Pote, born 9th February, died 15th August 1812, and Robert Leverett, died 20th May 1832, aged 44. Chitwarrah was managed from Shahpore Mircha in 1847. John Anderson was Sub-manager then. After him C. Strachan, then C. V. Argles. Then J. C. Muir became independent manager. It is now managed by George Blake.

Mr. J. V. Webb has turned Shahpore Factory into a Farm where he raises all kinds of produce. His Dairy and other farm produce, are well known and appreciated and anyone wanting to go in for Rhea or general produce could not do better than acquire this compact little place which I hear is for sale. It is close to the Tal Barcila, a grand place for wild duck shooting.

This concern was built in 1778 by Alexander Nœl or Nowell, afterwards Noel and Co. From 1816 to 1825 Contai was the head factory under which the following concerns worked:—*Belsund, Motipore, Amoah, Tatereah, Bhicanpore, Peepra*

Contai or
Kbanti
D. B.
C.

CONTAI HOUSE.

and *Secraha* in Chumparun. All accounts during the above years were kept at Contai. The proprietors were, in 1825, Messrs. Nœl or Nowell, Wood and Cahill. In 1832 Contai was leased to Alexander Fletcher for one year. In 1834 Messrs. Noel, Wood and Cahill sold to Messrs. Fletcher, James Alexander, and Charles Kerr. In January 1852 the above three sold to Messrs. Cullen, Henry Lumsden and Thomas Muir, and in May, same year, they sold to Dr. D. Begg.

In 1866, Contai and Motipore were sold to K. MacLeod and Charles M. MacDonald. In 1872, C. M. MacDonald sold his share to Neil MacDonald and Thomas Martin, and K. MacLeod his share to James Cox. In same year James Cox sold 2 annas to George Toomey and in 1881 T. Martin also sold 2 annas to George Toomey. In 1883 N. MacDonald's executors sold 4 annas to George Toomey and in the same year T. Martin and James Cox sold their remaining shares to Thomas Gibbon and George Toomey. In 1894 Thomas Gibbon sold his 4 annas to Mrs. Flora Toomey. I find in 1820 R. Cahil mentioned, and when the factory was built by Alexander Nowell. From 1776 to 1826 the names of Nowell and Cahill only appear as managers. From 1826 to 1832 D. Brown managed Contai, from then George Taylor, followed by D. R. Crawford in 1842 to 1852, then Charles Swaine and others. In 1869 to 1874 George Toomey became manager, followed by R. C. Brown in 1874-75, when Toomey again came in up to 1880. After him W. A. Cox to 1883, the A. MacRae, F. A. Shaw, H. E. Cox and again A. MacRae in 1893. The present manager, George R. Toomey, Junior, has been managing since 1894. The old Contai bungalow stood where the present *chota* bungalow stands and was not the fine house the present bungalow is, which must have been built by Cahill or George Taylor. The Contai outworks are Ragai, which was built about the same time as the head factory. Lowton was built 1884 and Narriar in 1887. The managers and proprietors of Contai have always been famed for their hospitality, and as the factory is only some 8 miles from Mozufferpore, it was a great *rendezvous* for picnics. George Taylor kept a four-in-hand coach and an English coachman who used to drive his guests out from Mozufferpore to a fine old banyan tree which stood a few miles beyond at Panapore. This tree was supposed to cover seven acres of ground, and it was here where picnic parties had their fun. George Taylor, report says, had a musical box in every bed-room, so that his guests might be soothed to sleep by dulcet melody. Gone are those days. "Where are those dreamers now."

There is rather a good story told about Mr. Cahill. He was staying at Contai with his manager, Mr. D. R. Crawford, and there was some trouble that necessitated a little *douceur*. D. R. Crawford suggested this to Mr. Cahill and named rather a tall sum as likely to be required. "Oh, no no," Mr. Cahill replied, "that is a thing I could never agree to." So they parted and went to bed. In the morning Cahill came up to D. R. Crawford and said, "About that matter we were talking about last night, don't you think the man would take less?"

The mokarrarie pottah for this factory is dated 1834.

Doomra
W. McG.
D.

The name of the gentleman in whose name it is given is obliterated, but the first letters looks like David, most likely David Brodie. In an old Persian document the name of Macrade or Mackay is given as being at Doomra in 1811; the signature is in English, but illegible. The outworks are Punchore and Butnaha. There is no trace as to who built Punchore. Butnaha was built by John Mitchell on his own account and was afterwards acquired by Doomra Concern. It is now again a separate factory and belongs to Mr. Moore. In 1844, or before a sugar factory was built at Doomra and a vacuum pan put up which made very good sugar, sugar and indigo were worked side by side. The Doomra concern formed one of many owned by the Tirhoot Indigo Association of London. I can find no records of who managed there before W. C. Baddeley in 1846-47, but have heard the names of David Brodie and John Mitchell mentioned. In fact there is a good story about Jack Mitchell, who must have had an interest in the factory and put down Rs. 10,000 of his own money towards outlay. The total outlay spent was a lakh for which he made enough indigo to fill a 500 cigar box. Some one remarked "What will the Agents say about the lakh?" When Jack retorted "Damn the lakh, it's my ten thousand I am thinking of." There used to be two very amusing old cash books signed by one De Josey. These books were very interesting from the free and easy entries contained, there was no cloaking anything, a spade was called a spade. These books were dated about 1815. Many wished to get these volumes as curiosities and they were kept under lock and key, but, alas! one fine day they disappeared and have never been seen since. To the North-West of Doomra stands Dynechuppra, a shut up factory and North of this Holoquarry, where many years ago troops were quartered. The old parade ground and sentry boxes, and some of the bungalows still exist. Here there is a grave-yard and some of the tomb stones that exist bear the following inscriptions:—

Sacred to the memory of Captain John Francis Blackney, of the 2nd Battalion, 22nd Regiment, N. I. Killed in an action with the Nepaulese on the 1st of January 1815. Aged 31 years.

This monument is erected by his affectionate brother.

Sacred to the memory of Lieutenant John Feryer Goad, Interpreter and Quartermaster to the 2nd Battalion, 25th

Regiment, N. I. An excellent officer. An amiable and upright man who died at this place after a short illness on the 14th of November 1816, much beloved and lamented. Leaving a disconsolate widow and infant family to mourn the premature and dreadful privation one of the best of husbands and fathers. A few sorrowing friends have erected this monument.

In affectionate remembrance. Age 29.

Here lies the body, of Major C. P. Hay, who died on 27th day of July 1820. Aged 38 years.

He raised and commanded the Chumparun Light Infantry, was an excellent officer, a good and upright man and deservedly regretted by all who knew him. He has left a disconsolate widow and infant child to mourn his irreparable loss. This monument is erected as a small tribute of tender regard for the revered memory of the best of husbands by his affectionate wife.

To the memory of Lieutenant-Colonel Edward Kelly, of H. M. Service, who died on the 6th of August A. D. 1828 in the 54th year of his age.

This gallant officer served His Majesty with distinction in Flanders, Spain, and at Waterloo, where he was severely wounded. He was present at the capture of the Fortress of Bhurtpore, and subsequently served in Ava, where he contracted the disease which proved fatal to him.

As a last mark of regard and esteem the Right Honourable the Viscount Combermere, G. C. B., Commander-in-Chief (on whose personal staff Lieutenant-Colonel E. Kelly came to India) and his brother officers on the staff have erected this monument.

Sacred to the memory of Charles Stewart Grant, M. L., Assistant Surgeon, 63rd Regiment, N. I., who departed this life on the 14th October 1833. Aged 37 years.

This monument is erected as a mark of respect by his brother officers.

There were many other graves, but before Government thought proper to step in and see to their being kept in repair, the villagers had gone off with many a slab to the memory of gallant men and used them to grind down curry powder, etc.

At Doomra Factory there are buried Robert Woodruff Stalkratt, who died March 1847, aged 29, and Charles Robert Pratt, who died 10th August 1851, aged 31. There are also the remains of two Dutch graves in a bamboo tope, but no inscription. Mr. M. J. Wilson had charge of Doomra and Pooprее in 1853-54 as well as Kurnoul, but in 1854 gave up Kurnoul and came to Pooprее still managing Doomra, and at end of 1654 came to Doomra which he managed till end of 1855 and to 1856, he managed from Shahpore Mircha Factory. Doomra Factory is situated to the north of the district, to the south of the *Seta Marhi* subdivision. After passing through many hands it now belongs to Mr. J. A. M. Wilson.

Doudpore D. B. D.

This factory was built in 1798 or before the mokarrarie pottah is dated 1st May 1798 and given to Mr. Powell. Arrigepore, the outwork, was built in 1829. The mokarraries stand in the names of Nœl and Company. Mousari, another outwork, was built in 1822. Chajun in 1864. The mokarrarie pottah of which is in the name of F. Collingridge, who built it. This concern was first a part of Contai. I cannot find out who were the sub-managers before C. Swaine in 1847, but I have heard the name of David Brown, *i.e.* Fat David Brown, to distinguish him from the other David Brown, a cousin in the same employ, nicnamed the Gooroo. To the north of Doudpore there is an old battle field, but no one seems to know much about it, or who were the opposing parties.

There are many Mahomedan graves, so I suppose it must have been between Moslems and Hindus.

In 1861 F. Collingridge, Dr. C. Macnamara and J. S. Begg bought into Doudpore. F. Collingridge taking the management which he held till 1867 when he went home. He returned to the country again and resumed management till 1876. His son Herbert took charge then. In 1882 H. Collingridge purchased a 4 anna share and managed from 1876 to 1893 when Mr. G. T. Collingridge became manager. The concern is now the property of the Collingridge family.

Doulutpore M. & S. D.

The oldest paper to be found is a receipt for rent, dated 1804, to one John Brown, manager, it is from Babu Dhuleep Sing. Rumour has it that Doulutpore was first a sugar factory. Megoul, an outwork, was built in about 1850. I cannot find out who managed between John Brown's time and R. Ronald's who was managing in 1847. He, poor man, was murdered by mutineers at Deogarh in 1857. He had left indigo and taken up an appointment of Deputy Commissioner in the Santhal Pergunnahs. W. C. Baddeley was manager in 1856, followed by F. H. Hollway, H. Spencer and C. MacDonald in 1865. He was followed by James Crowdy in 1872, then K. MacIver, C. Robertson, T. Robertson, and then the present manager, C. MacDonald, junior, who took charge again in 1901 after his return from South Africa with Lumsden's Horse.

When I came to the district Doulutpore was not considered a very good factory, but Mr. W. C. Baddeley improved the lands by mixing sand in the stiff clay soil and trenching freely, and so improved the soil that the factory lands are now looked upon by native cultivators with an envious eye. They offer as much as Rs. 40 per bigha for any of this land they can get for one year.

Dhurmpore J. M. B.

Dhurmpore was built by J. C. Muir when he was at Chitwarrah. How this came about was as follows: There was a certain amount of jealousy between Muir and George Smith, who was managing Shahpore Mircha. Muir thought George Smith was trying to encroach into the Chitwarrah dehat by building Kurhurrie Factory, so he started Dhurmpore, a great deal of money was spent and a good deal of ill-feeling shown. The strange thing was that both G. Smith and J. Muir were employees of the Tirhoot Indigo Association whose money they were spending to satisfy their own *zid*. Dhurmpore was built in about 1859. I do not know who was the resident manager; however, the factory was eventually sold by the Tirhoot Indigo Association to one Mukbull Hosain who sold to John Martin Becher. The place eventually went into the hands of Hajee Syed Mahomed Tukee Khan. His heirs sold the place to J. M. Wilson. The factory has one outwork, Chupta; this place was built by Mr. W. Llewhellin for Singia Factory and by exchange it eventually became part of Dhurmpore, which Factory was eventually purchased by J. M. Wilson and is his now.

A small Factory, Kootoopore, also belongs to Mr. J. M. Wilson; it is a place of recent date, and borders on Dhurmpore concern.

Dooria A. J. D.

The dates on the mokarrarie documents of this factory and its outworks are Dooria 1807. Bisoonpore 1808, and Karumbarie 1836. Very few records of this concern remain. In olden days saltpetre was a paying industry, and like several other places there are indications of this being one of Dooria's original industries. In the *Tackbast* map of days gone bye it is recorded as a saltpetre factory. As far as can be found out Dooria started indigo in 1780 I find, as will be seen in the preface to this, that in 1793 one John Finch, who came to the country in 1778, was put down as of Dooria Factory. As far as one can go back by documents and tradition Arthur Jones was among the first managing proprietors, thus the mark Arthur Jones, Dooria.

(A. J.)
(D.)

He was followed by Nicoll, then Finch, most likely John Finch, who was perhaps an ancestor of the proprietors of Shahpore Oundie (*see* Tirhoot and its Inhabitants of the Past). After him, according to factory records, came William, but that I take must be William Howell. There may have been a man between John Finch and Howell, but there is no record of this. In 1845-46, after the factory had passed into the hands of the Tirhoot Indigo Association of London, sugar was started, but was abandoned a few years later. In 1864-65 the Tirhoot Indigo Association of London sold to Messrs. E. Studd and Lauchlin MacDonald. During the proprietorship of the Tirhoot Indigo Association, after William Howell's death in 1848, the factory was managed by Charles Gale, followed by F. Collingridge and J. C. Muir. On Studd's purchasing, L. MacDonald took charge and was followed by several others, until the present year, 1905, when Sir L. Hay represents the management. The year Mr. A. MacDonald, MacRae managed the factory, made a record season, and as prices were high, the place made a very handsome profit. The Dooria indigo is noted for its beautiful colour and holds the head of the price list of Behar colour.

There is an old graveyard a short distance from the factory supposed to have been graves of Dutch people who lived at the factory, but there is no inscription left on the graves. In the Garden are the following three graves:—

Sacred to the memory of Mr. George Christy, son of Mr. James Christy, of Berhampore, who died on the 18th August 1812. Aged 20 years and 2 months. Sincerely regretted.

Sacred to the memory of William Maynard Howell, youngest son of the late Thomas Howell, of Cardiganshire, S. Wales, who departed this life on the 8th October 1847. Aged 34 years and 8 months.

Sacred to the memory of Janet Blackborn Whyte, who departed this life on 27th December 1867. Beloved in life and regretted in death.

I have just received the following from a friend which may be of interest as showing the expenditure of Dooria Concern in 1795. The total from January 1795 to December, including a balance of Rs. 908-2-9 for 1794 totalled Rs. 31-924-9-0. This includes expenses of Boggah Sooreah and Ghee concerns, but what these concerns are and where situated there is no indication nor is the manager's name attached to this account or how many bigahs of indigo cultivated. My informant remarks humorously: "Fancy, in your imagination, the manager of Dooria with his sleeves turned up pulling at his *hookah* a hundred years ago putting together his account of expenditure in peace and comfort far away from Europe and the bustle of the French revolution. No trains at Motipore, no worrying telegrams from bothering agents." Probably he never dreamt of the decay of the industry nor the heavy rise in factory outlays. He also gives the names of planters in the district dividing their advent into decades. These lists are open to corrections and additions, and the writer will be obliged if any one who can do so will correct any error. The following is the list of the first decade—1820 to 1830: P. Crump, J. Mackenzie, H. Sherman, David Brown, James Slade, T. Gibbon, J. Buck, J. Watson, J. Finch, F. Finch, J. Thomson Gill, Dr. C. Mackinon, Yule, Joseph Hill, Henry Hill, James Hill. In 1830 to 40, Morgan, George Drumoned, K. MacLeod, John Gale, James Cosserat, E. Willson, R. Willson, A. Roach, F. Collingridge, David Crawford, Andrew Crawford, James

Wilson, John Becher, Captain H. Becher, R. Taylor, George Taylor, W. Moran, Harry Brown, E. Harding, J. Mitchell, G. N. Wyatt, H. Holloway, Mons. De La Sene, C. W. Gale, Charles Swaine, A. Brown, L. Cosserat, James Cosserat, W. C. Baddeley, James Cox, Thomas Slade, T. Martin, John MacRae, E. Studd, W. Daunt, C. Baldwin, L. Cook, James Cook, J. R. Mackenzie, J. Anderson, R. Cahill, junior, James Cox, Ed. Studd. Between 1840 and 1850, H. Holloway, R. Beynon, Tom Cox, B. Anderson, G. Williamson, W. Williamson, W. Sharpley, G. Mitchell, R. Bradley, Arthur Crooke, G. Venables, C. Stachan, Archibald Inglis, Minden Wilson, Saunders C. Verpleugh, A. S. Young, James Sherman, E. Sherman, H. Sherman, James Mitchell, Buchanan. J. M. Becher, H. Hooper, F. H. Hollway, J. S. Smith, DeCruze, DePain, W. Garstin, Ogilvie, Afred Tripe, James S. Begg, P. MacFarlane, Goodenough, Curtis, W. Baldwin, John Stalkart, John Stalkart (of Bekenpore), De Mise, W. James, Hosmore, Ferrier, Falconer, David Brown, Charles Paterson. Between 1850 and 1860, Sir D. H. MacFarlane, H. Hudson, J. F. Mackenzie, F. W. Wingrove, L. MacDonald, J. C. Muir, A. Urquhart, P. Crump, junior, E. Urquhart, D. B. Whyte, E. T. Harrington, W. M. Stewart, James Wilson (Mhow), Mermaduke, G. Moore, Bluett Coulthurst, John Anderson, C. V. Argles, John Gale, junior, A. Howell, James Smith, Charles Oman, Hildebrand, W. H. Bullen, A. MacRae, W. Howell, J. Howell, M. H. Gale, E. Smith, M. Smith, R. Riddell, W. Riddell, H. Spenser, Joseph Tripe, T. Lethbridge, R. Lethbridge, T. Dyer, C. Pratt, George Pratt, W. Pratt, E. Lamb, C. MacDonald, Evans, E. Dalgleish, G. Mann, Joseph Finch, junior, M. Lloyd, R. Brooke, George Toomey, J. Neal, A. MacRae, Bolton W. MacQueene, J. Crawford, T. M. Gibbon, W. Gibbon, N. MacDonald, M. MacDonald, J. Reid, D. N. Reid, A. S. Tweedie, G. D. Blake, Alister Mackinnon, Blake (Ramkollah), W. Campbell, James Stewart, K. MacLean, Eneas MacDonald, W. MacDonald, George Deloy, George Llewhellin, J. Hamilton. From 1860 to 1870, George Hennessey, W. Oman, David Oman, D. B. Bullen, C. Sanderson, J. Forbes, T. Lamb, G. Bloomfield, R. Bloomfield, Hooley, J. K. MacIver, G. Mackenzie, F. Forth, W. Cooper (now Sir W. Cooper), G. Hamilton, W. Brooke, C. H. Webb, H. MacDonald, G. Smith, G. Wilson, C. Gale, junior, G. MacEven, N. Campbell, W. Moran, Bull, Jack Hollway, James Cosserat, junior, Arthur Cosserat, J. Hill, junior, R. Hill, junior, D. Begg, junior, R. Mackinnon, W. Cockburn, Simon Nicholson, S. Beacher, Hamilton, R. Irwin, W. S. Mackenzie, W. Macgregor, R. Wilson, A. Macalister, W M. Smith, W. Smith (Long), K. M. MacDonald, G. Pughe, John Fraser, G. Proudfoot, W. Buskin, G. Buskin, R. Robertson, G. MacEwen, Henderson, Chapman, W. Mackenzie, F. Hamley, Laddy MacDonald, G. F. Shaw, N. MacQueen, W. Gibbon (Shanghai), N. S. MacLean, W. Hickey, T. Hickey, B. Hickey, senior, Hugh Llewhellin, W. Llewhellin, Llewhellin (Moolvi), Cyril Irvine, Geo. Exshaw, E. Exshaw, Cooper, C. Pope, Wilkinson, K. MacIver, G. Williams, L. Coke, junior, G. Swaine, junior, L. Wilson, T. Fraser, D. Irwin, G. Irwin, D. Mackinnon, James Hogg, Henry Fraser, Hugh MacDonald, J. Inglis, F. Murray, E. Studd, junior, Pincher Brown, Tulloch, R. Brown, D. Reid (Black), Henry Studd, R. Waller, A. MacIver, S. MacIver, Adams, Angus MacEwen, E. Macnaghten, John Freeman, Pemberton, Trevor Lloyd, H. E. Abbott, G. Rennie, G. Nicolay, W. Nicolay, A. Edward, Arthur Ellis, M. N. MacLeod, F. May Fearon, Grant, Freeman No. 2, Wynns, R. Phillips, C. C. Smith, H. Manners, Borican, W. MacLeod, Cresswell, A. MacBean. From 1870 to 1880, E. Roberts, Llewhellin, Laurie, A. MacIntosh, W. MacGregor, W. Cavie, Carlisle, A. Abbott, Charles Mackenzie, Finch, Chalmers,

Holley, Pearce, Lindsay; Jones, Phil. Smith, MacIntosh, Sisson, N. MacLeod, J. Shortt, Farquhar Mackinnon, H. Dalgleish, Rennie, junior, Barclay, Bolton, James Wilson, C. Nicolson, Barlow, Coffin, Edwards, R. Hudson, Freeman No. 3, Phillips No. 2, Wood No. 1, Wood No. 2, Apperley, E. Manners, W. Thoms, Flavell, Campbell, John Grant, Sheffield, J. MacGregor, W. O. MacGregor, A. MacFarlane, H. Crowdy, James Mackenzie, D. Crawford, H. T. Kerr, E. Nicolay, E. Becher, F. Byng, G. Collingridge, M. Macenzie, B. Shortt, K. Shortt. In 1870 to 1880, H. Collingridge, junior, W. S. Irwin, A. Ogilvy, C. F. Ruxton, T. R. Filgate, G. P. Hume, R. R. Crookshank, T. Hodding, S. Becher.

Since 1880 I can find no account of new arrivals, but I fancy fully 30 to 50 new men must have arrived during 1880 to 1890 and as many more from 1890 to 1900 or 1905. This list is very defective, but gives an idea of how many men came and left, and of the lot, how few there are alive this day.

Dholi
C. McK.&E.S.
D.

There are no documents to show when this factory was first built, but natives say in 1203 Fasli, or A. D. 1796 which is probable, as we find Dholi mentioned in the Collectorate records as being managed by Mr. W. Orby Hunter, who, it appears, managed both Dholi and Doudpore in 1786.

Mr. or Captain Sloane, who the natives also name as the builder of Dholi, is most likely the first man there, though native tradition says there was an older factory built 50 years before Dholi. Mrs. Sloane, who had been a Mrs. Hopkins before she married Captain Sloane, seemed to be the managing spirit in Dholi affairs. She was always called Beebee Hopkins and is talked of to this day. She was a most masterful woman, good to her tenants and servants. She was supposed to have witchcraft powers and the natives feared her curse. She was also supposed to have the gift of prophesying. She went over the cultivation on a small elephant and was very energetic. By certain papers I gather that Mr. or Captain Sloane managed in 1823 up to 1833. Dr. C. Mackinnon came in as manager and proprietor in 1837, and most likely succeeded Captain Sloane. In 1848 Mr. E. Studd became manager and he was followed by James Cox in 1851. But Mr. John Stace Smith managed for a short time between Mr. E. Studd and James Cox, who managed up to 1861, followed by George Toomey, A. S. Tweedie, E. J. C. Studd, H. Spry, and then E. J. C. Studd, who made over charge to his son, E. Studd who is manager.

In 1854 Edward Studd bought from Mr. Richards, of Calcutta, a share in Dholi Concern, with its outworks, Berowli, Tharma and Sukri. This latter place, it appears, was an older factory than even Dholi and reported to have been a sugar factory. Berowli was built in 1825 and Sobnaha in 1890.

The Beebee Hopkins I mentioned above had been the wife of a Captain Hopkins at Pusa. She quarrelled with her husband and left him, and on his death married Captain Sloane. The following inscriptions may be found over the graves in the old graveyard near Dholi. Many others have been cut away into the river Gunduk:—

(i) Sacred to the memory of Mrs. Anne Sloane relict of Major D. Sloane. H. C. N. I. Died 7th November 1862. Aged 56.

(ii) Sacred to the memory of Charles Lauchlin Corry, beloved son of Charles and Henrietta Mackinnon. Born 18th January 1837, died 3rd November 1838.

(iii) Sacred to the memory of Harriet Augusta, second daughter of Thomas Insunda Shwood. Born 24th July 1824, died 2nd April 1831.

(iv) Sacred to the memory of Robert William Morgan,

who departed this life on 10th December 1836. Aged 65.

Dulsing Serai or Keonta. D. H. S.

In 1794 Dulsing Serai was built by Mr. Teare or Phaire, who was manager, and the mokarrarie stands in his name given by Dhanessur Chowdry, Mahunt Alak Ram, Ajab Sing Chowdry, Khoosi Chowdry, and others.

In 1802 Mr. Johnson managed, 1810 Morgan, then William Sherman. In 1837 Thomson K. MacLeod superintendent and Thomas Martin manager in 1851. In 1856 W. M. Stewart, 1862 C. Paterson, 1864 C. MacDonald, 1863 K. MacIver, 1866 H. Spencer, 1870 E. Dalgleish, 1881 E. F. May, 1882 R. Bloomfield, 1885 E. Dalgleish, 1894 B. Coventry, then F. Coventry 1903, who has gone home on leave. C. W. Spencer now manager.

In about 1847-48 the factory was sold by public auction in Calcutta and bought for a few hundred rupees by John Becher, who failed to pay up as he had to come up to Tirhoot to arrange for money and died at Shahpore Oundi, on his way. It was again put up in 1851 and bought by the brothers W. and Henry Poe, Solicitors, Calcutta, who placed the superintendence under K. MacLeod, who appointed Thomas Martin as manager, under whose management the factory did well and made a record season. Baddeley and Strachan and F. H. Hollway bought in some years after. The present proprietors are E. T. Harrington, H. Spencer's estate. C. Strachan's estate, F. H. Hollway, E. Dalgleish, B. Coventry, and E. M. Coventry.

The outwork, Pemberandah, was built by Thomson in 1837. The mokarrarie given by Babu Moorat Narien Singh; Chutra was built by W. M. Stewart in 1858, mokarrarie given by Babu Permeswary Persaud Narien Singh; Tubca was built by K. MacIver in 1866, mokarrarie given by Permeswary and Jagdeep Singh; Gobindpore built by Dalgleish in 1875, mokarrarie given by Permeswary Singh and Raj Koomar Mukerjee and others; and Shahpore in 1879 by Dalgleish, mokarrarie given by Goorpersaud Singh and others in 1858 in anticipation.

In 1895 B. Coventry built Kamlah. In 1904 F. Coventry built a Rhea factory with the Bengal Rhea Syndicate. There is but one old grave to the memory of a daughter of Mr. Thomson, who died in 1837. There are some new graves, mostly of children. In 1900 W. B. Carshore died and is buried at Dulsing Serai.

In 1898 Mr. B. Coventry, owing to depression in the indigo market caused by the introduction of the Badische Synthetic dye, started the agricultural and manuring experiments which have been appreciated by the Government and has resulted in his appointment to the management of the new Pusa Agricultural College the first stone of which was laid by our present Viceroy, Lord Curzon, in 1905. Mr. Coventry, under the auspices of Messrs. Begg, Dunlop and Company, employed Mr. E. A. Hancock as Chemist, and Mr. Bailey was sent to Java to study the indigo industry in that country. Mr. Bailey, after a short residence in Java, returned with the Java process and Java Indigo seed, Java process was tried in the Dulsing Serai Concern at an outwork, but was not a success. The merits of the Java plant were recognised, but it was difficult to get the seed to germinate owing to the hard husk shell, but in 1903 Mr. Leake obtained good results by scarifying the outer coat and the difficulty overcome, and since then a machine, designed by Mr. Watson and Messrs. Arthur Butler and Company, has been found most efficacious.

Gangowlie M & S. G.

Gangowlie was formerly an outwork of Doulutpore. The mokarrarie pottah was given by Babu Permeswary Persaud Norien Singh, of Nurhan, and is dated 15th November 1860, to W. C. Baddeley. It has one outwork, Allumpore, mokarrarie pottah dated 1874 given to C. M. MacDonald. These factories were bought by E. G. Stonewigg in December 1891, purchasing from W. D. Kilburn, Executor for C. M. MacDonald, and also from C. T. Robertson, junior. Gangowlie was built by C. M. MacDonald when he was an assistant at Meghowl while F. H. Hollway was managing Doulutpore in 1860. Allumpore was built in 1874, the foundations were put down by James Crowdy, and K. MacIver finished the building. There have been many assistants at these factories before they were purchased by E. G. Stonewigg, first Bishop, then R. Crookshank, then Browning, who died of enteric at Mozufferpore, then M. Halliday, Crichton, and several others. Later on Gangowlie was separated from Doulutpore and Farquhar Mackinnon took charge. It was he who built the present bungalow. It was before but a tattie house, R. Crookshank went from Gangowlie to Allumpore, followed by Robertson. Before Allumpore was built most of the indigo round where it stands went to Doulutpore by boat down the Bore Gunduk.

Mr. E. G. Stonewigg is now manager of his own Factory, 1905. He retired Home in 1907 making over charge to W. M. Vipan.

Hatti-Ousti
J. W. C. &
C. H. C.

All records of this factory were burnt during Marmaduke Stalkartt's time. This gentleman, in trying to shoot sparrows out of the verandah roof, set the house on fire. He would allow nothing to be saved as he said, he was going to start with a clean sheet. The factory belonged at that time to the Ganges Indigo Company. The factory must have been a very old one as tradition tells of indigo being carried in on donkeys and the Persian wheel worked by elephants. The only grave is that of J. Mitchell, who was manager of Herni (Bachouli), but there is no date on this to say when he died. In 1847 there was a sugar factory at Hatti-Ousti, but there is no record as to when built—perhaps in 1845. In 1847 Mr. Thomas Gibbon managed (*see* "Tirhoot and its Inhabitants of the Past"), since then the management has passed through many hands till at last it was purchased by the Crowdys, J. W. Crowdy being the present manager and proprietor. There is a good story about Mr. Stalkartt when manager. Having quarrelled with some of his *ryatts* he got their bullocks into the factory and chopped off their tails, and, as the Magistrate was to dine with him, he gave him what the *huzoor* pronounced to be excellent oxtail soup, which was much appreciated. A few days after a case was brought against Stalkartt by the *ryatts* for injuring their cattle and S., stepping into the witness box (with a wink to his friend the Magistrate), explained that he had (imitating the action of a pair of scissors with his fingers) only trimmed the hair at the end of the bullock's tail. The pleasant impression left on the Magistrate's memory by the soup softened his heart and he fined the culprit Rs. 50 to be divided among the offended *ryatts*. I do not vouch for the truth of this yarn, but it was one told in my younger days in the district.

Hattowree P. & O.

Hattowree Factory was built by John Anderson, but there seems no record of in what year Native tradition says once Anderson was going from Kumtoul with his indigo chests to send down the Ganges to Calcutta by boat. He was accompanied by his peon, Sunfoul Ray. Passing near where Hattowree now stands, he asked Sunfoul Ray whose land it was and the peon told him it was Fakeeranha, so Anderson on his return arranged to secure the land through Sunfoul Ray, whose house was at Korlahya ghat near the place. This was the beginning of Sunfoul Ray's fortune (*see* "Tirhoot and its Inhabitants of the Past"). Sunfoul Ray has been dead many years, but he became a big zemindar in those parts, his grandson, Chunet Ray, now reigns in his place. After John Anderson left in 1847, Hattowree was purchased by R. Taylor. There were two outworks, but who built them there is no record. Bunhar was one and the other stood at the confluence of the Bogmatee and Karaye rivers. At R. Taylor's death the factory was sold, but I can find no record as to whom. Charles Oman purchased in about 1858 and sold in 1864, but here again comes a blank in the record. I think, however, Tom Poe (Harrington) purchased and the place eventually went into the hands of Messrs. E. Dalgleish and H. Spenser who sold Bunhar to H. Dalgleish. Baghonie, another outwork, was built when C. V. Argles managed (I think for Mr. Thorburn) in about 1862-64. I believe Baghonie, too, has been sold, but I am not sure of this. Baghonie is to the East of Hattowree across the Karaye River.

Hursingpore S. & C.

Originally Bowarrah was the head factory and the mokarrarie document is dated 1793. This given to two sahebs whose names as far as can be read were Rech and Schum. Hursingpore itself was built in 1844, the mokarrarie pottah stands in the name of Mr. Johnson and was made head factory by C. Strachan when he purchased the concern in the early fifties. He built the present bungalow which was burnt down by a wild youngster who amused himself shooting sparrows out of the verandah roof, like M. Stalkartt at Hatti-Ousti. Strachan had to rebuild the house. He also built the outwork, Rahimabad, when C. V. Argles was managing in 1864. Bulampore, another outwork, was built by J. S. Smith in 1864. Bowarrah is mentioned in Hunter's *Gazetteer* as one of the oldest indigo factories in Tirhoot. There are ruins of a small indigo factory about 3 miles from Bowarrah on the banks of the river Noon or Bulan. It is curiously situated on a sort of island between two branches of the river. The remains of vats, Persian wheel and the floor of what must have been the press house are still to be seen. Tradition says this factory was built by a Frenchman and was abandoned as he considered the place unlucky. One man had committed suicide and another died of cholera. The following are the names of managers of Hursingpore since it became a head factory:—C. Strachan, C. V. Argles, James Bluett, A. Inglis, Maxwell, Smith, J. S. Smith, E. Dalgleish, George Bloomfield, and others. Its present manager is C. Mackay (1905). The proprietors now are J. S. Smith M. Smith's estate, W. Crowdy's estate and F. H. Hollway. The Factory stands to the south-east of this district. I add an interesting account gleaned by Mr. C. Mackay from a very old servant of the factory. There may be some errors as to date, etc., but that might be expected.

In the years 1175 Fasli A.D. 1728 a factory called Dogarrah (the old Bowarrah) was built by Dr. Mackinnon on the north bank of the Noon river. He carried on the factory for some 13 years from 1175 to 1187 Fasli, but owing to some superstition of ghosts, etc., he was compelled to remove the factory from Dogarrah to Bowarrah in 1188 Fasli. Mr. John Peller built Bowarrah Factory and worked it for some years. After he left Mr. Hamilton took charge and worked it for some years when he made over the factory to Mr. John Hill, being succeeded by Mr. Mackay and he by Mr. Ogilvie, who managed for five years and died on 16th May 1836 and is buried in the garden at Bowarrah.

After this gentleman's death the factory was left without a European manager for three years and the leases of the villages expiring only the mokarrarie remained. The maliks having resumed all the teekdaries the place was looked after by a moonshee, a responsible amlah. In 1839 Mr. Mitchell of Haloquary (most likely John Mitchell) bought the factory, including Hursingpore from Mr. Ogilvie's heirs for Rs. 32,000 and he after a period of 6 months (? years) sold Bowarrah and Hursingpore to Mr. C. Strachan for Rs.

40,000. Mr. C. Strachan, who had been managing Shapore Mircha, made Hursingpore the head factory and Bowarrah became an outwork.

Strachan managed for some years, and made over charge to C. V. Argles, who built Rahimabad, the outwork of Hursingpore in 1267 Fasli. After Argles came A. Inglis, etc.

This factory was originally an outwork of Jeetwarpore Factory. The mokarrarie pottah is dated 1851, given to John Mackenzie by Kewul Doubay. The factory was built in 1852 by John F. Mackenzie (son of John Mackenzie). In 1877 the Jeetwarpore Concern was divided and Illmasnuggur became a head factory and fell to the share of W. Mackenzie, who sold in 1884 to Messrs. E. S. Llewhellin, M. N. MacLeod, and H. Manners. Illmasnuggur has one outwork, Masina which was built in 1888 by H. Manners. At Mr. E. S. Llewhellin's death in September 1899 his share was purchased by Messrs. M. N. MacLeod and H. Manners.

Illmasnuggur H. & S. J.

Mr. H. Manners is the present manager.

Japaha was built in 1841 by John Becher as an interloping factory. It stands in the Jumalabad talka and the mokarrarie was given to Becher by the present proprietor's father. The building of this factory caused great friction between John Becher and David Crawford, who then managed at Contai and into whose management dehat he (Becher) had interloped, *i.e.*, the Bikanpore dehat. Things went from bad to worse till David Crawford, in an unguarded moment, spoke of Becher as a *bad potatoe.* On this Becher called Crawford out (for the results *see* "Tirhoot and its Inhabitants of the Past"). In spite of all opposition Becher held his own and the factory became an established fact. Becher died in 1847-48 and

D. B. B.

the factory passed into Messrs. MacKillop Stewart and Co.'s hands. To the Japaha Concern was attached a saltpetre factory at Burhampoora, near Mozufferpore. After John Becher's death John Stalkart managed, followed by others, and when Mr. Sharply was manager the concern was sold to John F. Mackenzie. He sold Burhanpora Bungalow to John Martin Becher, a son of John Becher's as he found the Indigo lands that surrounded the Burhampora Bungalow to far off, and it did not pay to work the saltpetre. Mr. J. F. Mackenzie sold Japaha in about 1872 to Mrs. Begg, and on her death Messrs. H. Hudson, E. Hudson, G. Richardson and Mrs. Begg purchased Japaha as part of Bikanpore. Mr. G. Richardson now is manager. In 1906 a sugar factory was started in Japaha village, and is now working and making good sugar. The proprietors the same as above.

Jaintpore
H. E. A.
J

This was an interloping concern. It was built by H. E. Abbott in 1872-73. It was built in dehats claimed by Dooriah, Seriyah, Motipore, Contie, and Dowdpore factories. The late Mohunt Raja Ram Dass, owned a large tract of country where many villages stood, and as he was all powerful, the suffering factories had to grin and bear, and Jaintpore became an established factory in 1873. Its outworks, Teekaha, Nirghee, Pukri, and Godai were built in 1875-76, 1880 and 1884. The mokarrarie stands in the name of H. E. Abbott, who managed for the mohunt and built all the factories. On Chowdry Mohunt Raja Ram's death, his brother, Mohunt Ragoonath Dass, became proprietor, and Mr. H. E. Abbott continued to manage. The estate having run into debt difficulty was found in getting funds to carry on with. The Mohunt Raghoonath Dass elected to try a change of management and after flirting with many Mr. M. J. Wilson was given charge of the business Mr. W. Vipan managing under him. A debenture loan was floated by Messrs. Begg Dunlop and Company and all the Mohunt's private debts paid off. Mr. H. E. Abbott is now again managing Jaintpore Factory and the estate, Mr. Hugh Urquhart managing Teekaha, Pukri and Godai for Messrs. Begg Dunlop and Company.

Jeetwarpore H. & S. J.

This factory was built in 1203 Fasli corresponding with 1795-96 by Noel and Company. Mr. Johnson was manager when the factory was built. There is a mokarrarie pottah of Jeetwarpore, Mordeba, dated 5th December 1795, given by Babu Gujraj Sing and Gonesh Dutt Singh in favour of Mr. Johnson. After Mr. Johnson came John Harrington, who managed from 1810. He was followed by Mr. W. Sherman, who managed for some 40 years. Sherman was followed by John Mackenzie in 1848. The mark H. and S. (Hogg and Sherman) would note that Sir James Weir Hogg of the Honourable East India Company was once a proprietor. There are two graves in the garden at Jeetwarpore—one that of Thomas Sherman, who died on 20th September 1844, aged 24, and the other that of William Bampton Sherman, who died on 16th July 1848, aged 31. The concern was bought by John Mackenzie and John Beckwith in 1848. John Mackenzie sold his share, 8 annas, to his son, John F. Mackenzie and son-in-law, M. J. Wilson in 1856-57. When his son took up the management followed by Mr. M. J. Wilson in 1857-58, later on M. J. Wilson bought Mr. J. F. Mackenzie's 4 annas and Mr. W. M. Stewart, Mr. John Beckwith's 8 annas. On the failure of the Agra Bank in 1866, Mr. John F. Mackenzie purchased with his brothers the 16 annas of the concern. In about 1884 the concern was purchased by Sir W. B. Hudson, T. Lamb, and others, and Mr. A. MacIver, who also had a share, took up the management.

There is rather a good story of what *occurred* in Mr. Sherman's time. The factory was in difficulty for money and the ploughmen were much in arrears. Colonel Apperley, then in charge of the stud at Pusa, went over to pay Mr. Sherman a visit and the fattened calf was killed to feast the Colonel: but just as dinner was ordered, the ploughmen turned out and formed line between the cook room and the house and declared that they would not allow any dinner to pass into the house till they received some of their long promised pay. Threats and promises were of no avail, they would accept nothing but cash, and of that there was none in Sherman's possession. Fortunately Apperley had a few rupees in his pocket and these turned into pice, being distributed softened the hearts of the ploughmen who retired and allowed the long wished for repast to be carried to the dining room. This story was told me by Colonel Apperley himself, and we had a good laugh over it.

Mr. MacIver, late manager, had to retire from the management this year 1905, and Mr. Dalrymple Hay, now manages. Jeetwarpore has two outworks—Husowli built in 1857 and Doodporah built several years later. Rewari, an interloping factory, was built by one Mahomed Baker Khan in 1856. He or his wife, Mussamut Ushruf Ollnisca, sold to Usuff Artin Bey and others and they eventually to Messrs. E. S. Llewhellin and M. N. MacLeod. The place now belongs to Mrs. E. Llewhellin. Rewari was an interloping factory into Jeetwarpore dehat, and is now managed by Mr. M. H. Mackenzie.

Kewan or Bachour

This factory was in 1847 a part of the Pandoul Concern, though I believe it was some years before that time a separate concern. The mokarrarie pottah is dated 1199 Fusli and given to a Mr. Watt. The mokarrarie of Bhakwa, an outwork, is dated 1230 Fusli and given to Mr. Brown. One reason I have for saying that Kewan was under Pandoul management is that I know Mr.

John Mackenzie's brother, Francis H. Mackenzie, was an assistant under his brother and I see by the tombstone on his grave at Kewan that he died in 1830. In 1847-48 when I first visited Kewan or Bachour, Mr. Hubbard was sub-manager under John Gale. He left some time in 1848-49 and I think went to China, but I have lost sight of him since then. Kewan also worked sugar for a time. It is situated close up to the Nepaul boundary, and one has a splendid view of the Terai and the lower range of the Himalayas out of the verandah. This factory and the surrounding dehat was once famous for the breed of cattle which came from round about. Report said that one of the old manager's imported English stock into the country and let all the bull calves loose as Brahmini bulls and thus the class of cow and bullock improved. The strain of good blood has worn itself out and now I do not think the cattle from about there are much better than any other. There are four graves at Kewan in a bamboo tope near the factory. Two bear no inscriptions and on the other two are as follows:—

Sacred to the memory of Francis Humberston Mackenzie, third son of John Mackenzie, senior of Galson north Britain. Died on 16th September 1830, aged 21 years.

Here reposeth the remains of Kennedy Huggins, who departed this life on the 5th February A. D. 1836. Aged about 58 years.

If my memory serves me true. Lewis Cosserat, followed Hubbard as sub-manager, but there seems to be no record. Kewan or Buchour, not many years ago, came into the possession of the Maharajah of Durbhunga who bought the factory from G. N. Wyatt. The present manager is Mr. R. W. Royds Birch. The Maharajah of Durbhunga has built a fine palace at Rajnugger close to Kemna or Buchour Factory.

Khan Mirzapore R. C.

Also called Mhow was originally a large saltpetre factory which belonged to James Wilson. In about 1851-1852 there was a great fouzdari between Messrs. Foster Rogers and Company, an American firm of Calcutta who had a claim over the Mhow saltpetre works. T. Martin, assisted by his assistant, F. Wingrove, held the godown against Wilson when they were attacked by a big force and badly mauled. I do not remember the result of the case. It was tried by a Magistrate who was nicknamed by the natives Samuel Misal, because his order for everything was "Samil Missal," or place with the *records*. In 1855 Mr. Wilson took a small mokarrarie in a village near Mhow and built a couple of small vats in which he used to manufacture the few bighas of indigo he cultivated. The present Khan Mirzapore is built some distance from the Mhow saltpetre works. This factory stands very near the banks of the Ganges, which river is constantly on the move. A factory, Behri, built by Macnaghten and Olpherts was cut away by the Ganges in 1891 and another factory built by Flavell was shut up in 1899, and also another, Monier, built in 1893 by Flavell. Begum Serai used to be one of this group of factories; the original Begum Serai was cut away by the Ganges; it was built by W. M. Stewart in about 1864-5. The present Begum Serai was, I think, built by E. Macnaghten. Mr. D. MacLeod manages here for Messrs. Gillanders Arbuthnot and Company, and it is reported he is selling up the factory piece meal, as the proprietors do not wish to carry on the place. Khan Mirzapore belong to Mr. F. Rawlins and he is working the place.

Khopee B. R. K. K.

This factory was built as an interloping factory by J. C. Muir, in 1865. It stands between the Shahpore Oundi and the Chitwarrah dehat. The place did not seem to flourish during Muir's time. It eventually became the property of Babu Nundun Lall.

Kurhurri
C. Mc K.
K.

This factory was built in 1859 by George Smith, who was managing Shahpore Mircha; his assistant, Mr. E. C. Lamb, attended to the building, Lamb was sub-manager up to 1863, then F. Wilkinson. The factory was then sold to Messrs. W. Campbell and others. The factory changed hands among its original purchasers till at last it stood in the names of W. Campbell, 8 annas and M. N. McLeod and F. Wilkinson 8 annas. A few years ago Mr. Campbell having died and his share being in difficulties his son made over the factory to the mortgagees. The factory now belongs to M. N. MacLeod and F. Wilkinson's estates.

Kurnowl
A. J.
K.

Kurnowl Factory, also called by the natives Sahebgunge and Purbulputti. There stands a very old bazaar. It is often mentioned in the records from which I drew my preface. Sahebgunge was evidently a great mart for saltpetre and grain and being near the big Gunduk these commodities were easily shipped to Calcutta. Kurnowl Factory was built in 1803 by Mr. Finch, who also built Doorea where he was in 1793, having come to the country in 1778. See preface to this history. Monine, the outwork was built by John Howell in 1836 Tajpore by C. Gale in 1862, and Gowra in 1884 by G. Robertson. Kurnowl, until purchased by Mr. F. Murray in 1878 from Mr. L. Macdonald, was a sub-management under Dooria. The present bungalow was built by John Howell. The original bungalow stands to the north of the vats and is now used as a residence and kacherrie by the amlah. Shortly after F. Murray purchased he took in G. Robertson as a partner. Mr. F. Murray is now manager, 1905. It is strange that though the factory bears the mark A. J. (Arthur Jones) no one seems to remember him or what he had to do with the place. I remember Cox, who managed at Kurnowl and was there from the early thirties, telling me that

Arthur Howell, a son of John Howell, was called after Arthur Jones. After Cox, W. Daunt managed, Cox having followed J. Howell, Daunt succeeded Cox in about 1846. M. J. Wilson took over from Daunt in 1852-1853 and was followed by A. Inglis in about 1854. Then several others came in till F. Murray took charge. He went home and G. Robertson and others managed off and on F. Murray now, 1905, manages.

Mea Chupra. Mea Chupra was built by Sir W. B. Hudson and the Hon'ble Francis Byng in 1883. These gentlemen had a difference with Baboo Guzraj Sahai and took a mokarrarie in the Shahpore Mircha dehat. The factory was eventually bought by Mr. Rudstone Brown, and now I understand, belongs to his brother, H. Brown. It is managed by Mr. H. K. Grey, who has lately become a shareholder.

Moktapore H. & S. M. This factory was orginally an outwork of Jeetwarpore. Most of the old papers connected with the building of this factory were burnt, but I believe the place was built shortly after Jeetwarpore. In about 1877, it was bought from Messrs. Mackenzie by C. Hay Webb and others. It had one outwork, Chuckmaisie, built in about 1862, but this was lately divided off from Moktapore and has since been purchased by Mr. Rawlins. It belonged to the estate of the late Mr. Campbell. During the time Sherman was proprietor of Jeetwarpore I cannot find out who was at the outwork, Moktapore, but during John Mackenzie's proprietorship, Mr. B. Anderson was assistant. He was a very powerful Scotchman and did not hit it off with the natives, and when they did not carry out his orders he would, what he called, "fetch them a chip" which meant a blow as from a sledge hammer and down they would go and so he was generally in trouble. However, the natives got the better of him at last, for one day as he was riding along (this was at Sebnuggur, the outwork of Kumtoul Factory), a tailor who he had illused crept up behind him and caught him a blow over the eye with a *lathie.* From this Anderson lost the sight of one eye, which cooled him down considerably. Anderson died in 1857-1858 at Mozufferpore. Another out-work built by Arthur Butler and Company still remains to Moktapore at Kalianpore. There is a gravestone in the Moktapore compound to Mr. W. Fleming, dated 1836, and an old malik told Mr. C. H. W. Debb that he remembered that saheb being in charge for many years. This tallies with the age described as 40 on the tombstone.

Mohwol W. R. B. M.

This factory stands in the Motipore dehat, it was built by Hajee Syud M. Takee Khan. The village belonged to him. As far as I remember he built this factory with the concurrence of the proprietors of Motipore. I cannot give the date when Mohwol was built, but it was, I think, some time in eighteen hundred and sixty. There is a small factory called Chowrghatta built by Alli Nawab, a son of the late Nawab M. Takee Khan. This latter place was sold up shortly after its birth and I do not know if it still exists or not. Mr. W. Wilson is assistant at Mohwol under T. Barclay, 1907.

Muniarpore M.

This was built as an interloping factory in the Dulsing Serai dehat by the Mahtas, bankers of Mozufferpore. This was resisted by the Dulsing Serai Concern, but eventually they came to terms and a boundary fixed. Muniarpore was carried on as an indigo concern, but is now leased to a Calcutta firm for the growth of cotton. I have not been able to get the year in which the factory was built by Mr. Corryton, but it is of recent date. Mr. Follettt is managing for the Calcutta firm.

Munjoul and Sessowni
F. H. & Co., M.
F. H. & Co., S.

I cannot get much information as to when Munjoul and Sessowni were built or by whom. Natives say the bungalow was built by Mr. Moorhead, but I can get no date. Mr. P. Crump was there as manager and proprietor in 1847 and had been there some years before and his son, P. Crump, was at Sessowni then also. The outworks, Bisumpore, Bundwar, Gumereah, Sowri, Beerpore were built by F. H. Holloway. The first in 1881-82, second 1866, third 1870 and fourth 1878. There are two graves at Munjoul—one that of James Thomson, died 27th September 1843, aged 41, and the other Mrs. M. J. Smth, died 6th August 1855. She was a daughter of Mr. P. Crump, senior, who married Mr. J. S. Smith. There is also a grave at Beerpore to the memory of Mr. Lindsay, who died in 1883. Messrs. Baddeley, Cox, and others bought the concern in 1862 or thereabouts and eventually sold to F. H. Holloway, who had acquired a small share and was managing. After he gave up the management Mr. L. Crowdy managed and after him the management passed into several hands. Mr. E. Dalgleish was managing early in 1905 and had been manager for some time before but had to go home. Mr. Danby, a grandson of Mr. W. C. Baddeley, is now in charge. Old Mr. P. Crump had his own ideas as to indigo planting and did not like a thick crop. He is reported to have weeded out a part of his crop on one occasion when he thought it too thick. For more about P. Crump *see* "Tirhoot and its Inhabitants of the Past."

Motipore
D. B.
M.

Motipore was originally built by the Dutch in 1789, as a sugar factory. In 1816 it became one of a group of indigo factories owned by Messrs. Noel and Co. (*see* Contai Factory). There are no records to show when the outwork, Chucklorn, was built. In 1871 Thomas Fraser built Morarpur. James Cosseratt managed from 1839 to 1844, R. Cahill 1846 to 1852, and then David Brown 1853 to 1855, when C. Oman bought Motipore and managed till 1858-59, he sold out and A. McD. MacRae took up the management, followed by George Toomey in 1866, then M. Smith, James Stewart, and in 1870 by Frank Hamley who had to go home ill and died in England. From 1888 to 1892, Tom Barclay and his brother managed. The factory is now, 1905, managed by Tom Barclay. There is one grave in the Motipore Garden thus: "Sacred to the memory of Lucy, infant daughter of W. E. Cahill, Captain, 40th Regiment, B. N. I. and Anna Jane, his wife, who died 25th March 1850, aged 3 months." Captain Cahill was a son of old Mr. R. Cahill. I believe he retired from his regiment which was stationed at Dinapore not long before it mutinied there. Tatereah was an outwork of Motipore, but was sold to D. R. and A. Crawford in about 1852-53.

Munghulgurh L. McD. & Co.

Munghulgurh Factory was originally an outwork of Dowlutpore and was built in the fifties by W. C. Baddeley. The proprietors now are F. Murray, C. Mackay and the estate of the late E. M. Murray. This factory was built within the last fifty years and is comparatively new. It is now an independent and flourishing concern. Mr. E. M. Murray, who had managed for many years, died suddenly and is buried at Dowlutpore 1905. Present manager Mr. Finch.

Ottur W. S. O.

The original factory stood on the banks of the river Gunduk, and as it was gradually being washed away the proprietors started building a new factory on a lake some little distance from the old factory. The original factory was built on milkiat which was acquired direct from Government many years ago. The new indigo factory is also built on milkiat. Husna is the oldest outwork and was, when I first remember it in 1847, a sugar factory. Mahomedpore Factory, another outwork, was built after 1851-52. Ghoserama built in 1880-81 and Misrawlia, near Mahomedpore outwork, a few years later. Messrs. G. Swaine and Lethbridge bought Ottur Concern from Messrs. Gillanders Arbuthnot and Co. in the seventies. Geo. Swaine managed for several years and was succeeded by R. F. Lethbridge, then A. MacIver, these managed for short periods. R. Hudson succeeded MacIver and has managed ever since off and on. While he was away in the nineties V. Hickley managed. Sugar operations were revived in 1900 and the property was transferred to the India Development Co., Ld., in 1904. Ottur Concern dehaut covers an area of some 83,000 bighas. Ottur is a very old factory and was in existence certainly in the beginning of 1800. Pooprie Factory was connected with it in early days. Mr. Sterndale was one of the oldest managers of Ottur I have heard mentioned. He must have been there before 1830, for Mr. John Mackenzie, who was an assistant under Mr. Sterndale, was manager at Pundoul in the thirties. I see by the collectorate records that in about 1793, Mr. James Gentil, who came to India in 1773, was manager of Ottur. After Sterndale I do not know who came, but in 1847 Mr. Holloway managed, succeeded by Ferrier; then for a short time James from Chupprah then Ogilvie, who very soon left Indigo (about 1851) for the Army. Then came W. Garstin, followed by Young; then J. MacRae and others till G. Swaine purchased. A daughter of Mr. Sterndale's married Sir Cecil Beadon, Lieutenant-Governor of Bengal.

A. M. Delasaire, a Frenchman, had something to do with Ottur in 1847-48 and was very keen on sugar manufacture; he dropped a good deal of money. Tom Martin was at Husna in 1847-48 with Monsieur Delasaire. The last I heard of Delasaire was that he was living in Switzerland, but that was many years ago. There is a good story told of Monsieur Delasaire. He was not overfond of soap and water; his wife persuaded him to indulge in a bath and this is what she described as having happened. Delasaire, he say, very brave I go to bath. Very good I say and he go. I hear plenty water fall on the ground. So I go and see. What I see, ah Delasaire pour the water on the ground. Ah Delasaire you cunning!!

Ottur Factory in the past used to build a *tazia* for the Moslem ryots living round, but that has been stopped for many years now.

Peerakpore M. W. H.

This was an interloping factory and was built in the Ottur dehat by Chummun Lall and Nuttoo Lall Chowdry, bankers of Mozufferpore. The factory was first put down at a village called Rowna, but this place was found to flood and only lasted one year, 1866, after that it was abandoned and Peerakpore built in 1867. Lewis Baptiste built Rowna and Ellis Peerakpore. Ellis managed for the Chowdries for some years, then James Stewart, after him Exshaw, W. Llewhellin, John Grant and H. Holloway. After the failure of the Chowdry bankers the factory was bought by Henry Hudson and managed by one of his sons for some time. Mr. W. J. Ross is the present manager, 1905.

Rajkund W. & M. M.

I can gain very little information as to the early days of Rajkund or Awrai Factory as the natives call it. A rather dilapidated cash book, dated 1817-19, shows that K. Huggins (I suppose the man who died at Kemna Buchour, in 1836) managed and that he drew his cash from Kumtoul. So that most likely Rajkund was an outwork of Kumtoul Concern in those days. During Mr. Huggins' time they grew indigo for the sake of the seed. Boats as well as carts were used to carry Indigo to the factory. In 1841-42 Lewis Cooke managed. His assistant, was Menzies, a very smart youngster, but unfortunately he took to drink and was sent home to his friends in Guernsey in 1849. William Forest was also assistant and died of cholera in October, 1845, aged 17 years. He is buried in the garden. He died when Andrew Crawford was manager. If I remember rightly Cooke quarrelled with his employers and left. He tried to establish a factory at Sydpore in 1845, but being opposed he sold his claim over Sydpore to Rajkund and the place worked as an outwork from Rajkund, but was eventually abandoned. In 1847-48, Williamson was assistant to Andrew Crawford; he was supposed to know something about sugar and either he or his cousin composed the sarcastic lines about sugar, beginning. "The Lion King stretched out his hand" and talked of cheapness of labour and richness of land (*see* "Tirhoot and its Inhabitants of the Past.") This was meant as a cut at Mr. Robinson, who pretended to know a lot about sugar. Williamson was followed by James Begg in 1851. D. H. MacFarlane followed A. Crawford and J. Begg. In 1852 C. Swaine managed from Contai and P. MacFarlane was assistant, and in 1853-55, J. S. Begg, P. MacFarlane and D. H. MacFarlane, all had a look in. In 1855-56 C. Swaine superintended and W. Oman managed for a short time. Then Harry Brown came in and managed to his death with the exception of a short time when he was sent up to Cawnpore in 1858 to look after Begg Christi's indigo seed business. While there he had to fly for his life from the Bareilly mutineers and seek refuge in the entrenchments. Wilkinson, another assistant at Rajkund, broke his neck riding in a steeple or hurdle race in Calcutta. He was followed by A. Grant. Then when Belsund and Rajkund became the property of J. F. and W. Mackenzie in about 1870 W. Campbell became their manager and managed till 1873. In 1874 A. R. H. MacEwen managed. In 1857, H. Spenser managed under John Begg;

he left in 1860, when W. Riddell took charge. The factory now belongs to Mr. M. H. McKenzie, is partially closed as an indigo factory. It is managed now, 1905, by Mr. M. H. Mackenzie, who pays the place occasional visits from Rewari Factory.

Rooni, Sydpor, J. M. & Co., S. R.

Rooni Sydpore was built in 1862-63 by Mr. R. P. Irvine. This factory interloped on the Belsund and Rajkund dehat, and after a good deal of fighting a boundary was arranged about September 1865. It stands near the site of Sydpore Factory, which Mr. Cooke tried to build when he left Rajkund. Mr. Irvine was followed by Mr. A. H. Rennie in 1889. He, poor fellow, was killed on boardship going home and was buried at Suez. *See* "Tirhoot and its Inhabitants of the Past." Mr. J. H. Smith took over charge from Rennie in 1883-84, and on his leaving in 1891 Mr. E. Stevens took charge, followed by Mr. De Vitse, the present manager, in 1903.

Shahpore O., J. F. S.

This factory again has no records to show and I can only refer my readers to "Tirhoot and its Inhabitants of the Past" for any information I can give them. Shahpore O. was built in 1790 by Joseph Finch, the head of the Finch family. In 1847-48 Justin Finch managed, succeeding his brother Frederick. Justin died in 1861, and was buried at Monghyr; his body was exhumed some years after and buried by the side of other members of the Finch family at Patna. After Justin Finch's death Frederick came back from England and took charge, Mr. M. J. Wilson having managed during the interval. F. Finch brought out C. Strachan, an old friend, but he getting into bad health returned to England, giving charge to M. Lloyd, who had been an assistant in the concern for many years. He managed the place for many years after to the great benefit of the concern. The management was then made over to W. Finch, a son of Joseph Finch and one of the heirs. After him came his brother-in-law Carshore, I do not exactly know to whom the place now belongs, but Mr. E. Abbott is managing, I believe, for Messrs. Kilburn and Co. Poor W. Finch died suddenly on the day of his daughter's wedding at Shahpore Oondie Factory and is, I believe, buried there. John Beċehr, who died in 1847-48 when on his way from Calcutta, is also buried in the garden. The lands belonging to the Factory are being sold off piece meal. A melancholy end to a fine old concern.

Shahpore Mircha, S. C. McK.

The mokararie pottah of this factory is dated 1799. It is on a one rupee stamp and bears the seal of the Kazi. Like so many of the other old Factories in Tirhoot there are no old records to show names of managers. The furthest back I can go and that is hearsay is that Cooke was manager in the early thirthies and James Cox assistant under him. The next manager must have been Drummond, and it was he who made Kalipersaud (whose wife is the present proprietress) *moonshee*. After Drummond came Sam Johnson, and he was managing in 1847, but died in 1848 when W. C. Baddeley took charge. Then C. Strachan, then W. C. Baddeley, again followed by M. J. Wilson, George Smith, and others till James Smith took charge on George Smith's death and eventually bought in in partnership with Kalipersaud. Byng and others purchased a share after and Byng managed. Then there was a quarrel and Musoonat Januk Koer, Kalipersaud's widow, became sole proprietress. Old Kalipersaud never forgot Drummond's having promoted him for many years after when Drummond was in distress, he asked me to offer Drummond some Rs. 10,000 which he had idle in the factory to use and repay him when better times came. Besides graves of children there are two graves without inscriptions and no one seems to know about them.

Then there is one sacred to the memory of Samuel Johnson, who died on 7th August 1848, in the 73rd year of his age. Another to the memory of George Smith, who died on 25th July 1862, aged 46. I do not know who owned Shahpore Mircha before the Tirhoot Association of London bought it, when they dissolved partnership in 1856-57 or thereabouts, Kalipersaud and James Smith purchased. I remember Kalipersaud telling me of a man who managed in his younger days. I cannot remember his name, but he was supposed to be a first-rate man, but Kali remarked he had one fault and that was every now and then he would retire to his room with a case of gin and would never be seen again till the case was finished. He was as Kali said "*Nehait Husiar, O burra zubberdust.*" E. D. M. Exshaw took up the management in 1895 and still manages for the present proprietor Babu Judoo Nundun Sahaie. This Factory has not been worked as an Indigo Concern for the last two years, Babu Jadoo Nundun Sahaie the present proprietor is the adopted son of the late Babu Gujraj Sahaie. A fine Hospital was founded at Baglie where the family reside. It was opened by Mr. L. Hare (now Sir L. Hare, Lieutenant-Governor of Eastern Bengal), when Collector of Tirhoot. The Hospital is called the "Gujraj Hospital." It was opened in 1895, the Hospital is endowed with sufficient property to support it for this act the Babu was thanked by Government and would have been made a Ray Bahadur had he lived a few months longer. Babu Judoo Nundun and the local committee take a deep interest in the working of the Gujraj Hospital where much good work has been done and an average of about 10,000 patients treated annually.

Sirsiah Indigo Factory was built in 1883 by Babus Mathoora and Hunooman Dass of Mozaffarpore in Sirsiah Buzrug and Mr. Birch was appointed as Manager. It was an interloping factory in the Kanti and Daudpore Dehats.

In the beginning of 1902 Rai Gunga Prashad Singh, of Durbhunga, got a decree over Mathoora and Hunooman Dass and sold up and purchased under their decree.

In 1901 Kanti Factory took over the place from Rai Gunga Prashad Singh in settlements of a decree for rents.

The factory buildings were knocked down and all the machinery taken to Kanti.

In 1905 Sirsiah was leased for 5 years to Behar Planters Association Ld., as a Research Station and is carried on with the Bengal Government grant by an advising Committee.

A considerable sum has been sunk in equipping an up-to-date Laboratory and Factory. The Staff consists of Messrs. C. Bergtheil (in charge) R. V. Briggs, J. G. Turnbull and R. Macgregor and already some practical and sound results have been obtained, and the future only can show what good and permanent benefit the work carried on there will be to the Industry.

This is another old factory where no records are to be
Surryiah found. Native traditions give Zeigler as the
C. K. M. Z. C. man who built Surryiah. He was a planter in about James Gibbon's time and owned Setalpore Factory, near Sonepore, in the Sarun district. In 1847-48 or thereabouts the late Edward Studd managed Surryiah. For further particulars *see* "Tirhut and its Inhabitants of the Past" and the history of Dholi Concern.

The Surryiah concern now belongs to the Maharajah of Durbhunga and the estate of the late George Llewhellin. It was managed for many years by the late E. S. Llewhellin, followed by R. Summers. It is now managed by Mr. Falkner. The only grave at Surryiah is to the memory of John Livingstone Neale, who died in July 1866. After writing the above the manager of Surryiah, who had been searching for information, very kindly sent me the following. First mokararie pottah was dated 1802, for 25 bigahs of land in Mouza Karara Dakli Rohna (Sirkar Hajeepore) from Chowdry Bhairo Dutt, of Bassantpore, in favour of Mr. Page, dated 1802. In 1811 Mr. Boldvaite got another 15 bighas of *Brit* land as mokararie from Divaladhari Misser. It appears Messrs. Colvin and Co. held the factory at one time but how they acquired it there is no record to show. They, however, sold to Mr. Leonard Zeigler, of Setalpore, in 1826. In 1830 Mr. Zeigler leased the factory to Mr. Henry Hill for one year and afterwards sold it to Messrs. Henry Hill and Dr. Charles Mackinnon in 1831 for Rs. 1,40,000 and subsequently Mr. H. Hill sold his 8 annas to Dr. C. Mackinnon, who became 16 annas proprietor. In the same year Dr. C. Mackinnon sold 4 annas to Mr. Fergusson. In 1835 Mr. Fergusson resold to Dr. C. Mackinnon for Rs. 45,000. In 1836 Dr. C. Mackinnon built Azizpore on 12 bighas of land acquired from Bhola Jha. In 1845 Mr. E. Studd purchased Coalporah village from Dr. C. Mackinnon for Rs. 50,000. Coalporah outwork was built, in 1835 by F. Collingridge, in this year Surryiah, Azizpore, and Coalporah with Dholi factories were leased to Captain W. Sloane for one year. The following are the managers from 1853, *viz.*:—E. Studd, H. Hudson 1856, E. D. Urquhart 1864, H. MacDonald 1869, who built Mahomedpore outworks, acquiring the land from Babu Pirti Singh and others of Gariba. In 1879 Mr. C. W. Thomas managed and in 1880. Henry Studd, son of Edward Studd. On the sale of Surryiah to the Maharajah of Durbhunga and Mr. G. E. Llewhellin, Mr. G. Llewhellin took charge then in 1882 E. S. Llewhellin followed by H. Manners, E. S. Llewhellin in 1885, R. B. Summers in 1897. E. Marsham in 1899, R. B. Summers again in 1900, and J. M. Falkner in 1905, who is still managing, Karnejee, another outwork, was built about 1883-84, but there is no record to show this. Mr. C. Bell is now managing 1907.

Singia G. I. Co. S.

This factory is interesting as it dates back to 1791 and originally belonged to the Dutch. The mokararie pottah being written in the Dutch character had to be sent to Hamburg for translation before it could be used in court. I now add an abstract of information kindly put at my service by Mr. Gordon, the present manager (1905): In 1791 the land on which Singia (or as the natives call it Lallgunge after a big bazaar in the vicinity) stands, *viz.*, some 14 bighas was put up for sale by the Dutch East India Company on the 29th of July 1791 and bought by a Bengali merchant by name Juggernath Sircar. The land was sold by an auctioneer called Hendrick Alleright Dalle for Rs. 100 sicca. In 1705 to 1801 it was sold by Juggernath Sircar to Mr. John Colliss on the 11th January 1795 at Patna for Rs. 435 as shown in the Bengali endorsement on the Dutch deed signed by Juggernath Sircar and witnessed by R. Dalatin. In the Statistical Account of Bengal by W. W. Hunter, B.A., LL.D., Vol. XIII, Tirhoot and Chumparun will be found "Singia" indigo factory situated close to the embankment of the big Gunduk river was originally a settlement of the Dutch East India Company for manufacturing saltpetre and was one of the first factories occupied by Europeans in Tirhoot. As early as 1812 the manager wrote that it had been the property of Europeans from time immemorial. In 1801-1803 it was sold by John Colliss to Mr. James Naysmith at Bankipore on the 21st March 1801, for Rs. 750 sicca. This is shown by endorsement on Dutch deed signed by John Colliss and witnessed by James Fallerly and Mathew Moran and also by an English deed of sale on stamped paper signed John Collier and witnessed by H. W. Wareham, junior, and Mathew Moran. Registered in the office of zilla Tirhoot on Saturday, 13th June 1801, at 3 o'clock in the day and entered in page 297, etc., etc. It was sold by James Naysmith to

James Gibbon at Patna on 18th January 1803 for Rs. 750 sicca. Singia consisted of three factories in 1824 to 1835, *viz.*, Singia, Bhyropore, Anarpore, and was sold by James Gibbon described as planter at Calcutta to John Abbott in trust for Mesrs. Alexander and Co., of Calcutta, in 1824. H. Fizgerald as of Singia obtained a transfer of all right and title in Chayton Pursa on the 15th December 1828 from Joseph Simon Finch. A boundary agreement was made between Jalalpore Joseph Simon Finch and Chayton Pursa. H. Fitzgerald 12th January 1829.

H. Fitzgerald seems almost immediately after this to have conveyed Chayton Pursa to Messrs. Alexander and Co., 23rd and 24th February 1829. In 1736 a boundary agreement was made between Chayton Pursa by H. Fitzgerald and Ramkolah. This is shown by an old parchment deed dated 31st December 1836, which recites that the above conveyance had been made and also that on the 23rd and 24th February 1829 Harold Fitzgerald of Singia and Eliza, his wife, had conveyed to John Abbott in trust for Messrs. Alexander and Co., factory of Chayton Pursa in 1835-1836 all right and title in Singia. Bhyropore, Anarpore belonging to H. Fitzgerald were made over to assignee for insolvent estate of Messrs. Alexander and Co. The assignee to the insolvent estate of Messrs. Alexander and Co. sold Singia, Bhyropore, Anarpore, and Chayton Pursa to George Folly Hodgkinson, merchant, Calcutta, for Rs. 50,000 sicca in 1836-1837. In 1837 to 1852 George Folly Hodgkinson sold Singia. Bhyropore Anarpore, and Chayton Pursa, *i.e.*, the Singia Concern to Richard Austen Fitzgerald for Rs. 50,000 on 7th July 1837

From mortgage deeds to Gisborne and Co., dated 29th June 1837, it appears that R. A. Fitzgerald owed them Rs. 30,754 and from Singia deeds, dated 1838-39, it appears he only mortgaged four-sixteenth of Singia. Between this and 1848 there are transactions between Gisborne and Co. and Baring Brothers and between 1848-1852 there are five deeds leasing and releasing several factories including Singia (described as indigo and sugar between Baring Brothers and J. Farm and Co.)? In 1852 the Ganges Indigo Company was formed as from 1st October 1852. Besides Gisborne and Co. and Baring Brothers a Mr. George Brown is a party to the document and seems to have sold an interest in some factories in Bhauglepore, Dehri, and Allahabad, Hattiousti and Singiah, Tirhoot, to the people belonging to the Company. The Ganges Indigo Company consisted of 110 shares. The following were the shareholders:—

Baring Brothers	55	shares,	Rs.	27,500
T. M. Gisborne	34	,,	,,	17,000
John Dougal	12	,,	,,	6,000
George Dougal	9	,,	,,	4,500
		Total	,,	55,000

The Company went into partnership for five years. Gisborne and Co., were appointed managers in India. Singia was described in the schedule as consisting of four factories and 40 vats. Mr. James Gibbon, mentioned as a purchaser of Singia in 1803, is the same as afterwards had charge of the Burhamporah Saltpetre works in 1847-1848. He had a large family of daughters and I believe only one son who was wounded during the Mutiny and died. Old Mr. James Gibbon, I believe, died at Burhamporah, near Doudpore Factory, Tirhoot. Of his daughters one married John Anderson of Hatowrie (*see* "Tirhoot and its Inhabitants of the Past.") One James Cosseratt, one Pell Cosseratt, and one Colonel C. Smith. There were other daughters, but I forget who they married. Old Mrs. Gibbon lived to a good old age. I remember seeing her when she was about 90, and it was wonderful what an active old lady she was. Here is a translation of the Dutch document, but it seems very imperfect. "The witness whereof appeared before us the Acting Secretary of the Honourable Council at this place, James Vonder Brock, and made known to us that on the 29th of the past month of July by order of the Honourable Isac Fitsough, member of the Defence Council at Baland and Director at this settlement with the aforesaid member of the Court, of Judicature, had been publicly put up for sale to the highest bidder the undermentioned pieces of ground the property of the Dutch East India Company, *viz.*:—First, the factory at Singia, consisting of a house building of two stories with two halls above as well as below, two rooms and verandah, battle-khanas, cook-room, peons' house, and two godowns. Second, the appertaining grounds near the house in 13 bighas bearing summer house standing on it and a number of fruit and other trees as also two tanks. Third, another appertaining piece of ground containing one bigha and two cottahs planted with divers trees over which goes a public road, so that these two pieces of ground contain 14 bighas and two cottahs. Fourth, a piece of ground half a mile from Singia called Naginabagh and contains two and a half bighas. That all these parcels be sold by the auctioneer Hendrick Alleright Dalle upon and for account of a Bengal merchant Juggernath Sircar for a sum of Rs. 100 sicca rupees. He also for the Company declaring having been by his aforesaid quality expressly authorized for it and therefore in the name of the Honourable Director and Council for and were during the said general Dutch East India Company to own over and transfer the right of property of which the said Company has been in the mentioned possession to and for use of the aforesaid by Juggernath Sircar, who by the said public purchase became the lawful proprietor of it and for which having duly paid the sum of one hundred sicca rupees do promise therefore in the name aforesaid this transfer at all times to free and indemnity at the place where it ought to be done. Actum Hooghly in Bengal this 29th day of October 1791—Signed H. Demaffe, C. J. Van Neorap.

Of the Singia outworks Nawada was built in 1871, Chukdowlut 1864, Ponra in 1890. Bhyropore stands down to the east of Hajeepore, near the Ganges and was shut up many years ago. Chayton Pursa, a factory on the west side of the big Gunduk in the Sarun district, has passed into other hands.

The following tomb stones and inscriptions are to be found at Singia:—To the memory of Eliza Fitzgerald, died 27th May 1827. Mr. George Dolly, died July 1828. Mrs. Eliza Fitzgerald, died 28th June 1880. Edward Fitzgerald died 4th October 1881, Barbara Finch, died 9th February 1840. Henry James Neale, died 5th November 1864, Mark Lines, died 28th April 1900.

In 1847-1848 or later the Singia Concern was placed by the Ganges Indigo Company, under the late Edward Studd's superintendence. It was afterwards purchased by W. Riddell, F. Collingridge, and Dr. Booth and was under several successive managers. It is now (1905) managed by Mr. Gordon. Since then the Factory has been sold up piece meal and is practically shut up 1907.

Tatareah.

Tatareah was originally under Motipore. It stood to the north of the Boer Gunduk and not far from the Bagmatti. It became a separate concern in 1853-54, when it was purchased by D. R. Crawford and A. Crawford. I can find no record as to when the factory was built, but it is among the old ones. It is here that in the early 1800 in one of those mad frolicks planters went in for, they set fire to a man I think called "James" by pouring a bottle of spirits over him and setting him alight which killed him. There was an outwork near the Bagmatti river now closed. I forget the name. Bala, an outwork near the Boer Gunduk, was built by T. O. B. Norman in 1880. Andrew Crawford took up the management shortly after the purchase of the factory but he died of cholera in 1857. Shortly after his death his brother, David, came out and James Smith was installed as manager. When James Smith left, the factory was sold to Bullen and eventually to G. Swaine and Lethbridge. Then Mrs. Power, *nee* Miss Alice Swaine, became proprietress with the Macqueens, Norman, and A. W. Wyatt. Mrs. Power finally parted with all her share. W. Macqueen managed for many years and then retired home. W. King came in lately as manager and now B. S. Hickey is manager in 1905. There are only two graves with inscriptions—(1) to the memory of George Medicott, who died 19th October 1842, aged 43; (2) to the memory of Andrew Crawford, who died 30th June 1857, aged 42.

Urneah.

Urneah was originally an outwork of Shahpore Oondi. It was built by Justin Finch in the early fifties. It was sold not many years ago to Babu Nundun Lall, who owns the village the factory stands on, *viz.*, Jhandaha. Urneah stands to the north-west of Shahpore Oondi, and to the west of the Tal Bareila, that fine piece of water which is crowded with every description of wild duck and thousands of snipe. The Tal is so long that a shot fired at one end is scarcely audible at the other. The shooting is done from dug outs and sportsmen often bring home grand bags. The native shikari with his matchlock has, however, made the birds very wild.

I find I have not recorded Pundoul, Nurharh, Joynuggur, or Kumtoul. All these factories belong to the Maharajah of Durbhunga. There are no records as far as I remember, but what I give from memory which does not date back much further than 1847. Pundoul existed well back into the thirties, for we know Kemna or Buchaur was working then as an outwork of Pundoul. John Gale put down a good part of the concern into sugarcane in 1845 or thereabouts. John Gale sold to G. N. Wyatt, he, Gale, having I think bought out R. Cahill's estate share. After John Gale left, his two sons, John and Marmaduke, followed each other as managers. Then Wyatt bought and sold to the Maharajah of Durbhunga. I can find no records of who built Narharh. Natives say that a Mr. Long took a mokararie in Narharh in 1825, when the village belonged to the Rajah of Tirhoot. It was working as a sugar factory in 1847-48, when it was managed by L. Cosseratt. Joynaggur was also working as a sugar factory, managed by James Cosseratt, but both these concerns had been indigo factories before sugar started. Narharh afterwards fell into the hands of John M. Becher and others and then became the property of Durbhunga, who had large landed properties round about. Joynaggur also became Becher's, but before then Mr. A. Christian built a house there; he was then doing a big timber trade, selling sleepers to the E. I. Railway. Kumtoul was purchased in about 1848 by Mr. James, Wilson and then was bought by Mr. George Anderson from Mr. James Wilson's estate in 1856-57. It after that became the Rajah's property, and when Mr. George Anderson retired from the country and Durbhunga purchased the place from him, the late Maharajah gave Mr. George Anderson a handsome pension, which he enjoyed till his death a few years ago. This pension was given in recognition of Anderson's services as manager to the Raj during the minority of the two young Rajahs. Of the above factories, Narharh and Joynaggur still do indigo in a small way as also Pundoul. But Ibelieve Kumtoul has shut up as an indigo factory and is kept purely as a zemindari. Mr. Summers manages Pundoul and Mr. Birch Kewan, or Buchour. I do not exactly know who are at Narharh or Joynaggur, but the indigo from Joynaggur comes to Narharh. Kumtoul we know was where Mr. John Anderson used to be, but we have no record who built it. Before 1845 a Mr. Richardson managed; he had been at Kumtoul for some years and was a proprietor, but had to leave in about 1846. He saw a good deal of this country and had a son and several daughters. One married Bob Taylor and one Guinness, a relation of the Irish brewers. The son got into the English army, served through the Sikh war. The Tommies called him "Black Daniel," but at one of the battles and when the regiment got into a tight place, he is reported to have rushed to the front and called out "*Who'll follow Black Daniel?*" and with a roar of applause the men flew after him.

The following factories have been completely shut up and some of them hardly exist: Amoih, where old Mr. Lethbridge (*see* "Tirhoot and its Inhabitants of the Past" used to command the show and lead a peaceful life after his experiences as a middy at Trafalgar. Jamoih, where Arthur Crooke hoped to make a fortune but never managed to get his sugar machinery across the sands of the Bagmatti. It is all buried in the sand there to this day. Pooprее, the factory that in about 1835 was classed as one of the finest in Tirhoot, as by a memo. made in 1830 or so which was shown to the writer in 1859. The estimated value being much above any other factories in the district. In those days men looked upon low lands as the best. They gave it a scrape with the plough and sowed a few seers of indigo seed per bigha; if the season was dry it meant a fortune, if wet the *dhan* crop paid for rent and the seed and perhaps gave a small profit. Nawada, where poor old John Anderson died of a broken heart. as his old servant had failed him in helping him with money to buy the place, is now a ruined and shut up factory. There is no trace as to who built it, but many tried it and struck on rocks and were wrecked. Beerpore and Balaha and one or two other small places cease to exist except in name. I often wonder if the ghost of old George Mitchell or Alfred Tripe are to be seen at night wandering among the ruins of Amoih, where they passed so many years of their youth, or does Joseph Tripe's spirit moon about the remains of Dynechappra, where he lived for so long before he was called away to ioin the great majority. Dynechappra was an old factory; it is near Majorgunge, the old military station on the Nepal boundary. The old sentry boxes are there still and the wells. There is also the ruins of several of the officers' bungalows and mess house. The graveyard, which had been much neglected, was put into repair some years ago by Government, but a number of tablets had been removed. For a memo. of the few old tombstones existing, *see* "Doomra Factory." Mr. F. Collingridge, who managed Dynechappra in the thirties died in 1905, aged 91. A fine specimen of an old English gentleman. I think I have given the history of nearly all factories in Tirhoot, excepting Burgong *alias* Bouchoulie *alias* Hirnie. I believe this place with its outwork, Pie, were built by Mr. Alexander Drummond Mitchell, who died at Hatti-Oustee in 1845. He built a sugar factory near Hirnie called Bisereah which has been closed many years. The Factory Hernie was closed when I came to Tirhoot, but in the fifties was bought and re-opened by Mr. Lauchlin MacDonald, who, after a good deal of fighting and worry, managed to get a cultivation. He sold towards the end of the fifties, the factory passing into several hands and not doing much good to any one. It now belongs to the brothers Crowdy, who have wisely elected to make it into a zemindari, and as the factory possesses valuable khastkari zeerats and grows fine tobacco and other crops it should pay. To the east of the outwork, Pie, there is a plain for miles as far as the eye can see which is used for grazing cattle and half the poor conditioned cattle of Tirhoot go there during the hot weather to get a little grass.

Ryam used to be an outwork of Pundoul Factory and has been bought by Mr. Daubeny, who still grows indigo there. Tewarah or Burrarie and Munkowlie its outworks were purchased for a small sum of money by Messrs. H. Hollway and K. Shortt and they are working these as zemindaries. Munkowlie has been sold to a native. Tewarrah is an old factory, but who built it I cannot say; one Paddy Medlicott was there in the early thirties. He died in 1842. In 1847 it was purely sugar, though there were indigo vats also. The sugar machinery was put down by Mr. Robinson; the engine was an enormously powerful one which planters round named *Goliath of Gath*, while the engine at Kumtoul was called Rattletrap and another Blowhard. A place called "Monkey" was another outwork of Tewarrah for sugar, but it shut up long ago. A new outwork for indigo was lately built at Tewarrah, but I do not know what has become of it, if it is working or shut up. Thurma is another factory I have not named. It was in olden days an indigo and afterwards a sugar factory. It was attached to Dholi at one time and became a separate factory some years ago when it was purchased by C. Hay Webb. It was then bought by Nickolls, to whom it still belongs. It stands to the north of Suckri Factory, an outwork of Dholi. Paharpore and Banday, interloping factories built by Teg Ali and his brothers flourished for several years, but are now almost extinct. Bokraha or Chucksecunder was built by the late Mr. M. Lloyd. I believe it has now closed as an indigo factory and lapsed into its old position as zemindari. After Mr. M. Lloyd's death his heirs sold the property, which was bought by Babu Vishnath Persad Mahta, who kept it as an indigo factory for a short time, but treats it as a zemindari;

now I believe cotton has been attempted there, but the Calcutta firm who leased it were met by the good old Tirhoot *lattee* and had to beat a retreat. Pokerairah Factory built by Abdul Ali and after bought by Ray Gunga Persad is also shut up and worked as a zemindari. Begoo Serai was purchased by James Hennessey in 1864, from Lala Ram Nareen Singh. He, James Hennessey, sold to F. H. Hollway in 1869, who continued sole proprietor until the property was sold to C. H. Crowdy a few years ago and he sold to Mr. L. O'Reilly who at present is proprietor and manager. Niagong was purchased by L. J. Crowdy and C. J. Feron from Roy Luchmipal Singh, Bahadur. L. Crowdy in 1892 purchased Mr. C. J. Feron's share and sold the whole concern to Mr. R. J. Carruthers. This place is, I understand, now closed. If I have left out any factory I hope my readers in the *Indian Planters Gazette* will put me right. If I have omitted anything of interest or if any one can give me any data where I have failed to get them I need not say how obliged I will be for information. Many have given me great help and I thank them. I yet hope to succeed in making this as perfect a history of factories as one can expect from the meagre records to be found, but I must be helped.

This ends my History of Tirhoot Factories and I will begin on Sarun Factories in my next. But before I begin on them I would like to make the following corrections and additions; Contai and Motipore were bought in 1866 as one concern by K. MacLeod and James Cox, 8 annas each; of this Cox gave G. Toomey, senior, 2 annas, George Toomey, senior, was then manager of Motipore. Tom Martin went to manage Contai about this time or a little later. Then Toomey, senior, went to Contai, being succeeded at Motipore by Maxwell Smith, who was succeeded by James Stewart and he was succeeded by Tom Fraser, one of the present proprietors of Motipore. The old outwork of Contai, Ragaie, is nearly as old as the head factory; there are three graves in the compound of Regaie, one to the memory of Charles Holman Swaine, who died in 1845, another to Alexander Mitchell, who died in 1843; on a third grave there is no inscription, but the natives say a man, called *Necknam* Saheb, who was a planter visitor, was killed by a Brahmini bull which charged his dog-cart, upsetting it and killing him on the spot. The name of Johnson will be noticed as having been at many factories and I find that he was at Dowlatpore in 1837 just fitting in between John Brown and R. Ronald. A friend of mine writes me as follows:—"A Mr. and Mrs. Johnson are buried near Tollygunge, Calcutta; they died about 100 years ago; he is noted as having owned an indigo factory in Tirhoot. Can he be the same man?" Begoo Serai was built by Hennessey some years ago and became part of Munjoul. But was sold by the concern and bought lately by the brothers Crowdy who again sold, it is being worked, I understand, as a zemindari. Purorie or Monjie, another shut up factory, was built by F. Collingridge and Dr. Macnamara in the Doulutpore Dehat. There was a good deal of unpleasantness and fighting in court over it; Baddeley was very angry, but could do nothing. The place has since died a natural death. I would strongly recommend to my readers who take an interest in the statistics of the districts to read with this the Statistical Account of Bengal by W. W. Hunter, B.A., L.D., compiled by W. A. Mackie, C.S., Vol. XIII., Tirhoot and Chumparun. This book can be had from Trubner and Co., London. It was lent to me by a friend and I have found it very interesting and useful. I see mentioned in it that Bowarrah was worked by Messrs. Fich and Schum in 1793, and it goes on to say that ten years after Mahomedpore, Balsor (Belsund?) Pipra, Dulsing, Serai, Jeetwarpore, Tewarrah, Kumtoul came to life. Before these Daudpore, Suryah and Dhoolie—worked by William Orby Hunter, Duria by Mr. Finch and Shahpore by Mr. Purvis—existed. Chitwarh, Pupri, Shahpore, Oondie were started in 1792. About them the Collector of Tirhoot received orders that no European was to hold land. until he had received permission of the Governor-General in Council.

The following will also be found in *The Statistical Account* written in 1877 :—" Under the heading *Capital* will be found an estimate of the annual outlay of the factories in Tirhoot. " It is difficult to foretell the future of indigo. The practical command of the market which Indian indigo has at present, depends on no cheaper substitue being discovered by chemists' Mr. (now Sir S.) Bayley thinks that prices must continue to rise, and to rise considerably, before the system is on a satisfactory footing. It will then depend on the European market whether the rise can be borne or whether it will destroy the trade. Such a destruction would even under the present system be an unmitigated calamity to the people. But for the present at all events I think we need apprehend nothing so serious as the margin of profit is large enough even after a considerable rise in rates to allow of prudent men working on their own capital getting ample returns from indigo." Surely there were prophets in those days.

In 1877 a very black cloud hung over the Indigo industry in Behar.

The Lieutenant-Governor of Bengal, Sir Ashley Eden having noticed that a large number of criminal cases had occurred in the three districts of Sarun, Chumparun and Tirhoot, wrote to S. C. Bayley, the Commissioner of Patna, asking him to collect the opinion of some of the leading planters and officials as to the unsatisfactory relations existing between planters and ryats in respect to indigo.

His Honour was anxious to avert any general disturbance while at the same time " he is not prepared to tolerate a state of things in which cases of illegal disposession and illegal retention of land are causing breaches of the peace of a more or less serious nature. His Honour was afraid that a Commission might excite men's minds and be followed by a general refusal by the ryats to grow indigo, pay rents and cause much litigation and distress to both parties. His Honour therefore suggested that the opinion of competent officials and planters be asked to consider the defects of the present system and see if remedies can be applied." Mr. S. C. Bayley on this addressed Mr. Thomas Fraser on the subject and he consulted with the late Mr. George Toomey. They having put their heads together called a meeting of planters on the 2nd April 1877, which was very largely attended.

This meeting was to the following effect, its object being to form an association to take into consideration any matters brought before it and to protect the planting interest.

The following is the notice of the meeting and the names of those present, etc.—

On Monday, 2nd April 1877, at a meeting held at the Planters' Club, Mozufferpore, it was proposed by Mr. F. Collingridge and seconded by Mr. R. Wilson that an association of indigo planters, managers and proprietors be formed to protect the interest of the planting community. The object of the association should be to take into consideration any matters or subjects affecting planting interest that may be brought before them. The following gentlemen were present:—

F. Collingridge	representing	Doudpore.
R. Wilson	,,	Joynugpur.
J. M. Becher	,,	Dhurmpore.
E. Dalgleish	,,	Dulsing Serai.
W. Mackenzie	,	Belsund.

W. B. Hudson	representing	Pursa.
R. Hudson	„	„
C. H. Pope	„	Poopri.
Geo. Toomey	„	Contai.
T. Lloyd	„	Nurharh.
H. Thorpe	„	Bahas.
A. MacIntosh	„	Dooria.
Fred. Wilkinson	„	Singiah.
E. W. Llewhellin	„	Rajapatty.
M. Gate	„	Pundoul.
W. R. Llewhellin	„	Japaha.
John Gale	„	Pundoul.
John Grant	„	Peerakpore.
M. N. McLeod	„	Peepra.
J. J. McLeod	„	Lalseriyah.
A. Edwards	„	Motihari.
E. S. Freeman	„	Loheria.
W. Riddell	„	Singiah.
W. Macgregor	„	Doomra.
Geo. Swaine	„	Ottur.
J. F. Fraser	„	Motipore.
E. G. Williams	„	Behrowlie.
E. J. C. Studd	„	Dholi.
F. Murray	„	Burhogah.

On the 7th June 1877 Mr. S. C. Bayley in reply to Mr. T. Fraser writes that His Honour the Lieutenant-Governor sees nothing in the resolutions of the minutes of the meeting of the Association touching khooski indigo which would bring the planters in direct touch with the ryat and do away with the ticcadhari system. But this matter was dropped.

On the 21st June 1877 a General Meeting of the Association was held at Mozufferpur, when it was settled that the Association be called "The Indigo Planters' Association" and that all interested in indigo cultivation be asked to join, also appointing a committee etc.

The Association started with Mr. Thomas Fraser and the late George Toomey as Honorary Secretaries.

On the 29th August 1877 the Lieutenant-Governor of Bengal wrote to the Secretary Indigo Planters' Association as follows:—" In reply to final para. of your letter, I am to say that as long as the Association show their present willingness to eet the Lieutenant-Governor's views and to get rid of the obvous blots on the system, the Lieutenant-Governor has no intention of interfering in any way or of doing anything which can hamper the planters in the conduct of their business, all he desires is that the law should be strictly obeyed and that indigo planting should be carried on like other commercial enterprises without the frequent complaints and the necessity for executive interference which have hitherto characterised it."

On the 17th December 1877 the Secretary to the Government of Bengal, wrote that His Excellency the Viceroy approved of the Lieutenant-Governor of Bengal's action which he considers very judicious. His Excellency also cordially acknowledged the praiseworthy efforts made by leading planters in the direction of reform and concurs with the expression of the Lieutenant-Governor's satisfaction.

On the 15th May 1878, Mr. (now Sir W. B.) Hudson was appointed Secretary and the Association became a recognised fact.

The Committee of the different districts took up and looked into all complaints made by ryat and planters and up-to-date matters have progressed smoothly.

It was a fortunate thing for the Behar planter that they had in the Lieutenant-Governor a man who had experience in dealing with similar abuses carried on by the planters of Lower Bengal and the disastrous results it had on the industry when the Government of Bengal stepped in between planter and ryat.

Having this experience in view and to avoid a recurrence of such a calamity His Honor went direct to the leading planters and was happy in his choice of picking out such an open minded pair of men as Messrs. Fraser and Toomey.

The district owes these gentlemen a great debt of gratitude.

I have been asked by some planters to give my ideas as to why sugar proved a failure in Behar in 1845-50 and to say what I think of the prospects of its proving a paying industry under improved methods of cultivation and manufacture. My experience of sugar during the early years of sugar manufacture in Tirhoot did not impress me much in favour of its turning out a success, and its eventual abandonment showed that this was the general idea. However, I have had reason after reviewing the faults committed in the growing of cane in those bygone days to change or modify my views considerably.

My short experience in the Mauritius was not much help to me in advising on the cultivation of cane. There the soil is volcanic, and cane was grown year after year in the same fields, and such a thing as rotation of crops is seldom tried—the finest results in that island were got from virgin soil where forests had been cut down—and the average result from such lands was about 8,000lbs. per acre.

The soil of Behar is as a rule light, and a cane crop easily exhausts it. The soil north of the Bhagmattee river in Tirhoot proper is stiffer and better for cane, but the lands there are liable to inundation. In 1845-50 little or no attempts at manuring were tried. Most factories grew indigo side by side with sugarcane, but the valuable "seeth" (refuse) manure was not made use of. In those days saltpetre was a very paying industry and the "seeth" was used for fuel in the saltpetre refineries—men who had started sugar were utterly ignorant of what was required to make the industry a success. All they knew was that Tom, Dick or Harry had put down some bighas of cane. They never considered that these bighas were small plots of the very best and richest lands and that they had got an enormous outturn of what they called sugar, and they calculated that if this sugar sold in Calcutta at a certain figure, fortunes were well in view. What was the result? From want of manure or change of lands, the produce per bigha fell yearly from, say, 60 maunds per bigha to 2½. The sugar granulated after a fashion, but after it had been bagged became a sticky mass and the consequence was that it sold in Calcutta for next to nothing—whether it was the climate affected the stuff, or that it was underboiled no one seemed to know. The sugar would not show a dry clean grain. Factories had invested in expensive machinery and plant—principally open pans. Mr. Robinson, an engineer, who had been in Mauritius, introduced his machinery and boiling plant and, though he professed to be an expert, he knew as little about how cane was to be grown successfully in Behar as those who were already working at it. In Tirhoot one factory had set up vacuum pans, and the sugar made from these was all that could be desired, and as good as any of the sugar now sold as Cossipore No. 1, but though those vacuum pans made good sugar the lands were exhausted, and production falling to zero they had to be shut up. That cane will grow in Behar there is no doubt, for I find, in documents of 1793 and after, nearly all the old indigo factories in Tirhoot are spoken of as being sugar and saltpetre, as well as indigo manufactories. In some parts of Behar cane grows better than in others. The reason why the sugar industry was abandoned after 1849-50 was that prices of indigo began to run up and the dye sold at very profitable prices, so men did not bother their heads about sugar. Before sugar was started in 1845 prices of indigo had fallen very low, some of the best marks selling at Rs. 110 per maund, and I have seen a paper bearing date 1837 where minutes of a meeting were recorded to settle whether indigo should not be abandoned, as prices had fallen so low. The cause attributed was over-production; for Bengal was in full swing in those days. The introduction of first, aniline dyes and then the synthetic and the consequent fall in the price of indigo has now set men thinking of the reason why sugar failed in days gone by.

Planters who generally grew a few bighas of cane as fodder for their bullocks knew from this experience that indigo grew well in lands where cane had been sown and *vice versa*, and they therefore did not see why cane should not be made a success, and after some study the conclusions come to were that cane to be a paying crop must be grown in new lands. Those lands must be well manured, every kind of manure available and suitable for sugarcane lands to be used. Indigo refuse (seeth) must be looked upon as the most valuable of all manures and be carefully guarded and used as well as all bullock, horse and stable refuse.

The new machinery worked by the India Development Co. has been found to make excellent sugar, none of the old defects coming out. The sugar sells readily at good prices, and they also find that the molasses sells so well and readily at paying prices that it is better to sell it than make rum. At Sakri, a sugar factory near Durbhunga, the molasses was found to be unsaleable and a nuisance, but the Development Co. find no difficulty in selling. There has been a good deal written lately about sugar and cane cultivation, and figures given to work out for or against. Figures, we know can be made to show anything. But I think the practical planter will hold with me that given a picked cultivation, well manured, and then after two years of rest in other crops, cane and indigo, then a rest or a crop of Indian corn; and then after two years of rest in other crops cane again will give good results. The boiling plant must be of the best and newest.

In this way a good and profitable business may be secured, if the industry is worked in a rational and economical way.

The soils in Behar, as I say above, are not volcanic nor virgin, and have not the strength of soils found in the Mauritius.

The uncertainty of rainfall is a drawback, but now canals for irrigation are being made, and when this is added to high manuring and careful selection of land, why should not cane succeed where tobacco and chillies do so well, for tobacco and chillies are a very exhausting crop? We have also a ready market at our door, and we are protected against dumping by the countervailing duties. I may say that those who have tried sugar making in Behar outside the Development Co., are well pleased so far. Under the rotation and manuring system, indigo side by side with cane should show great improvement, for where produce is good the colour of indigo is ditto. I am writing this principally in the interest of sugarcane cultivation. But I cannot help mentioning that the indigo industry has great hopes from the results of trials made with plant got from Natal and Java seed. These trials, only so far made in a small way, showed great results. This season larger areas have been sown in some factories, and some of these have already started manufacture, and the planters are anxiously awaiting reports of results.

In writing the history of Chumparun factories I have been disappointed in getting information as to some of the larger and older concerns; however I still hope to get what I require, which I can add later on.

A friend sent me lately the following which may interest my readers. It is a biographical sketch of the first indigo planter in India, the late Monsieur Louis Bonnaud, by H. James Rainey, and is dedicated to William Bonnaud, Esq., the eldest and sole surviving son of the subject of this sketch.

Some historical facts, not generally known regarding indigo and its manufacture in this country, will probably interest the reader and may be given by way of introduction to this sketch.

The popular opinion appears to be that the manufacture of indigo dates some time subsequent to the advent of British rule, and Mr. James Westland thus gives expression to this view in his excellent report on the district of Jessore. He then states that "from the absence of indigo in the 1791 list of exports we may justly conclude that no indigo was then manufactured." He further on says that it was introduced by Europeans in India.

Indigo, it may be stated, is the product of an indigenous Indian plant (*Indigofera tinctoria*, Linn.) and was known to the ancient Latin authors. Pliny and others write of it as Indicum, which designation *per se* sufficiently indicates that it was produced in India and we are indebted to the Roman naturalists just mentioned for a curious method of distinguishing superior from inferior indigo. He says to quote his words as translated:—

"The proof hereof is by fire, for cast the right indigo upon live coals it yieldeth a flame of the most excellent purple."

This test, it may be stated *par parenthese*, is worthy the attention of indigo brokers and others interested in the produce, but we regret we cannot add *probatum est* to it as we have not yet given it a trial.

In Germany, in the seventeenth century, indigo was denominated "The Devil's dye," and by an imperial edict its use was prohibited in A. D. 1654 as it appears to have decreased considerably the sale of woad, and Bancroft tells us that the Nuremburgers exacted every year a solemn oath from the dyers to the effect that they would never have recourse to indigo as a dye. So little was the nature of indigo known at the time in Europe that the Elector of Saxony denounced it as a corrosive substance not fit for man or devil.

Now to turn to India itself. From Abdul Fazil's "Ain-i-Akbari" we learn that excellent indigo was produced near Ahmedabad in Guzerat, and that it was regularly exported thence to Rum or Constantinople and other remote marts. From the same source we gather that the highest price realized per maund for superior indigo produced at Biana, near Agra, was only Rs. 16.

In a footnote to page 156 of the appendix to Journal Assoc. 1836, we find it stated of indigo that in 1631 there was a large contract for its supply to the English at Agra and much loss was sustained as it found at that juncture no ready sale either in Persia or England.

In 1863 Bernier mentions of the Dutch that the purchase of a nil or indigo gathered in the neighbourhood of Agra, particularly at Biana, no doubt the same place referred to, in the Ain, two days' journey from the city whither they go once every year having a house in the place.

Whilst residing at Gondolpara Monsieur Louis Bonnaud had an encounter single handed with some dacoits or gang robbers who used then to carry on their depredations even within the precincts of the Maharatta ditch in Calcutta. His courage and presence of mind saved his life and property on this trying occasion. One of the dacoits was killed and several were wounded. When all was over as usual in this country the police came to investigate into the matter. The

Governor of Chandernagore appears to have had a grudge against adventurous indigo planters and thought this was a favourable opportunity of injuring him. According to the French law then in force no European French subject could be tried and punished in this country for any criminal offence, and it was the intention of the Governor to send Monsieur Bonnaud to France for trial on a charge of murder. This, however, he was prevented from doing or for taking any other steps in the matter owing to the judge, magistrate, and other influential friends of the accused gentleman coming forward and stating that they would go to France if necessary to testify that the act was one of pure self-defence and in no wise constituted murder.

The next act we find the subject of our sketch taking an active and prominent part in, was a political event at Chandernagore of some importance and the history of which is very imperfectly and incorrectly known, according to the information supplied to us. It is commonly stated that the French populace at Chandernagore followed the example of their countrymen in Paris in 1792-93, and when news was received that the mob had proceeded to Versailles and led the King captive to the capital the French mob at Chandernagore determined to do the same with the representative of their deposed sovereign. The Governor is said to have been seized at Geretti, where he had retired and brought back to Chandernagore in triumph and subjected to gross insults. This at least is in substance the account given by the historian, the late Mr. J. C. Marsham, in an article contributed by him to the *Calcutta Review*, Vol. IV, p. 510. We find it, however, stated in the notes given to us by Monsieur Bonnaud and referred to before that France having become a republic the republic Government was declared at Chandernagore. The Governor was directed to give over charge of the place to the republic Government, but this Monsieur LeChevalier refused to do in positive terms and then proceeded to the Government house at Geretti south of Chandernagore. Here he was a prisoner so he managed to effect his escape by the southern gate of garden door and sought refuge in Calcutta.

From Chandernagore Monsieur Bonnaud appears to have proceeded to the Maldah district, where he in connection with three wealthy Englishmen, one of whom was named Adam, built an indigo factory, and as lime was a scarce article in that locality he exhumed human skeletons from a neighbouring Mohamedan graveyard and converted them into that necessary material. While residing in his garden house at Hazinngar in Chandernagore on the Rue de Paris he established a large canvas and twine factory which flourished for some time, but unfortunately it was at last burnt down by which the owner suffered considerable loss. In 1814 he joined the Bankipore Concern and he was for some time proprietor of Nayahatti Indigo Concern in the district of Jessore. Lastly he was managing proprietor of the large indigo concern of Kalna in Burdwan, including the Mirzapore Indigo Factory not far from Krishnaghur. He terminated his connection with the Kalna Concern in 1819 when he made no less than 1,400 maunds of indigo, the largest quantity of produce yielded by probably any single concern in Bengal up to that period. His being part owner of it, however, caused him much loss, trouble, and anxiety owing to the principal proprietor, Mr. Edward Majoribanks of the Bengal Civil Service, who was deeply involved owing to losses on the turf, having mortgaged the property to Messrs. Fairlie Fergusson and Co.

This misfortune is said to have hastened his death which occurred in 1821 at the advanced age of 84 years. He left two sons by his second marriage. The eldest is William Bonnaud, who was long chief accountant of the well-known Union Bank and has been secretary of that Bank in liquidation since its memorable failure. The youngest, Mr. Peter

Bonnaud, died in 1873, and was for some time Assistant Collector of Customs, Calcutta. Their mother, Madame Louis Bonnaud, died in 1860 at the great age of 93 years.

In the "Report of the Proceedings of the East India Company, in regard to the culture and manufacture of indigo," it is stated that it was a well-known article of importation during the first century of their trade with this country; and in 1779-80 the Directors thereof used their best endeavours to increase the quantity and improve the quality of indigo, entering into a contract for the purpose with Mr. James Prinsep. That gentleman wrote to Lord North, in a letter, dated 25th January 1780, that he wished to introduce "Indigo sugar, and tobacco. into Great Britain from the East Indies" and in a subsequent letter to the same nobleman he stated he had "with the utmost trouble and expense" collected round him Europeans bred to different arts and science, as well as the most intelligent mechanics and planters of the East.

Although it must be admitted, as will be evident from the above collection of facts, that indigo was produced in India from ancient times, Yet there can be no doubt that the manufacture of indigo according to the system practised in the West Indies, was introduced by Europeans in this country some time after the establishment of the British Government, and previous to that they do not appear to have had any connection with it as planters or manufacturers. A work on indigo planting published in 1835, and now out of print, written by Mr. John Phipps, states, and we believe quite correctly, that the first European indigo planter in India was the late Monsieur Louis Bonnaud, and as, doubtless, any particulars regarding the life of one who introduced this great industry in its present form in this country will be interesting to all, more especially indigo planters. We venture to put together in a connected narrative, information derived from certain notes kindly placed at our disposal by the eldest and sole surviving son of the gentleman referred to, with free permission to make such use of them as we may think proper. This gentleman is now in the 75th year of his age, and takes a commendable pride in being a son of the first European indigo planter in India, and in this respect it may aptly be said of him *primus in Indis.* We have dedicated this slight biographical sketch to Mr. William Bonnaud as he is best entitled to have his name associated in connection with it, specially as he has been good enough to supply us with materials for constructing it.

Louis Bonnaud appears to have been descended from a good French stock and he was born, in what year is uncertain, but probably in 1737, at Marseilles, where his parents resided at the time, and where his mother was also born. His father, who was an officer in the French Army, died leaving several children to the care of his wife, namely, two sons and two or three daughters. The eldest son, Francois, took to a seafaring life and rose in due course to be the chief officer of a French corvette; and Louis, the youngest son, proving intractable, as boys of spirit usually are and beyond the power of his mother, Madame Bonnaud, to manage, he was at a rather youthful age apprenticed to the sea. He was posted as a midshipman in the same vessel in which his brother was second in command, and they sailed together in several voyages to different parts of the world.

In one of the voyages of the corvettes to the West Indies she encountered a terrific gale on that coast and went down. Some of the officers and crew of the ill-fated ship managed to reach the shore in safety, and among them were the captain and the midshipman Louis Bonnaud. The brother of the latter unfortunately perished. The brothers were swimming close to one another, when Lous, heard Francois call out to him by name twice, but he was utterly unable to render any help, and Francois immediately after sank to rise no more.

The shipwrecked mariners were treated kindly by the residents of the place where they landed, and were well cared for. After staying there for some time the young midshipman returned to his native country, and having made a few voyages in some other vessel he appears to have grown tired of a sea life, and went back to the West Indies, where he had learnt that trade could be profitably carried on. With some little money he had managed to save, he had launched out in trade and speculation. He appears to have been there initiated in the processes of manufacturing indigo, and by success in his various dealings he contrived to amass in no great time a moderate fortune.

Then, for some reason unknown to his son, but probably simply from that restlessness and love of change, inherent in all who have roamed the sea for any length of time, he shifted his abode, (after visiting Marseilles on the death of his mother and finding his sisters married and well settled in life), from the Western to the Eastern Hemisphere, and settled in the Island of Bourbon as a merchant, where he established a considerable mercantile firm, and occupied a large and well-known house there called the "Maison Rouge," which was standing some thirty years ago, and it is probably still in existence. His commercial ventures prospered for some time exceedingly, and at one time he was possessed of considerable wealth, but eventually misfortune overtook him. Three of his ships laden with valuable cargo were lost on their way from Bourbon to France, as they were not insured he became a poor man. He then determined to remove from the French isle now known as Reunion to Bengal to mend his fortunes by turning his knowledge to indigo manufacture acquired in the West Indies to account.

Accordingly we find Louis Bonnaud coming out to Bengal in 1777 or thereabouts and residing at Chandernagore.

Soon after his arrival he took the house at Taldanga in the Hooghly district and built there a small indigo factory.

The place is situated to the north of Chandernagore and as the road thence to Hooghly turns to the right or east it will be found immediately to the north and is merely separated from the boundary of the French settlement in that direction by the road itself. Here, however, he found that no great quantity of land could be obtained and it being inconveniently far from the river he leased a larger garden at Gondolpara on the banks of the Hooghly near Telinipara to the south of Chandernagore, where he built a pair of small vats and a press house. A fine avenue of beautiful bokul tress used to line the road leading from the gate to the dwelling house in this garden, but they nave entirely disappeared. The sites of both factories at Taldanga and Gondolpara are, however, still in existence and can be identified. Mr. Bonnaud undertakes to point them out to anybody desirous of seeing them as his late father carefully showed them to him several times in the walks they had together about Chandernagore.

CHUMPARAN FACTORIES.

Barrah M. and H. B.

This concern, according to what can be found out from old men (natives) was built by a Mr. Stewart in about 1820. Mr. M. Moran bought from him, and Henry Hill, who was proprietor of Rajpore, bought a share with Moran selling out of Rajpore. One can hardly understand why he sold out of so fine a factory as Rajpore to buy into Barrah. The following are the names of the managers as far back as I can find out:—Mr. Stewart, Moran Henry Hill, Captain Hickey, Henry Hill, Joseph Hill, H. L. Hollway, A. S. Urquhart, December 1857 to September 1858, W. Gibbon, from October 1859 to 31st January

1865, H. L. Hollway, 1st February 1865 to 28th February 1865, C. W. Dyer, March 1865 to June 1865, B. S. Hickey, June 1865 to June 1866, J. N. Macqueen, June 1866 to June 1871, James Begg, 4th June 1871 to 31st October 1872, F. J. Nicolay, November 1872 to October 1874, James Begg, November 1874, W. Scobie, November 1874 to February 1875, J. Begg, February 1875 to March 1876, E. A. Hickey, March 1876 to May 1877, J. H. Dixon, May 1877 to March 1878, A. D. Bolton, March 1878 to October 1879, E. A. Hickey, November 1879 to December 1880, John C. Gale, December 1880 to March 1892, D. R. Crawford, March 1892 to March 1895, G. H. D. Hay, March 1895 to December 1895, D. R. Crawford, December 1895 to November 1903, G. R. Macdonald, November 1903 and is still managing. The following are the outworks:—Jagoulia built in 1848; this outwork was rebuilt some years after on a higher piece of land. Mohowah built by John C. Gale in 1881-82, Gowandrah by Gale in 1882-83. Russelpore by D. R. Crawford in 1892-93. Stewart sold to M. Moran and Moran to Henry Hill and James Hill, executor for Henry Hill to D. R. Crawford and others in 1896-97. The following graves are to be found at Barrah:—Sacred to the memory of Mrs. Wiffen, 27th November 1843; Henry Hill Young, 1849; Hanna Alladin wife of Henry Leadbeater Hollway, 6th May 1867; Julian Maclaine, wife of John Cherry Gale, November 1888; and C. W. Dyer, year illegible, and others of modern date. Here is what a clerk in the Rajpore Concern writes; he is a very old servant of some 40 years' standing. I give it in his own words:—"I have heard and afterwards it fall to my look that one Finch obtained mokererie, but worked for a few years and then transferred it to one Hill, most probably the father of Joseph and James Hill for in the first period of my service, I have heard both the Hills born at Rajpore and after some time they transferred the right to Bell. One of the Hills remained at Turkoulia and the other at Seeraha. As far as my recollection runs I may also have heard from Shib Baboo that in past days Barrah was dependent to Seeraha and was belonging to family of Hills.

"These are topics general amongst everyone that two big wealthy companies started Indigo business in Chumparun and Tirhoot, Newell and Co. and another rival MacKellop Stewart and Co., starting manufacture of saltpetre and sugarcane.

"The former making Kanti head concern upon other twenty-three big concerns and the latter their head-quarters at Burhamporah with a large golah.

"On the side of former, Falkner and against him Becher and they '*Fighted*' ruined both, but M. S. and Co. has a house in Calcutta, and when N. and Co. failed in connection of indigo, Dr. Begg started mart and house of Begg Dunlop and Co. In evidence of above-mentioned statements you will find the Barrah old chimneys standing and waste materials of machinery lying and the indigo manufacture were performed by human hands till first of the period of our time."

This history of Barrah is rather crude, but it gives one an idea of what happened. There was a row between Captain Becher and Falkner. When Captain Becher came into Mozufferpore to swear the peace against Falkner, the magistrate asked Becher to swear he was in bodily fear of Falkner. "What!" cried the indignant old salt, "Captain Becher in fear of any man. No Sir! never!!" So the magistrate could do nothing and the row died a natural death.

Byreah. H. W. H, B.

This factory was built in 1884 by C. F. Carlton. The following were managers:—1884 to 1890, C. F. Carlton; 1890 to 1891, Hume; 1891 to 1893, C. F. Carlton. In 1893 this factory was sold to H. Hudson and H. W. Hudson managed to 1897, when W. Cox took up management to 1899 when H. E. Hudson managed till 1901. From 1901 Mackay, 1905 H. E. Hudson and C. S. Delafosse. Dokraha and Munjhowlia Proprietors, J. F. G. T. Barclay and J. Barclay, Manager R. Yate Lee.

Koriah McD and F.

Kooriah was built in 1884 by H. W. Freeman. Freeman managed till he died and was buried at Motihari. After his death Kooriah became an outwork of Lohereah, but afterwards a separate concern and was sold to J. Lowis, who, on getting the management of the Bettia Raj, sold to Elliot and A. Elliot took up the management. Hardea Factory was built by George Boule while manager of Moorla Concern then belonging to T. M. Gibbon and W. Macqueen, George Swaine being assistant at Hardia.

This factory was built in 1862. Up to 1885 Hardia was an outwork of Moorla. T. M. Gibbon eventually exchanged a 4-anna share in Tatereach of McQueen's 4-annas in Moorla and became 16 annas proprietor in about 1873. Later the Lethbridge brothers bought 4 annas in Moorla and in 1885 they divided their 4-anna share from T. M. Gibbons 12 annas, taking Hardia as an equivalent. Up to this time G. Swaine continued assistant at Hardia. Then Mansfield, Godfrey, Freeman, H. Thorpe then F. Blechy nden who managed about 10 years. After 1885 H. Thorpe managed but resigned after a month and F. A. Hudson took charge and managed for four years. Then H. Thorpe resumed chaarge and continued so except for 9 months during which time H. Hollway acted for him, *i.e.*, 1890-91 to 1896.

Several years prior to this the concern had been acquired by Roland Hudson, who sold half in 1895 to Messrs. J. F. Barclay and they resold again in 1900-01 to R. Hudson. Since 1896 F. D. Fletcher has been manager. Under present management the concern has shown satisfactory results. This concern is situated some 3 miles from the Nepal Frontier. The lands are chiefly paddy. There are no graves at Hardia.

Lohereah McD and F.

This factory is of recent date; it was started by Brouke of Bugaha in about 1859 or 1860. He carried on the factory for a few years when he sold to A E. McDonald and W. L. Freeman. McDonald managed till 1875, when he left the country, selling his share to Freeman, who then took over charge till 1877. H. Fraser purchased Freeman's share and took up the management which he kept till 1892, when he went home. J. Barclay purchased Freeman's other share and managed till 1902, when he went home and H. Fraser again took up the management and still manages. There are no graves at Lohereah.

Mo rla T. M. G.

Moorla was built in 1864-65 by T. M. Gibbon, H. L. Holloway and W. F. Gibbon.

The following were managers:—From 1864 to 1867 G. Boule; 1867 to 1872 Lethbridge; to 1875, R. Lethbridge; to 1876, Edwards; to 1885, H. Thorpe; to 1890, A. E. Macdonald. In 1891 the factory was managed by the native amlah and 1878-79 T. M. Gibbon, and from 1892 to 1905 A. L. Harman. There are no *graves* at Moorla.

Motihari Moran.

Motihari was built by C. Moran in 1817. Of its outworks, Sougong and Meerpore, there is no record as to when built. Poornahee was built by Baldwin in 1859, Bhelwa also by him in 1861, Huraj in 1863, and Cheyhaia in 1890 by Edwards. The following were managers: Charles Moran in 1817, followed by W. Moran and he by Gill. Then in 1858 to 1870 by Baldwin. Then C. Moran for a few months in 1871, when he died. Then came in Edwards in 1872 till 1891, after him E. Thorpe 1892 to 1894. Then Miller 1895 to 1897, when W. S. Irwin took up the management and is still managing. Originally the Motihari Concern belonged to Messrs. Moran and Hill, but early in the sixties Mr. Miller, of Hoare Miller and Co.,

PEEPRA HOUSE.

bought six annas. In the Motihari Factory compound there is a grave in the memory of Charles Moran, who died in 1851, and in the garden at Sougong one sacred to the memory of Miss Mary Martindale, who departed this life on the 4th September 1858, aged 53, and another sacred to the memory of Henry Finch, who departed this life 18th August 1839, aged 30. Mr. John Mackenzie relieved M. Finch of the charge of Meerpore Factory (which is a part of the Motihari Concern) in about 1840.

Mathew Moran, an uncle of M. Moran, was one of the original proprietors. The C. Moran, who died in 1851, was one of the younger branches of the Moran family.

Mullayah
D. H. S.
M.

Mullayah was built in 1883 by E. W. Dixon and started manufacture in 1884. Sirsealy, an outwork, was also built by Dixon in 1886. Dixon managed from 1880 to 1886, then Hill for a few months when Dixon returned in 1886 to 1888. In 1889-90 C. Hill again managed and Dixon returned in 1891-92. He was succeeded by H. E. Cox. Then in 1896 Dixon again and 1897 H. E. Cox, 1898 C. J. Mackay, 1899 H. E. Cox, 1891 Dixon, 1902 and to present time H. E. Cox manages.

Peeprah
G. N. W.

This concern was built by the Dutch, but there is no record of in what year. In 1835 to 1838 Peeprah was one of a group, consisting of the following factories which belonged to Messrs. Noel or Newell and Co. as per a memo. in factory books:--Contai, Motipore, Doudpore, Bhicanpore, Peeprah, Belsund, Tetereah and Seeraha. But the factory was built in 1807 by a Dr. Gibb, who sold to John and Edward Brown, who admitted Richards as a partner. In 1831 the concern was sold to Messrs. Nowell and Co. They mortgaged the factory to Fletcher Alexander and Co., and in 1854 the latter sold the Peeprah Concern to George Neville Wyatt. The managers, as far as I can go back, were Yule, G. N. Wyatt, Daunt, Macqueen, Gibbon,

Hudson, MacLeod, A. W. Wyatt, and at present J. B. Norman. The outworks are Dinamut, Jaghira, Decaha, Mudhoban, Daboulie. Dinamut was built in 1812 by Mr. Yule's assistant, Bailey. Mudhoban by M. N. MacLeod in 1885; Jaghira in 1854 by W Daunt, assistant B. Anderson, Daboulie in 1888 by A. W. Wyatt's assistant, Lamb of Dinamut.

Many successful men had their early training at Peeprah, apart from the well-known names of the managers, Mr. Gordon Canning, now managing proprietor of Pursa and Charles Still, who was manager of the Battiah Raj, started life at Peeprah as assistants.

The Peeprah indigo mark G. N. W. is, I believe, used as the standard test for comparison in London. Peeprah was also selected for experimental trials conducted by Mr. Rawson and his staff in 1901-02.

Pursa, T. G. and S.

Pursa was built by Tom Gibbon and Tom Lethbridge some time in the sixties, but I cannot get dates. The plan of the factory was drawn out by A. Butler. Dokraha was an outwork of Pursa but subsequntly became an outwork of Lallseriyah in 1871-72. Pusa was sold to the brothers Sir W. B. Hudson and R. Hudson in 1872-73. They built two outworks, Hurpore and Sirkia. R. Hudson eventually sold his 4-anna share to Mr. Scott and Sir W. B. Hudson his share to F. A. Shaw. Since then I believe Mr. Gordon Canning, A. Butler and Dixon have become proprietors. Pursa was managed for some years by that good sportsman R. Hudson; he found it a grand place for sport. He stuck some 33 boars there single handed as he had no near neighbours who cared for piksticking. He found it also a good place for black partridge and quail. He there trained in the seventies the following winners:—Black Eagle, Kilmore, Miss Bertram, Talisman, Piccadilly, Amethyst and others. I understand that a sugar factory is about to be built there, and as the lands are fitted for cane it should prove a success.

Rajpore T. S. and Co.

This factory, as far as I can find out, was built in 1801 by Mr. Jeffry Finch, who held a share with a Bengali gentleman. The mokararie pottah for the land on which the factory is built is dated 2nd October 1807, but from the wording of the document it is evident that the factory itself was built some five or six years before, *i.e.*, 1801, Hossenie, the head outwork, was built by James Slade in 1856, Puckrie by Geo. Richardson in 1887, and Jamudpore by M. N. Macleod in 1894. The Hills purchased from Jeffrey Finch and Ball purchased from Hills. James Slade inherited from Ball, his uncle, Tom Slade getting a share also. James Slade managed with a short interregnum till 1857. Then Tom Slade to 1860, H. W. Hudson to October 1862, E. Hudson to 1872, F. A. Shaw and E. D. Urquhart, L. Wilson, Geo. Richardson, M. N. MacLeod followed. Then E. H. Hudson, junior, who is still manager. H. W. Hudson bought in 1857 and his brother E. Hudson in 1862. For further particulars about Rajpore *see* "James Slade in Tirhoot and its Inhabitants of the Past." The late H MacDonald was also a partner and he and E. D. Urquhart sold out in late years. The place now is owned by the brothers H. and E. Hudson.

Satti S. H. C.

Satti was built by Sir W. B. Hudson and was looked after by Carlton, who managed for some time about 1874. Sir W. B. Hudson sold to Coffin and Still. They built an outwork and A. Butler became a proprietor. It was about then that Kooriah was built.

Seerha Factory M, & H. S.

The first mokararie lease is dated 1807 given to Mr. John Taylor for the purpose of building indigo works. In 1818 another mokararie lease was given to one John Sims Saheb. About a mile to the east of Puttaihi, one of the outworks, there are some scanty remains, of an old sugar factory and near Nawada, another outwork, a Dutch factory; this place existed before Seeraha was built. Near Poornahee it is said that there was a small outpost where a regiment or part of one was posted, but excepting for two mounds in the village there is no trace of the cantonments. There is a single grave by the road side said to be that of an officer, but it is only marked by a mound of earth. Poornahee was built by Edwards in 1856-57. Tradition says that two regiments were posted at a place called Line tolah Ghoresari, during the first Nepal War. Seeraha had the following outworks: Parewah, Puddumkair, Puttaihi, Nawadah, Murpah and Tillara. Sir W. B. Hudson on purchasing the Seeraha Concern in 1889 for over 8 lacs sold Nawadah to F. Walker, Tillara to Bloomfield and J. H. Smith, Murpah to May and Coventry, Puddumkair to W. and H. Cox, Puttaihi to Freemantle. I have tried very hard to get more information about Seeraha. We know at one time it belonged to Noel or Nowell and Co., and was one of a group of factories under Kanti, where John Taylor had his headquarters. From what I have heard from old planters, Mr. Wood was one of the first managers. He was rather a wild man. He had a wooden leg and went by the nickname of *Laknee* Wood. He had a peculiar habit when visiting his assistants when he was in his cups, of smashing all the crockery and glassware on the table and when he had done this he went home and sent the sufferer a new set of everything. This was all very well, but rather a nuisance. The man who told me this was John Watson who lived to be a very old man; he was from Yorkshire and had been brought up on a farm there. He came out to India and got employment at Dinapore with people who cured pork and fattened turkeys, which they sold to planters in Tirhoot on festive occasions, and in this way John Watson got employment at Seeraha Factory. After he had been some time employed in indigo he got leave to visit Dinapore and while there got engaged to a young lady. On his return he told Wood of what he had done when Wood suggested that he better get his bungalow in order and arrange for his wedding, old Watson took fright and said. "Oh I never thought of marrying her and bringing her over here. I don't want her here." So it ended in old John writing to say so and the young lady ran him in to the tune of Rs. 2,000, which John Watson did not like. He said he would never get engaged again as it was too expensive.

Turcoolea.

I can get no information about this concern, though I have been promised what can be found out, and when I receive this, I will add after. What I remember of Turcoolea is that it was shut up for several years; then suddenly Joseph Hill determined to open it out and in a very short space of time Turcoolea was working with a very big cultivation.

Since writing my history of Sarun factories I have heard from a Sarun planter the history of a few small concerns, most of them built in later years. Zummunpore was built by Moonshee Jawad Hosain, who was the Judge's Sheristadar at Chapra, in about 1864-65. After his death Dost Mahomed sold it to Angus MacEwen in 1888 and after he died Donald MacEwen took the place over.

Gopalpore was built by Opendro Narain Singh in about 1867; he was one of the Chainpore babus. He worked it himself for some years and sold it to Malcolm MacLeod and Booth, who managed for some years. The place is now owned by Mr. J. Karpeles.

Jatepur was built about 1870 by Arthur Harman for a banker at Patna, Seeree Ram, who still owns it. Harman managed for some years, after him came E. Chardon, I believe this factory was closed as an indigo concern.

Koohunia was built by A. Buskin in 1878. He was part proprietor with his brother Mark and Colonel Roberts. *Gour* was one of its outworks, built a year or two later. After A. Buskin went to Australia, Ferguson took charge, he was a nephew of Buskin's. This place is now shut up for indigo but makes sugar in small way.

Turcowlia and Seeraha, etc.

"It is almost impossible to give an approximately correct idea of who the managers of the various concerns were in olden days. Old Henry Hill went to India towards beginning of 1800 and it seems pretty clear that he was at Rajpur at any rate from 1810 to 1814, as he had three sons born there. He probably went to Turcowlia when that concern was bought in 1816, at any rate he was there in 1824 and he probably remained there till I. M. Hill had charge. I think there is no doubt that was in any case not later than his marriage in 1836. Old Henry Hill then probably went to Barrah (it may have been a few years earlier), where he remained till his death there in 1848 (he is buried at Barrah) and Joseph Hill looked after the work there for him. James Hill remained at Turcowlia until a few months after he came home very ill in 1851. Joseph Hill went to Seeraha when that concern was purchased in 1848 or 1849; he remained there till he came home in 1857 when H. L. Holloway was left in charge of the three concerns of Barrah, Turcowlia and Seeraha, with A. S. Urquhart under him at Barrah. Holloway lived at Seerah, old Tom Gibbon at Turcowlia and K. Hill and T. M. Gibbon at Ghyree and Mukwah. Joseph Hill went out again to Seeraha for a year or two in 1858, but I don't know what changes that made in the management. In March 1859 J. M. Gibbon left Ghyree and Mukwah, John Justin Holloway (a nephew of H. L. Holloway) taking his place. Until old Tom Gibbon's death in 1860-61. Turcowlia concern formed two divisions under Seerah, but on old Tom Gibbon's death T. M. Gibbon came back as manager of the whole Turcowlia concern under H. L. Holloway at Seeraha. In 1863 G. M. Gibbon went to Peeprah and John Stace Smith took his place as manager. On Smith's leaving in 1865 T. M. Gibbon returned to Turcowlia, remaining there till 1867 when he went to Bettiah as manager of the Raj and was succeeded at Turcowlia by his cousin W. F. Gibbon, known commonly as Barrah Willie. James S. Begg succeeded A. F. Gibbon in 1869 and Hill succeeded Begg in 1871. At Barrah A. S. Urquhart was succeeded (whether immediately or not I cannot say) by W. F. Gibbon (the Gibbon above referred to) and when Hill went to India in 1865, the manager then was Charley Dyer, who died soon afterwards at Seeraha and was buried at Barrah. After Dyer came Blayney Hickey, John Neville, Macqueen and then I think J. S. Begg. H. L. Holloway remained at Seeraha till 1866, succeeded by W. Macqueen, then by R. H. Hill, Ted Hickey, Dixon, and W. F. Gibbon (Shangai).

In 1818 Mathew Moran and Henry Hill acquired the 16-anna of Barrah, Motihari, and Rajpore factories. Mathew Moran was the uncle of the late William Moran (the founder of the firm of W. Moran and Co., Calcutta). Mr. Moran was buried in the Motihari Factory compound. In 1818 M. Moran and Henry Hill purchased 16-anna of Turcowlia. In 1836 H. Hill bought 16-anna of Barrah, Jugalia, Turcowlie, Lallseriah, Sukwah, and Ghyree, and in 1838 a factory called Burhurwah, but I can find no trace of when Lallseriah was sold. Report says that Lallseriah was sold for 1,000 maunds of oats. Sir W. B. Hudson bought Seeraha from the Hills in 1888. I also now add a few memos for the History of Chumparan factories belonging to the Hills.

1810 2nd June.—A deed records that William Warren Wood and Richard Cahill, as attorneys of Alexander Nowel, agreed to sell Barrah Factory to Mathew Moran.

1812, 5th October.—Conveyance of 7/16 Barrah to Henry Hill. The deed recites that Mathew Moran and Henry Hill had been several years past interested in the Factories Barrah, Motihari, and Rajpur, they having borne the expense of carrying on the factories 9/16 and 7/16 proprietors.

1816, 12th July.—A deed of this date records the purchase of Turcowlia by Mathew Moran (9/16) and Henry Hill (7/16) from William Wood, Indigo-planter of Mirzapore.

1829, 31st July.—Records that Mathew and Henry Hill were proprietors of Barrah, Jugalia, Turcowlia, Lallseriah, and Sukowah. Rajpur must have been sold some time between 1812 and 1829. It must have been after 1814, as Henry Hill's seventh child was born at Rajpur on the 12th August 1814.

In 1849 J. M. Hill and Joseph Hill were the only partners in Hill and Co. in equal shares. Seeraha concern was bought by either the Executors of Alexander Powell and Co. or from John Taylor I am not sure which in 1848-49.

1880, 1st November.—From this date Joseph Hill became the sixteen-anna proprietor of Barrah.

1889, 1st October.—Henry Hill and Co., sold Seeraha concern to Sir W. B. Hudson.

Note.—Motihari concerns must have passed to Mathew Moran some time between 1812 and 1829. As far as I can make out Henry Hill was at Rajpur from 1810 to the beginning of 1815, at any rate probably for some years before 1810, and he may have remained at Rajpur later than 1815, perhaps till the place was sold. He may have gone to Turcowlia in 1816 when it was purchased, for his youngest child was born there in 1824.

I may mention before I end, that the following are the Turcowlia concern outworks: Chileram, Ollaha, Burhurwah, Jallaha, Mukwah, Doodhi, Fairwa, Ghyree, Serine and Tejpoorwa. I can find no trace of when the older outworks were built.

Turcowlia has agreed to grow 1,000 acres of rhea, and rhea factories are being built at Chileram and Mukwah. The following are the Assistants at Turcowlia: R. L. Marsden, zemindari manager; F. H. Murdock, personal assistant; J. B. S. Hill, Burhurwah, Ollaha and Jallaha, and T. A. Hodge, Mukwah; E. E. Fraser, Serine and Tejpoorwah; J. A. Collier, Ghyree; F. H. Manistry, Kharrwat; J. H. Hill manages the concern.

The following are the Managers of the Turcowlia concern since 1860:—

Names of Managers.	Seasons.
T. M. Gibbon, Esq.	1860-61
J. Holloway, Esq.	,,
J. Smith, Esq.	1861-62
J. Holloway, Esq.	,,
J. Smith, Esq.	1862-63
T. M. Gibbon, Esq.	1863-64
Ditto	1864-65
Ditto	1865-66
Ditto	1866-67
Ditto	1867-68
Ditto	1868-69
J .S. Begg, Esq.	1869-70
Ditto	1870-71
Dr. J. H. G. Hill	1871-72
Ditto	1872-73
J. Lewes, Esq.	,,
Ditto	1873-74

Names of Managers.	Seasons
W. F. Gibbon, Esq., Senior	1873-74
Ditto	1874-75
Dr. J. H. G. Hill	„
Ditto	1875 76
Ditto	1876 77
Ditto	1877-78
W. F. Gibbon, Esq , Senior	„
Ditto	1878 79
Dr. J. H. G. Hill	1879-80
Ditto	1880-81
Ditto	1881-82
Ditto	1882 83
H. W. J. Hill, Esq.	„
Ditto	1883-84
Dr. J. H. G. Hill	„
Ditto	1884-85
Ditto	1885-86
J. H. Dixon, Esq.	„
H. W. J. Hill, Esq.	„
Dr. J. H. G. Hill	1886-87
Ditto	1887-88
G. D. Campbell, Esq.	„
H. W. J. Hill, Esq.	1888 89
Ditto	1889-90
Ditto	1890-91
J. H. Dixon, Esq.	„
H. W. J. Hill, Esq.	1891 92
J. H. Dixon, Esq.	„
H. W. J. Hill, Esq.	1892-93
Ditto	1893-94
W. F. Gibbon, Esq., Junior	„
H. W. J. Hill, Esq.	1894-95
W. F. Gibbon, Esq., Junior	„

NAMES OF MANAGERS	SEASONS.
H. W. J. Hill, Esq.	1895-96
W. F. Gibbon, Esq., Junior	"
H. W. J. Hill, Esq.	1896-97
W. F. Gibbon, Esq., Junior	"
Ditto	1897-98
H. W. J. Hill, Esq.	1898-99
F. M. Coventry, Esq.	"
Ditto	1899-00
Ditto	1900-01
Ditto	1901-02
J. L. Hill, Esq.	"
Ditto	1902-03
F. M. Coventry, Esq.	"
J. L. Hill, Esq.	1903-04
R. L. Marsden, Esq.	"
J. L. Hill, Esq.	1904-05
Ditto	1905-06

Telbara M. & H. T. L.

This factory at one time was an outwork of Seeraha concern, and was bought by Robert Bloomfield and J. H. Smith in 1892. There are no graves. Present manager Robert Bloomfield. Poor Bloomfield was cruelly murdered by some natives on the 13th February 1907, and Mr. Severs now manages.

Lallseryiah, J. F. and G.

This factory was built by one of the Hills (James). It was built as an outwork of Turcowlia in about 1822; about 1846 the Hills abandoned the factory, native report says they sold the place to Geo. Falkner for a thousand maunds of oats. Falkner established a hide depot, but that not thriving, and another man, whose name is not readable (seems like Oman), started indigo in a small way. When he gave up the place Kenneth MacLeod and James Cox bought in 1856-57 and Lewis Cosserat managed for a few years. Cosserat was at Lallseriah when the 12th Irregular Cavalry mutinied and killed Colonel Holmes, his wife, and the Doctor and his wife, the only one escaping being the Doctor's little child, saved by an ayah. Cosserat saw the regiment passing from Segowlie after they had committed this murder, but knew nothing of what had happened. It was strange they did not attack him, but they seemed in a great hurry; they were off to Delhi. Some natives took the bodies of Colonel Holmes and his wife (they had decapitated Colonel Holmes) to Motihari, and W. Daut, who was managing at Peepra Factory, hearing this pluckily drove in to Motihari and read the burial service over them. The Doctor and his wife were burnt in their bungalow. Strange to say, several years after the murder, one of the men who fired on Colonel Holmes and his wife appeared at Segowlie. He was recognised by Colonel Holmes' syce, who informed the police, the man was taken, he confessed and was hanged. L. Cosserat, after the mutiny, was made an Honorary Magistrate and held Kachery at a place still called *Fauzdari Chakta*. His lockup still exists.

The concern was lastly purchased by Messrs. Freeman and Gibbon, then James MacLeod purchased Gibbon's share in 1867. J. MacLeod worked up the concern and made it a valuable property. He built the outworks Rajghaut. Furrwah and Madhupur. Jimmy was the essence of hospitality and all knew him as a hard rider and his stables were ever full of horses.

There are two soldiers' graves at Madhupur, regiments used to march past and bivouacked roundabout those parts during the Nepaul war. Segowlie, where a regiment of Native Cavalry used to be stationed, is only 24 miles from Lallseriah and the officers attached to these regiments always found a welcome at the factory, joining in any sport or pastime going on. The senior officers preferred a quiet life and remained at home.

Good old Colonel Robarts, who kept a pack of hounds and some racehorses, was a man after Jimmy MacLeod's own heart.

D. C. Reid is now manager of Lallseriah and, if I mistake not, Apperley (commonly called Apples) his assistant. He, Apples, is the son of Colonel Apperley, who many years ago had charge of Pusa, a right good fellow he was, and like father, like son.

This ends my History of Indigo Factories in Tirhoot, Saran and Chumparan. I would have wished it to have been more elaborate, but such as it is, it will be an introduction of the past to the *present* generation. Since writing the above I have received the following from a friend:—

SARUN.

I now start on indigo concerns in Saran. Most of the factories in this district were built after 1847. Those as far as I remember working before then were Ramcollah, Rajahputtee, Chaitanpursa Jullalpore and some others. We find these two latter mentioned in the history of Singiah as having entered into boundary bonds with that concern in 1829 between Joseph Simon Finch and H. Fitzgerald. I cannot give the factories alphabetically as there has been some delay in getting certain information, but I will give each factory as I have received the information required.

Arrowah
A. K. R.

There are no records of when Arrowah was built; some of the factories forming part of the concern date from before 1830. In the fifties, Kazee Ramzan Ali was owner. He had many European managers, among them W. James and Tom Martin, who managed from Tilpah house, where old K. Macleod lived and which later on became the Sarun Planters' Club. Old Kazee Ramzan Ali was a very plausible, popular, and knowing man and there are many stories told about him for the truth of which I will not vouch, but *sinon e vero*, etc. There is no doubt he had great say and power with his brother Mahomedans, in fact with nearly all the respectable landholders and bankers in Chupra. He was always hardup and greatly put to to raise the wind. One story goes that, being very hard pushed and not knowing how to raise cash, he got up from Calcutta several iron money chests and put them up in the four corners of a room where he lived. He then invited a number of wealthy friends to have a talk; while the conversation was going on, men came in, opened one chest, put in a bag of money. then another would come and take out this bag of money and this went on till the curiosity of the guests was raised and they asked him what the business was he had got hold of and he said. I am agent for a big company who receive and keep money for constitutents and pay a large interest for deposits. Money can be deposited to-day and taken out when wanted, etc., etc. This took the minds of the friends who immediately sent in large cash deposits. With these deposits, Kazee Ramzan Ali worked his factories and, I hope, paid back what he borrowed. The story went that the bags of money which were put in and taken out of the chests was but one solitary bag and a man brought it in and locked it up, then another man came in, unlocked the chest and took out the bag; immediately after from another door another man brought in the same bag and locked it up in another chest and so on. Another yarn was that when W. Taylor, Commissioner of Patna, started a model farm the old Kazee was asked by Taylor to help to get the native zemindars to help with subscriptions. The Kazee went round with the hat but let zemindars know that a little private tip to the Kazee would very much reduce the amount required by the Commissioner saheb from each zemindar. The old Kazee was a most genial old boy, he was always ready to help anyone. If a planter had a rotten factory for sale the Kazee was on to buy and, what's more, pay up, and the next thing you would hear was that he had sold it at a profit to some native friend. The Kazee was trusted by the Government and during the Mutiny, when the Commissioner ordered all Europeans out of Chupra, the Kazee was put in charge and, as far as I know, acted to the perfect satisfaction of the Government. See Buckland "Bengal under the Lieutenant-Governors"—Halliday. The Kazee getting into money difficulties over Arrowah his creditors put the concern under the Civil Court in 1864-65, nominating E. D. Urquhart as receiver. On his leaving Arrowah, John MacRae succeeded in 1869. In 1874 Ashburner and Co., bought the concern at public auction and greatly improved it. At this time Chaitanpursa and Jullalpore were sold and Urna, Owrah and Pygumberpore purchased. Tajpore was also sold, but after a few years bought back. For the most part of the time Arrowah, Tehati, Tajpore, Dungerah, Urna, Jullalpore, Owrah, Chaitanpursa and Pygumberpore composed the Arrowah Concern. J. MacRae continued to manage with a share from 1874. J. D. Macgregor joined in 1871 and W. O. Macgregor in 1877. On J. MacRae's death in 1881, the concern was jointly managed by the brothers Macgregor, one at Arrowah and the other at Urna, the concern being made into two divisions. W. Macgregor, one of the brothers, sold out in 1887; his brother, J. D. Macgregor, becoming sole manager and taking up his residence at Arrowah and from 1896 became proprietor of the whole concern.

Mr. J. D. Macgregor is anxious to visit his native home and is ready to sell the concern or any part of it for cash. Anyone wishing to acquire this fine property or part of it at a very reasonable figure should apply to J. D. Macgregor, Esq., Arrowah Factory, Naga P.O., Sarun.

Bans-ghaut
E. G. W.

This factory is now closed. I believe it was built by W. Wilson in 1869; he died in 1872. The superintendence of the factory was then given to Malcolm MacDonald (Callum) and he (M. MacDonald) in partnership with G. Williams bought, he holding 6 annas, G. Williams 6 annas and R. Phillips 4 annas and the management. The place proved a bad speculation, though old W. Wilson had done well here and had made some splendid indigo. Gwatkin Williams sold his share to James Murdoch of W. Moran and Co., and M. MacDonald made over his share to Messrs. Schoene Kilburn and Co. Phillips left as his management was not successful and was followed by F. Forth and then by G. Nicolay in 1880. The place was then bought by R. Berril, C. Boileau and MacElroy from Messrs. Kilburn and Co., and J. Murdoch, but they came to grief and the factory now belongs to Messrs. Begg Dunlop and Co., who had financed them. I believe there is an outwork belonging to the place built by W. Wilson called Dekowlie. As far as I can find out the whole concern is shut up.

Balla Barhoga
K. McL and
J C

These factories were built in the early fifties, Balla by W. James in 1854. Tom Slade bought 8 annas of Balla Barhoga from K. MacLeod in 1858 and went to manage Balla. In June 1858 Tom Slade and L. MacDonald started from Chupra for Pertabpore *via* Balla. They were accompanied by a youngster called Biddell, who on account of rebels being all about the Gorakhpur district where his factory was, could not get back to his place. Starting on the 18th June 1858, the following day they reached Balla. The receipt of no post made them anxious, and on the following day they heard the mutineers had burnt Ramghur Factory, and that they had a skirmish with the Sewan Dazzlers (a corps raised in Chupra) at Ekma. The Magistrate had left Sewan and the rebels were between them and Sewan, so they could not go to Pertabpore, they had to wait at Balla, which they did till the 27th June, when a man came, there in great haste to say the mutineers, foot and horse, had started from a place called Bisanpore, three miles off, on their way to burn Balla factory, Slade and MacDonald were having their mid-day *siesta* at the time. Slade wished to stand to his post, as he said he did not wish the natives to think he was afraid. But hearing there were ladies at Sudowah, he thought it his duty to go to their assistance, and so off they set for that factory, and arriving there found E. Wilson had boats, ready to drop down in the big Gunduk. They at once drove the party consisting of, among others, Mrs. E. Wilson and family, and got all safely on board, where they were very comfortable. They got on board about 6 P.M. The night soon set and they could see the blaze of burning factories and thanas which the rebels were setting on fire. They remained on the river for a couple of days. On the 30th June Alex Urquhart and J. C. Crawford came from Rajpore Factory to their boat, and Slade, Biddell and MacDonald went with them to Ranjpore; E. Wilson, his wife and daughter remaining in the boats and returning to Sudowah the next day as the rebels had cleared out of the district as suddenly as they came in. On their return to Balla they heard from the factory servants that just after they had left the mutineers appeared, firing several volleys into the house at a good long distance, as they were not sure if the *saheba* had gone and had heard that they were armed and had been practising with their rifles. The rebels burnt the Balla Bungalow, also a dog-cart of L. MacDonald's, heaping up straw over it and setting this on fire. Fortunately some six horses of his escaped their notice. They smashed every bottle, empty or full, and they scattered all the clothes they found about the compound. This shows that the rebels entered the house, which they first looted and then set on fire. I mention the above to show the narrow escape that many planters had in the exciting days of the Mutiny. L. Cosserat and Colonel Robarts bought Burhoga in the early sixties. Cosserat managed till 1872, when F. Murray took charge with a share and managed till 1877, when A. MacIntosh managed for a short time. Then J. Hodding came in as part proprietor. The place is now leased, I believe, to the Sugar Development Company.

Bhamo was, I think, built by R. Berril in partnership with C. Boileau and MacElroy. It became an outwork of Bansghat Factory afterwards.

I have but one or two factories left and about these I hope to get information in a few days when I will come to an end of my history. I am rather disappointed in not getting more particulars. But only a few factories possess any record of the past. However, I hope the little I have got together will prove interesting to men of the present day.

Bubnowlie
E. S. and Co.

Bubnowlie is situated in the Gorakhpur district. It is an old factory and must have been built by one of the Finch family, most likely Joseph, as I find him recorded as manager in 1829 to 1859. After him came Mr. Meyer in 1860, R. P. Brooke from 1861 to 1873. The factory about this time changed hands, being purchased by the brothers MacDonald, E. Studd and A. MacRae. A. MacRae took charge in 1874. J. MacDonald became manager from 1876 to 1878, when MacRae returned and remained to 1879. In 1879 C. E. Mackenzie became manager and J. MacDonald returned. In 1880 to 1883 C. Mackenzie managed again and in 1883 John MacDonald took over charge again. In 1885 F. Mackinnon became manager and continued so to 1888, when A. Macfarlane took charge till 1889 when F. Mackinnon returned and continued to 1897. John Mackinnon then took up the management to 1899. In that year F. Mackinnon managed to 1905 and still continues as manager. The outworks are Bykuntpore Domath and Sepaha. There are the following tombs:—To the memory of Isabelle wife of R. P. Brooke, born 16th January 1833, died 20th January 1873; George William Mackenzie died 8th October 1882; Gustavus Vernon Hume was drowned at a pigsticking party. Born 2nd July 1861. Died 19th March 1885; Thomas P. Lynch, aged 52 years, died 31st October 1891. There are also tombs to several children, etc. In 1887 F. Mackinnon built two outworks called Bulichi and Bagwanpore. Kinderputi also situated in Gorakhpur District was built by E. T. Sealy, R. Fenton and R. Sealy in 1885; manager W. Brouche 1886 to 1888; R. Fenton 1888 to 1891, R. Sealy 1892 and is now manager. There are no graves.

Behrowlie I. F. C.

This factory stands on the Changaree river, about 26 miles from Chupra. The mokararie pottah was given to H. Curtis of Ramcollah by Mahunt Ram Churn Dass of Pusa and was for 51 biggahs 10 cottahs, dated 2nd February 1861. The first vats were built by George Llewhellin, who was then an assistant at Ramcollah. The factory and dehat were purchased by E. Gwatkin Williams and Syud Abdool Ghyas. Williams later on bought his share and owned the 16 annas of the place until November 1886, when he sold to the Bengal Indigo Company, who in turn sold to T. R. Filgate in 1896. Owing to bad seasons and fall in prices the factory was closed in 1901. The managers of Behrowlie were E. G. Williams to 1885, R. C. Phillips to 1893, T. R. Filgate to 1901. There were several managers who held billets for short periods during the absence of other managers. Williams was the first planter to introduce into Behar the purchase by weight of plant in 1884. Williams was also very fond of horses and for a time kept up a racing stable at Behrowlie; he raced under the name of Mr. Cresswell and for a time trained the Nawab of Dacca's horses. There are no graves at Behrowlie factory. The rents of land round Behrowlie are high. The factory as a going indigo concern is, I believe, at present closed.

Hariharpore and Nawadah F. C. I

This belonged to Kazee Ramzan Ali, who was porprietor of Arrowah. He sold it to MacLean in the early sixties. MacLean seems to have abandoned the place and the Maliks of the mokararie on which the factory stood sold it for rent due and took possession. They sold to Stephen Cooper, but as soon as Cooper went there, MacLean returned and succeeded in ousting Cooper. Cooper then started Nawadah factory close by Hariharpore, and the two places were at feud for some time. Eventually MacLean cleared out and Hariharpore shut up for a time. When Cooper died, his brother, Sam Cooper, who was in the Opium Department, took over Nawadah and ran it for a year or two. R. Phillips managed in 1872, then Tulloch for one year. Laurie bought in 1874-75 and managed till 1885. The owners of the land on which Hariharpore was built again got possession and sold the place to Jones, who got a few biggahs of cultivation. Laurie took it over from Jones in 1876-77 and amalgamated it with Nawadah. Laurie left in 1885, to go to Bunsghant and Elliot went to Nawadah, where he managed for three years. After him came Exshaw, then Bonner Hodding to 1892, Ellis to 1894. In 1894 Laurie became 16-anna proprietor and took charge of Nawadah. Finding the factory did not pay, Laurie put in H. Walker to manage and took up another appointment. In 1901 Laurie sold to Granville, who worked the place till 1902-03, when he finally closed the Concern.

Jogapore
K. MacL.
J.

This factory was built by Mr. James in 1863, his manager, a native, called Mahomed Yakoob Khan. In 1864 they built two outworks, Bansopally and Kahalla, Cyril Irvine being put in as manager by James, and his brother W. Irvine assistant at Kahalla. In 1866 K. MacLeod found James in financial trouble, and took these factories over. On K. MacLeod's going home Tom Martin became manager and put Donald Reid in charge with Walter Mackenzie as his assistant at Bansopally and John Reid at Kahalla. In about 1867 K. MacLeod sold Bansopally to Jawad Hossain, Donald Reid getting the management of Suddowah Factory. Tom Fraser came as manager to Jogapore in about 1867, and Frank Hamley as his assistant at Kahalla. Fraser built the outwork, Choukey, in 1868. In 1869 Fraser left and took over the management of Motipore. W Smith became manager with Harry Fraser as his assistant at Kahalla, and Hugh MacDonald at Choukey. W. Smith continued to manage till 1878 when Angus MacEwen, who was then assistant at Kahalla, became manager. Martin taking MacEwen's place at Kahalla, and M. Hutchins going to Chowkey. Martin left to join the Purtabpore in 1881, when M. Hutchins went to Kahalla, and Hugh Macdonald went back to Chowkey where he remained till 1883, when he went home ill, and never came out to this country again. In 1882 Malcolm Macdonald managed for a short time while MacEwen was at home, and when MacEwen went home again in 1884 M. Hutchins managed for a year, D. MacEwen (brother of Angus MacEwen) going to Kahalla, Angus MacEwen took over the management again in March 1885, and remained on till December 1887, when he went to manage his own Factory Zamapore, he made over charge to M. Hutchins. M. Hutchins on going Home in February 1888 made over charge to M. M. Macdonald, he left for Home in July of the same year making over charge to D. MacEwen. M. Hutchins came out from Home in April 1889, and took over charge of the Concern which he still holds. The Assistants in 1889 were D. MacEwen at Kahalla, A. MacGillwray at Chowkey, D. MacLeod at Madhopore. D. MacEwen left to take up the management of Zamapore in 1890, MacGillwray left in 1891 to join the Purtabpore Concern, and MacLeod left for Champarun in 1895. Since then the following Assistants have been in the Concern: Herman, J. MacGillwray (Bourneo), G. H. Hodding, D. P. Macdonald, L. Bean, J. D. Campbell and R. Macdonald. Madhopore Factory was bought from a native in 1885 and opened out as an outwork of Jogapore the same year. The first assistant there was J. Christian.

Portaubpore K. MacL. P.

W. James has the credit of building a few pairs of vats and starting this fine Concern, but as he had got into money difficulties K. MacLeod took it over from him and put in John Anderson, late of Chitwarah, Tirhoot. Bunkut was an old shut up factory and was opened as an outwork in about 1857-58. This outwork has now, 1904-05 been turned into a sugar factory with the latest and best machinery. In 1858 Lauchlin MacDonald got an 8-anna share and took over the management. John Anderson leaving, L. MacDonald continued to manage till 1863, when his brother Neill was put in charge and managed till 1866, then M. MacDonald managed. During Neill's management he built Chuckea in 1864, Arthur Cosserat being assistant. In 1865 Jugdispore was built A. MacAlister being the assistant. When M. MacDonald took over charge of Purtabpore, Jugdispur was made a sub-management, MacAlister, sub-manager of Jugdispur, and the assistant at Chuckea. G. Proudfoot, who was there till he was relieved by Waller. In 1869 Gumour was built and J. Tulloch was

PERTAUBPORE HOUSE.

assistant there. This outwork was sold in 1871 to Jawad Hassain and his brother Golam Hossain. In 1871 Rattaseah was built and J. Tulloch went there. On the death of MacAlister in August 1871, Tulloch became sub-manager of Jugdispore until November when Buskin took charge making Chuckea his headquarters, Waller going to Jugdispur and Tulloch back to Rattaseah, M. MacDonald continuing to manage the concern till January 1882, when he left and made over charge to John Robertson who managed till 1893, when J. A. M. Wilson became manager, followed by Jack Campbell; since then there have been several managers. Chuckea was made a separate concern. After Buskin died Minden Mackenzie managed till he went to Dooria, Sealy getting Chuckea. MacAlister was buried at Jugdispur. Martin died at Rattaseah and was buried there in about 1885. Miss Annie Robertson died of typhoid at Chuckea in April 1887; she was buried in Chupra, John Fraser also died that year and was also buried in Chupra. M. MacDonald managed Purtabpur for 16 years off and on; M. MacDonald was also an assistant in Arrowah Concern in 1863 under James. Purtabpur Concern is at present broken up into several managements. G. Hay at Purtabpore and W. Mackenzie at Chuckea. Neil MacDonald also had a share in Purtabpore.

Rajahputtee
G. W. L. & Co.

This factory, now managed by J. B. Rutherford, was also built by Wilson in the same year as Ramkola. After passing through many hands, it became the property of the Llewhellins and was managed lately by M. Mackenzie, and I have not heard if it is being carried on now or what has happened to it. In 1852-53 one Monsieur La Roche was there; he was relieved by Wingrove. I don't know if he was a proprietor or not. He was a very amusing old gentleman, could sing a good French song after dinner.

Ramkola J. F. C.

This factory was built by one of the Wilson, either A. C. E. or E. Wilson, brothers of W. Wilson. It will be seen (*see* Singiah) that in 1836, H. F. Fitzgerald made a boundary agreement with Ramkola, so that the factory must have existed then. They were Irish and had been in Sarun ever since they came to India, and, as far as I understood, from what they told me, neither of them had seen an ocean-going steamer or a railway till W. Wilson went to Calcutta to sell his indigo in about 1870-71. The elder brother, A. C. Wilson, died at Ramkola and is buried in the garden; he died on 22nd September 1827 aged 27. Josephine Adelaide Curtis, wife of J. F. Curtis, was also buried here in 1868, aged 32, and J. F. Curtis in 1879, aged 52. Hugh Llewhellin took over charge in 1865-66. H. Macnamara built an outwork called Gorgaha in 1878, which has since been demolished.

Sadowah Concern K. McL. and C. McK.

Sadowah Concern which includes the following factories, *viz.*, Sadowah built by E. Wilson in 1819. Sepaiah by his brother W. Wilson in 1824-1825, Muniarah by Cook in 1867 and Tirbeenie which was built in 1887-88. All these factories formed one place called Sadowah Concern. In 1888 the Concern was divided and managed by D. N. Reid. The following are the managers of Muniarah:—1867 J. W. Pughe, 1868 L. J. Cooke, 1874 D. C. Reid, 1875 A. Buskin, 1877 J. A. Reid, 1880 Hugh Johnstone, 1881, J. A. Reid, L. D. Reid, 1883 C. D. H. Wilson and C. A. Mackenzie, 1883-87, Hugh Johnstone, 1888 D. N. Reid, 1892 C. A. Mackenzie, 1893 G. R. MacDonald, 1898 J. S. Dodd, 1899 G. N. MacDonald, 1899 to date 1905 John Mackinnon. I have not so far succeeded in getting the managers of Sadowah Factory, but I remember in 1852-53 and for some years before that Edward Wilson managed there and his brother William Sepaiah. Old Bill was a jolly old chap. He did love a rollicking party and could stow away a power of liquor. I remember once suddenly quoting the evidence taken by a Parliamentary Commissioner on the subject of drinking the question was—"Ever had D. T." and the reply "once or twice rather liked them." On this being quoted suddenly poor Bill thought he was being addressed and replied, "I have only had them once and that was from bad liquor." Ned Wilson was a very steady old chap. After his death Sadowah was sold and he left his widow over a lac of rupees. Mrs. E. Wilson adopted C. V. Argle's daughters and took them home and on her death left them all her money.

Seereepore.

The proprietor of this Concern was Indra Pertah Sahai, Maharajah of Hutwa. It was built by Malcolm MacDonald, who was sub-manager under Neil MacDonald. He was called on one fine day from Chuckea while fighting the caterpillars which swarmed in 1865 to go off and build Seereepore for the Rajah at a place called Dularpore, nine miles from Chuckea. So leaving the caterpillars to have their feed in peace off he started, taking up his abode in a tent and before long uprose a factory with a fair cultivation. The first year a small place with a small cultivation, *viz.*, two pairs of vats and 250 bighas of indigo from which as the crop was sown late he made 75 maunds of indigo. The next, however, he had 18 pairs of vats with press and cake house and bungalow and 2,900 bighas of indigo and made 700 maunds of indigo and should have made more but was short of carts.

In 1866, November, Neil MacDonald took over charge and M. MacDonald went to Purtabpur. In 1867 an outwork was built to Seereepur called Amakapur, Yankee MacDonald going there as assistant. He was followed by Mark Buskin. Neil MacDonald managed till February 1869, when he went home and Mark Buskin was put in charge during Neil's absence. Neil again took charge on his return from home, but left the country for good in 1871, when M. Buskin got the management and Pincher Brown became assistant at Amakapore. In 1875 M. Buskin got the management of Hutwa estates and Pincher Brown got the management of Seereepore and Adlam of Amakapore. In the early eighties this fine Concern, although paying handsomely, was closed by the Rajah as an indigo concern, as the Brahmans told the Rajah no son would be born to the Raj as long as he cultivated indigo there. Seereepur is now kept up as a farm only.

Zumunpore, Bhamo, Gopalpore, Geurs, Jatepore Kehumia.

The factories in the margin are all of recent date; some are closed and others going on in a small way. I can get no information as to who built them. Kehumia was for some time used as a sugar factory, but I don't know if it still continues this industry. Setulpore, a very old Sarun Factory is said by the oldest native inhabitant in the place to have been built by one Wall Saheb, in 1801. This information is corroborated by old records in the Collector's Office at Chupra. Where Mr. Wall prays that the brothers Chamfrain may be restrained from building in his dehat close to Sonnepur. Wall sold to Finch as the title deeds disclose him as first proprietor in 1818. Zeegler purchased from Finch many years afterwards and gave the Factory to his nephew De Meiss, who sold to J. Stalkart and he to K. MacLeod in about 1865. Geo. Toomey going to manage for a short time. K. MacLeod sold to Abdul Ali and Kazee Ramjan Ali, they in 1870 sold to Gonesh Lall and Gopal Das Bankers in Chupra. Rooney Dougal Coffin and Lockhart purchased from them. Rooney Dougal a few years after sold his share to Coffin and Lockhart. The Concern was closed as an Indigo Factory in 1900 and Coffin and Lockhart disposed of their interests to Mahomed Khan and Syud Iltaf Hasain Bankers of Patna.

This ends my history of Sarun Factories. If I have made any mistakes I hope my friends over the water will correct me.

Pertabpore.

Since writing the above I have received the following about Pertabpore Factory :—L. MacDonald sold 4 annas in Pertabpore Concern to Neil MacDonald in 1863, and afterwards another 4 annas more to him. L. MacDonald had become the 16 annas proprietor in 1861. He purchased his first 8 annas for Rs. 5,000 and eventually the second 8 annas at Rs. 1,50,000; this shows how greatly the place had improved in value. The representatives of the late Neil MacDonald still hold this 8 annas share and Lauchlin MacDonald the other 8 annas. Bunkut, one of the outworks was an old Sugar Factory and was opened out in 1851 by Mr. W. James as manager on account of K. MacLeod the proprietor. In 1854 Pertabpore was opened out by Mr. James as an outwork to Bunkut, K. MacLeod selling 8 annas of Bunkut and Pertabpore to John Anderson. Mr. James then went and opened out Burhoga, where he got into difficulties and Kenneth MacLeod had again to take over this place and sold 8 annas to Tom Slade. Mr. James was then out of work and went to manage Arrowah and from there he started Jogapore Factory. Here, too, he failed and K. MacLeod again came to the rescue. In these days the three leading indigo men in Sarun were K. MacLeod, Kazee Ramzan Ali and Mr. James. K. MacLeod financed them and between them they made the Sarun district the flourishing district it was in those days.

REMINISCENCES OF BEHAR.

PREFACE.

Some old friends have suggested to me the idea of publishing my experiences in Tirhoot from 1847. The following pages give a brief sketch as far as my memory serves me. Dates may not be always accurate; but they are not far out. Events have been jotted down as they came to mind; and if the occurrences of 1857 come tumbling in when my reminiscences are of 1847-48, I must ask my readers to remember that these pages have been put together hurriedly during leisure moments.

September 1887.

CONTENTS.

PAGE.

CHAPTER I.

Arrival in Calcutta—Journey Up-country—Sugar Planting ... 105

CHAPTER II.

Tiger-shooting—Midnight Alarm—Death by drowning of H—— ... 114

CHAPTER III.

House-keeping in Olden Days—Killing a Cobra—Daily routine at an Outwork—Ryots and Rent Laws 121

CHAPTER IV.

My Visit to Tiwarrah—I go to Sukree—A Haunted House and Ghost Stories—Poosah: a Government Stud Nursery—A Fauzdhary ... 133

CHAPTER V.

Ride over to Dooriah for Christmas—"Dulcinea del Tolboso"—Return to Work 144

CHAPTER VI.

Go to Kurnoul—Fatteued Ghainies—"Many a Slip 'twixt Cup and Lip"—How Cattle are treated—Brahmini Bulls—Narrow escape of J. S.—False Case 149

CHAPTER VII.

Journey down the River in charge of the Indigo—Sonepore Fair and Sonepore Race Meet 154

CHAPTER VIII.

Lord Mayo and Jung Bahadoor at Sonepore—Bargaining "à lá Oriental"—German Missionaries 161

PAGE.

CHAPTER IX.

My Christmas Party at Kurnoul—Wild Buffaloes—Shooting an Alligator—Visit of my Brother—Get the Management of Doomrah—My Assistant keeps Snakes as pets—Revival of the Mozufferpore Race Meet 175

CHAPTER X.

Another Shooting Expedition to Nepaul—Mud-imbedded Elephant—A Nepaulese Collector 185

CHAPTER XI.

I take charge of Shahpore Mircha—Journey and visit to Calcutta—Outbreak of the Mutiny 192

CHAPTER XII.

We fortify the Doctor's House—The "Vieille Guarde"—Taking a Prisoner—False Alarm—Murder of Major and Mrs. Holmes—Mutiny of the Native Infantry at Dinapore—Defence of Arrah—The Mutiny over—Homeward-bound 199

INDEX OF PROPER NAMES.

Baddeley, Wm., 203.
Becher, Capt., 112, 208.
Cox, James, 113, 115, 118, 133, 135, 141, 185, 207.
Crump, Phil., 107.
——, Mrs., 107.
Daunt, Paddy, 149, 150.
Drummond, F., 183.
Ferrier, 138.
Gale, John, 113.
——, Charles, 144, 185, 188.
Garstin, 138.
Gordon, 117, 118, 119.
——, "Fatty" (nick name), 134.
Grant, Gregor, 108.
Holgate, 114, 117, 118, 119, 120.
Hollway, Fred., 123.
Howell, Arthur, 179.
——, John, 151.
"Jimmy," James McLeod, 166.
John, Mr., sporting name of above, 166.
McLeod, Kenneth, 148.
McDonnell, Fraser, 138.
Mangles, 159.
Ogilvy, 138.
Pauling, Wm., 123.
Paxton, 111.
Ronald, 108, 109.
——, Mrs., 108.
Russell, Alex., 183.
"Simmy" Simpson, H. B., 184.
Slade, J., 151.
——, Tom, 119.
Stalkart, John, 117, 118.
——, J., "mad Jack," 123, 147.
Studd, E., 135.
Tindal, Jack, 133, 134, 135.
Vincent, Frank, 184.
Young, 138, 148.

REMINISCENCES OF BEHAR

BY

AN OLD PLANTER.

CHAPTER I.

ARRIVAL IN CALCUTTA—JOURNEY UP-COUNTRY—SUGAR-PLANTING.

In the year 1847, towards the end of September, I bade farewell to my people in Mauritius, and sailed in the good ship *Albatross*, an American vessel of over a thousand tons, Captain Coffin, commanding, for Calcutta, which we reached, after a prosperous voyage of five weeks, early in November. I was met on arrival by a very talkative Bengali Babu, who despatched me in a palkee to the house of Mr. Alfred Gouger, to whose care I had been consigned by my father. He lived at that time in Tank Square, and was of the firm of Gouger, Jenkins and Co. I was most hospitably received by him; but soon found that I had made my first acquaintance with Calcutta at a very inauspicious moment; the great firm of Cockerell and Co., having just failed for an enormous sum of money, and the Union Bank as well, spreading ruin and dismay amongst thousands of people. Every business man's face bore an anxious look, for no one knew when some big bill might be returned protested. Money could not be raised on the best security, and business was at a standstill. Things were in this condition when I steamed out of Calcutta down the Hooghly round by the Sunderbunds bound for Monghyr. As we passed in the steamship *Benares*, my good friends in the *Albatross* hoisted her colours, and dropped them in a parting salute to me, a stranger in a strange land, and I felt not a little downhearted, as I waved them back my last adieu.

The voyage from the Sunderbunds to Monghyr took over a week, and to a young griff, as I was then, became most exciting, the herds of deer on the low-lying lands bounding away into the thick woods, and the large alligators lying like logs of old timber on the muddy banks, and gliding into the water, when disturbed by the noise of our paddles, were a source of constant interest to me, and I only longed for my gun to have a shot at them. When we got out of the jungly part of the Sunderbunds, we came again on signs of civilization and soon passed the large concern, Maharajgunge, an indigo-factory, which, when Bengal was in its palmy days, used to sell for one lakh of rupees an anna share! Now, alas, it is a case of Ichabod!

The vessel had hardly touched the shore at Monghyr before we were boarded by hundreds of natives selling every conceivable kind of wood and iron-work, desks, boxes, pistols, knives, etc., and ornaments of all descriptions in buffaloe horn and ebony, all exceedingly cheap; a double-gun by a Monghyr Manton, could then be bought for Rs. 5. Now-a-days you may go to Monghyr and hardly find any of the people who used to work so well, and at such moderate prices; the iron horse and the march of civilization have pretty well cleared them all out.

Dr. Hastings, Civil Surgeon at the station, was kind enough to meet me and take me to his house—that in which Mr. Fitzpatrick afterwards lived—just outside the Monghyr Fort Gate, and close to the Railway station. I remember the present neat little public gardens were being laid out—those which have been brought to such perfection under General M—'s care, and are now the attractive rendezvous of society. Of course, I did not fail to visit the Sita Koond (hot springs), just below Peerpahar (Mountain of the Saint) where Mr. Alonzo Money then resided; he was Magistrate of Monghyr, and lived to distinguish himself during the mutiny when he marched to Gya. He was afterwards Commissioner of Bhaugulpore. After a short stay I proceeded on my journey to Tirhoot, my ultimate destination, crossing the Ganges in a very ricketty boat to where stood my palkee, awaiting my arrival with the usual quantum of bearers, musalchee, etc. Having spread my *razai* (quilt), and settled my pillows to my satisfaction with a cheroot to beguile the time, I started on what proved one of the most unpleasant journeys I ever made. I shall never forget the monotonous "h'm-h'm" noise of the bearers, or the almost unbearable smell of the *masal* (torch), which was lighted when night fell, or the agony of stiffness in my back, when I awoke from my first doze! The cold was intense on the lands between the banks of the river and the higher ground, and as no mattress had been put in the palanquin, there was nothing between me and it but the quilt, which was not as large as could have been desired, and consequently, I was nearly frozen. It was a most merciful dispensation when, at last, the bearers put down the palkee, and lit a huge fire round which we squatted together till the time came to get under way again. That was a night of misery!

We reached Munjowl Factory, where P— C— was manager and proprietor, about 6 A.M.; and never shall I forget poor old C—and his "get-up" of black velvet cap, knee breeches, and top boots, and over all a bright, coloured dressing gown. I was most kindly received by him, and Mrs. C—, and their little daughter, and observing his costume, I fully expected that he was just setting out to ride; but for the two days I stayed at Munjowl, his dress never varied, and never a horse did he bestride. Again betaking myself to my palkee, I reached Dowlutpore in the early morning, and giving my bearers one rupee as *buksish*, I dismissed them, but they had spotted me as a griff, and one of them shortly after returned with a long yarn in which the words "rupee" and "crab" were often repeated, and of which I did not understand anything, till the English-speaking factory Babu coming to my assistance, it was explained to me that the rupee I had given was a bad one, and that they were asking for another, which I gave at once. R—, who was managing Dowlutpore, was away at the time, and was highly amused at my simplicity in believing them, for, of course, they had swindled me. I spent two very pleasant days with R—and his wife, who were most kind to me. Both have been dead many years,—he, poor fellow, was one of the many victims of the mutiny. He had left indigo and gone into the Sonthal Commission. He and G— G— were paying a visit to some officers in charge of a detachment of sepoys stationed near the Grand Trunk Road. They had dined, and passed the night with their friends, when, in the early morning, they heard shots fired G— G— immediately understood what was up, and bolted straight way, getting into the jungle, where he was hidden by a Pasi woman. R— was following G— when a sepoy called after him: "What are you running away for, Sahib? There is no fear." Poor R— was foolish enough to turn back, when the sepoy bayonetted him. Thus died poor R—. As it may interest my readers to know about the two officers, I will go on with their story: They, finding their men in a state of mutiny, ran for the house, and locked themselves in. One of these officers was reported to be a very kind and considerate master, the other a man of a most violent temper who never had a civil word to say to a native. They had not been long in the house when a sepoy came to the door and called to the bad tempered man to come out. Though bad tempered, he was brave, and he told his brother officer that he would go out, and the sepoys would, no doubt, shoot him, and in the meantime he could escape. What was his astonishment, when, on his stepping out of the house, four men formed round him, and marched him off to Bhaugulpore. A purse was got up by the residents of Bhaugulpore as a reward for these men who had saved their officer. One of the old Eurasians, however, questioned the sepoys as to why they had not saved both officers. "Oh," they said, "this man is a mad man; and if we had killed him, the devil in him would have gone into one of us!" In the morning when the station residents went to present the purse, they found the sepoys gone. The other unfortunate officer was shot. I may as well relate another instance of a marvellous escape during the mutiny which happened about the same time. Some irregular cavalry mutinied and ran off from Bhaugulpore. They had to pass by a factory where a young planter was living: and expecting some loot, they fired a volley, and made for the house. The planter was just going to bed. He told his bearer to run to the stables and bring his horse round to the back of the garden and hide it in the ditch. The sowars were close to the house, so he had to make up his mind sharp as to where he would in the meanwhile hide. He suddenly remembered that he had had a big earthen vessel called a *mutka,* made to hold water, lately dug out of the floor of one of the rooms, so he felt his way in the dark and got into the hole where the *mutka* had been. He had barely settled down when one of the *sowars* entered the room. He dropped a gun cap, and bent down to try to find it by groping about on the floor with his hand. As the sowar got nearer and nearer to him, the young man felt his blood run cold. The sowar shortly after went out of the room, when the planter jumped out of his hiding place, ran along the garden hedge, got into the ditch, and finding his horse waiting there, jumped on it, and rode off.

I must now go back to Dowlutpore, and continue the thread of my story. From R—'s hospitable roof, I again continued my journey to my next stage, Hattowrie Factory, and arrived, as on previous occasions, in the early morning.

As a matter, of course, my palkee was put down at the door of the bungalow, and looking out, I saw a lady and some children, but having no letter of introduction and being unaccustomed to the ways of the country, I felt rather as if I were intruding, and not very happy. However, she came forward in the kindest way, and asked me in, making me so welcome that I soon forgot my shyness. I was very desirous of testifying my gratitude by an offer of my palkee and bearers, as she wanted to leave Hattowrie, her husband having sold out; but nothing would induce the men to take her—they would only carry me to my journey's end, and with many regrets at my inability to assist her, after a few hours' rest, I again set out on my weary way. How thankful I was to find myself some twelve hours after grasping my brother's hand, and my wanderings ended. It was late at night when I arrived, and he had got out of bed to receive me, so, saying, he should reserve all he had to say till next morning, I very gladly "turned in," and was soon in the delightful arms of Morpheus. I don't know how long I had slept when I was awakened by some one singing in the room next to mine, really most beautifully, and then the same voice addressing an audience—which I found afterwards was an imaginary one—in these words: "What do you think of that for a song? "Oh, you encore me? Well, I will sing you something this time that will bring down the house;" and off he went again, song after song, till, worn out with his exertion, as I was with mine, sleep overtook us. Next morning I made the acquaintance of my eccentric next door neighbour. He was standing, looking into a drain, as I approached him and said: "Good morning." "Do you hear her, poor thing?" he asked, for a reply. "She says she has not been washed for a week." I was rather taken aback by this remark, and still more so when pointing to some water, out of which something stood upright, he asked. "Do you see that boa-constrictor?" I thought him stark staring mad, as indeed he was not far from being, and was very glad when at this moment my brother made his appearance. The gentleman in question was a Mr. P—, who had charge of machinery at Purhehar Factory, who having imbibed too freely *en route* had been put down at Kumtoul to recover himself before continuing his way to Mozufferpore. He had been a professional singer before he took to engineering, which accounted for the midnight entertainment he had favoured me with. He only remained a few hours my brother's guest, and that was the last we ever heard of him.

After breakfast the factory *amlahs* (office servants) came in a body to pay their respects to me, the "*Burra Sahib's*" brother, each offering his gift of one or two rupees, according to the donor's position, laid on the corner of his clean *chudder* (sheet worn over the shoulder) with a low *salaam*. I was rather puzzled as to the wherefore of this ceremony, and inquiring what I was to do under the circumstances, learnt, to my surprise, that I was to take the coin, raise it to my forehead in token of acceptance, and pocket it, a not unpleasant and easy occupation as I found by the evening that I had added to my slender fortune not less than fifty rupees. The custom prevailing at that period was, if you were a *Burra Sahib* (great man) to touch the rupees with your fingers, and then your forehead, and the *sirdar* bearer (head bearer), who took care to be present on such occasions, pocketted the money. Since the time I speak of this and other respectful practices have nearly died out in India, times have changed —not altogether for the better.

Before leaving Mauritius, I had been employed as a sugar-planter with the view of learning the work it was proposed that I should follow in Bengal, but within two years sugar-planting in Tirhoot, was pretty well given up, and many a good man ruined. The soil was found to be unsuited for it, and the cane degenerated,—then it was that I took to indigo; but before that time arrived, many jolly days were spent with my brother at Kumtoul and other places. One holiday at Kanti, in 1848, is very fresh in my memory, at my cousin, Russell Crawford's house—a very pretty place, situated on the border of a large semi-circular lake, well raised off the ground. The drive up to it, meandered through hedges of lovely roses, and the grounds were enclosed by clumps of enormous bamboos, whose graceful feathery heads seemed to wave one a welcome. Flowering shrubs were dotted all about, and banyan trees with wide spreading branches roomy enough to take in a regiment of soldiers, were to be seen every here and there. We spent New Year's Day in shooting. Breakfast was sent out to us; and we had a charming picnic after making a capital bag of black partridge, hare, and quail. In the evening we danced; to my extreme confusion it was discovered that I alone of the men could waltz, and I was, therefore, led up to the "Spin." of the party who danced "round dances," and we did "the light fantastic" together, to the admiration of the spectators. Quadrilles and country dances followed, and fun became fast and furious till the small hours chimed. Happy bygone days! Captain B— was one of those I met for the first time during my visit to Kanti. He was quite a gentleman of the old school, and most courteous in manner. At one period he had been in the Hon'ble East India Co.'s Navy, which he had left tolerably well off. Unfortunately, he invested all his fortune in indigo, and lost it, and was at that time managing a saltpetre manufactory, near my cousin's place for Mackillop, Stewart and Co., of Calcutta. I was back at work at Kumtoul early in January, and found that it was becoming pretty hard. The west wind had begun to blow, and so violently in the day time, that the sparks from the furnaces were carried for miles around, endangering the villages, and we had, consequently, to do the cane-crushing at night, which was a very cold and tiring business, and I was thankful when at last it was finished. The engines had been very trying to the nerves of everybody—" Blowhard " and " Rattletrap " by name—the boilers of both being in such a crazy condition, that they were always on the point of bursting, especially " Blowhard," which actually did come to pieces, and killed a young blacksmith. Happily, I was absent when the accident took place, but it did not contribute to my peace of mind when I returned. I had been with my brother to Pundoul, Mr. J.— G—'s factory, where sugar was extensively manufactured,—a very pretty place with grand mango groves all about it. Mr. G— was devoted to gardening, and showed great taste in the way he had laid out the grounds. It was said that his pineapples were so plentiful that he fed his pigs on them, and that every fruit and flower that India could produce might be found in his gardens.

Shortly after this, I was asked to make one of a tiger-shooting party, and having obtained leave to go my delight was unbounded. For a week beforehand every spare moment was spent in seeing to the state of my guns, casting bullets, and getting the howdah gear in order, and it was a red letter day when about the end of March, Mr. J— C— picked me up at Kumtoul and carried me off to Doomrah.

CHAPTER II.

TIGER-SHOOTING—MIDNIGHT ALARM—DEATH BY DROWNING OF H——

OUR escapes were narrow and many during the drive to Doomrah Factory, for neither the roads nor the horses were of the best; of the latter, one was given to backing, another to gibbing. However, we arrived safe and sound at last, and the perils of the way had been so exciting that they added just the zest needed to make our journey most amusing. Our host, a jovial merry-fellow, had assembled a large party of friends; and although I was a stranger to most of them, I soon felt myself at home, and burning with ardour for the early start, we were to make on the morrow.

Long before the peep of day, we were up and away to S—, where H— lived, not far from Purhilca Factory: H— carried on some farming business in connection with villages belonging to the Soorsund Babus. Resting there till the afternoon, we again set out, and, crossing the Nepaul boundary at a place called Sirrecpore Kablassa, we shortly came upon our tents, ready pitched, and every preparation made for us.

I was astonished and much impressed to hear from the villagers that big game was so numerous, and that tigers were running all over the place like cats, but I was soon to find out that a Nepaul Shikari (hunter) is not to be quite depended on, and tells a "good one" when he wishes to keep the thing going. We were to be ready to start at four o'clock next morning, and long before then were astir, getting our properties in order, rubbing our guns, and preparing our powder and shot. The elephants, with howdahs strapped on, appeared on the scene at the appointed time, and, I must confess it was with some trepidation I approached the huge, restless monster on whose back I was to take my first lesson in elephant-riding, as well as tiger-hunting. J— C— was made Captain of the expedition, and having reached the jungle, we were placed in a line, he in the centre. Between each howdah animal there were several pad elephants to do the work of beating, and in this order on we marched, the elephants stamping and crushing down the trees in their path by putting their foreheads against them, and bringing the whole weight of their bodies to bear. We, on the tiptoe of expectation, ready to fire at "Stripes" the moment he showed himself. However, our first day out was doomed to be a blank, as far as big game was concerned. In spite of the story of the *shikaris*, that tigers were as plentiful as cats, we beat the thick jungle till midday in vain. Then the order to fire only at tiger was withdrawn by our Captain, and we turned our attention to deer, hare, and pea and jungle fowls, of which we made a large bag before night fell. As the elephants with the tiffin (luncheon) basket hove in sight, we called a halt, and, getting into a piece of magnificent sal forest, we were not long in setting to. Near us ran a lovely river, the rippling water of which was as clear as crystal, and on its banks we pitched our tents. How delicious it was after many hours jolting to dip in the stream, and refresh our tired limbs! Elephant-riding had reduced me to one great ache in every part of my body; and, I think, the slumbers of all our party were pretty sound that night, when, soon after our evening meal, we turned in. Early morning we were again afoot and away, the day opening with brighter prospects, for having reached some marshy ground in which tall reeds were growing, the elephants began to show signs of uneasiness, and all at once there was a rush and a regular volley of shots. I saw nothing but the tip of a tail over the reeds. Following in line, I suddenly came on a tiger dead, or dying in about a foot of water. My animal pulled up with a jerk that nearly threw me out of the howdah, and the *mahout* shouted to me to fire, or the elephant would go down on his knees to crush the tiger. There was a tremendous hubbub, natives shouting, elephants screaming and trumpetting, sportsmen scolding, so I blazed away, expending all my barrels on the brute, which I believed was already dead; however, there could have been no doubt about it when I had ceased to fire, and we gathered round our trophy. It proved to be a tigress over nine feet long from tip of nose to end of tail. She was handed over to the *chamar* (tanner) to skin and partly tan; and we afterwards found that the natives had boned all the whiskers and several of the claws as charms, which was very amusing. I have shot several tigers since those days, but have never succeeded in recovering the skin with its full number of whiskers, the natives will have *one* at any cost. As may be supposed, we were excessively proud of our first tiger, for we were nearly all griffs and new to the work. Late next day, when some of the party had dismounted and gone after florican a long way from the rest of us, a *mahout* called out: "There goes a tiger," and, sure enough, about half a mile away in the middle of a big plain, we saw his royal highness quietly walking off towards a wood on the opposite side. We halted to collect our scattered forces, and they too seeing the beast, got on their elephants sharp, and gave chase. As we advanced, we watched with intense interest a native who was crossing the *maidan* (plain) within a few feet of the tiger, the animal passed almost close to him, but he never increased his pace, it was *kismet!* Our elephants, unfortunately, were not of the best—they were not howdah elephants—and were very slow, so, we did not get up with the tiger as rapidly as we ought; but S— got a long shot at him, as he was entering the wood, and thought he limped as he went away, but it was too late to follow him that night, and we returned to camp. At dawn we were off again in search of the *bagh* (tiger) which S— thought he had wounded; but, though we beat every possible bit of jungle, we did not see any signs of him, and we had almost given him up, when, returning to the ground we had shot over the previous day, H— and G— saw a little patch of grass ahead, which they thought they would try. Hardly had they entered it when out jumped a big tiger. G— in his excitement fired two barrels loaded with shot, but H— sent a bullet after him, as he disappeared into the jungle, and declared he had hit him. Next day we moved our camp, and beating down a stream that ran through the wood near where H— had fired at the tiger, I came upon him dead. He must have been the same animal that S— had hit as there was a wound on his hindleg. Our "find" was another tigress about the size of the first.

During the night that followed, when we were all sleeping the sleep of the just after the fatigues of the day, we were aroused by the most frightful yells I ever heard. To jump out of bed and seize our guns was the work of a moment; but in the dark all was confusion and hubbub at first. I had never heard horses screaming from terror till then; and a very horrible sound it was, mingled with the shrieks of the *sirdarjee* (underservant) who, asleep outside the tents, had opened his eyes to find a tiger standing at his feet, it was only a wonder that he had not been carried off by the brute. The poor horses were perfectly paralysed with fear. We were soon afterwards in pursuit, and very anxious to come up with the gentleman who had so nearly polished off our bearer. Following the footprints in the sand, we got into a piece of jungle thick with an undergrowth of grass and briar plum, which we beat carefully through without result. Then we sent the *shikaris* to see if there were any footprints in the dry bed of the river which might indicate an exit that way, but none were visible. We felt certain that the animal could not be far off, and wheeled round to beat back again. About half way, I observed a tuft of grass, too small, one would have thought to conceal any large animal, but "every stone must be turned" in tiger-hunting, so, I called to the driver of one of the pad elephants to go through it, when, with a growl, out jumped our midnight visitor. The whole line fired, and she rolled over just outside the jungle in the sand. A pad elephant had been told off to carry her, when she was observed to blink one eye as much as to say: "I'll give it to *you* now," and in a second up she sprang with a roar, and made a kind of semi-circular charge on us.

Away sped the elephants, S—'s howdah was smashed against a tree, and knocked to pieces, and his guns thrown on the ground. Fortunately, he managed to spring at C—'s elephant as it passed, and hold on to the howdah. S— and H— disappeared on theirs down the dry bed of the river, and did not return for over an hour. G— was on a blind animal, which did not run far, and mine stood still after a short scamper. C—'s, with S— hanging on behind, rushed into a thick forest, where the gigantic creepers half-skinned the wretched *mahout*, and C— himself, who had ventured to peep out from a secure position in the bottom of the howdah, got such a crack with one that he looked for some days after, as if he had been having a round with Heenan. S— escaped easiest in the end, squatting behind the howdah, though his clothes were nearly torn off his back, and he got a scratch or two. It had been the last dying effort of the tigress; and when our scared elephants had recovered their lost equanimity, we bore her triumphantly home to the camp. It was on that eventful day I despatched my first cobra. A very demon he looked, with his wicked little eyes gleaming and his hood extended, disputing the right of way. We had hoped to have had a few days more hunting, but that night brought us our marching orders in the advent of a heavy "nor'-wester."

The wind roared through the neighbouring trees till the tents seemed as if they would be blown to shreds, and the rain came down in torrents. As it is considered dangerous to remain in the jungle after wet weather on account of malarious fever, the order was given to pack up and be going —some of our party started at once, and the rest followed later, of which latter number I was one. The heat and mugginess of that night were fearful, added to which our senses were invaded by a most horrible stench, supposed at first to be the dreaded malaria, but which proved to be pieces of tiger-flesh, which the servants had kindly attached to the outer fly of our tents, intending to take the savoury morsels home with them as charms. We struck camp early the following morning. On lifting the floor-cloth in our dining tent, the ground was found to be literally alive with little snakes, about four inches long. I never saw such a sight!

How sorry I was when our expedition was over! Though it is six and thirty years since those happy days, every incident of them is vividly before me still, and I look back to that time with the liveliest pleasure. Of the jolly few, gathered together then, only two remain; H—, G—, T—, S— and J—, S— are dead. Poor H— was drowned shortly after our return. He was staying with my brother at Kumtoul; and one day having nothing more amusing to do, we borrowed a boat from one of the big crafts that were shipping saltpetre on the riverside for the purpose of having a row, but, finding the stream heavy to pull against, and the breeze favourable, I suggested getting a sheet and improvising a sail. My bungalow was not far off, and I ran home to get one. As the tailor was working in the verandah, I waited a few minutes to get him to sew it on a cross bar of wood for a yard, and then returned to the river, but could not see anything of H—. Thinking he had got tired of waiting and strolled on, I hoisted my sheet and sailed up the river, expecting to come on my missing friend. Not doing so, I returned the boat to its owner, and started in search of him on foot. I looked for him everywhere, but could see or hear nothing of him. All night I sat up waiting and watching for his return, very anxious and much distressed, for we were great friends. Three days passed, and then the village-watchman came and gave us the information that the body of a European was floating in the river a little way down, and this was poor H—. We got him out and buried him under a tree to the North-West of the big bungalow on the border of the factory *zerat*. Greatly to my annoyance, no sooner had the police got wind of what had happened, than I found myself an object of suspicion, the *Darogah* (Police Inspector), through others, kindly giving me to understand that he suspected foul play, but that a tip would put all right. Fortunately, my brother was at the factory, and my evidence was taken in his presence, or I might have found myself very awkwardly placed. The following year when some of the river boats returned, we learned how it was that poor H— was drowned. Having probably got tired of waiting for my return, he took up a long bamboo, and tried to pole the boat up stream. Either the water was deeper than he anticipated, or the bamboo stuck in the mud at the bottom, for, he was pulled off, and went down before the men who saw the accident, could rescue him. Seeing that the *Sahib* did not rise again to the surface, one of them, they said, swam to the boat as it was floating down the stream, and moored it where I had originally left it under H—'s care. Why the boatmen did not speak then and tell what had occurred, it is impossible to say. Either they were afraid of suspicion attaching to themselves in the first instance, or they were paid by the police to keep silence, when the hope suggested itself of making out a case against me, and being well "tipped" to hush it up.

CHAPTER III.

HOUSE-KEEPING IN OLDEN DAYS—KILLING A COBRA—DAILY ROUTINE AT AN OUTWORK—RYOTS AND RENT LAWS.

Shortly after this, I was sent to an outwork and set up house-keeping on my own account. A few tables and chairs and a couple of beds formed the not very elaborate furniture of my bungalow. My crockery was of the most miscellaneous kind, and would have realized a small fortune in these days of China mania, so battered and mained was it: but in the days when I speak of, it had its value for me, for my means were limited, and I had picked it up cheap. How well I remember the first smash! Not long after getting into order, a cobra had presumingly established itself in my kitchen, and the cook arrived in hot-haste to desire me to come and kill it, or it would devour the only fowl there was to be had for my dinner. The appeal touched me so nearly that I forthwith set out with my gun, but finding I had no caps, I seized a thick stick, and made for the enemy. He was full of fight, and came at me the moment I put my foot over the side of the door with such viciousness that I had to beat a precipitate retreat. While I was taking counsel with myself how best to rout the intruder, the factory *jemadar* (head cultivation servant) came on the scene, poising aloft in his hand, a manyheaded spear used for killing fish. With this he entered the kitchen; the cobra, which had coiled itself up in a corner, charged again, and he let drive, jumping as he did so on to a wooden chest that stood conveniently by. It was that in which my dinner service and cups and saucers were kept; the original lid had been broken, and replaced by some ill-fitting pieces of wood, which gave way under the *jemadar's* weight. There was a fearful crash, and

I knew that my china was no more. The greater part of it was demolished; but the cobra was writhing on the spear heads, and victory was with us, so I had to put up with my loss as well as I could. Just afterwards a snake-charmer, who had heard of what was going on, appeared, and was much disgusted to find he had arrived too late to take the reptile alive. I suspect this one would have given him some trouble, for though I have seen many since, I do not remember any other as vicious as this cobra.

My household consisted of a *khitmatgar* (waiter), a cook, a sweeper, a *dhobie* (washerman), a bearer, (valet), a waterman, and a tailor. For these one pays now just about twice as much as I paid then. I was never a clever house-keeper, and do not quite remember the prices of things, but I think I am right in saying that then, you would get eight very fine fowls fit for roasting for a rupee, or sixteen chickens for the same money; a small lamb for four annas; rice twenty seers, and milk twenty quarts for a rupee. Country-bottled beer, the only kind sold and used then, could be procured from Calcutta, if bottles were sent down by the boats, and the ale bought in casks, at Rs. 4 to Rs. 4-4 or Rs. 5 a dozen. English bottled beer is the only kind that is drunk now, brought by steamers from England in a month's voyage, whereas three to six was formerly the passage round the Cape, a length of time that was quite destructive to English beer. The price it sells at is not much higher—from Rs. 6 to Rs. 6-8 a dozen in Calcutta, and Rs. 7 to Rs. 7-8 in the district. Formerly, beer was universally drunk; and some men had a wonderful capacity for taking it in. New-a-days, this has been exchanged for claret or whisky and water, and certainly the Tirhooteans of the present day are much more abstemious than those of the past generation, who, in the good old days, if a man got up a case or two of beer immediately assembled from the surrounding neighbourhood, and remained his guests till every drop was gone. This was called "giving him a party," though it might be defined the other way.

At Sibnuggur Factory, I was allowed two riding horses. My house was a thatched bungalow containing three rooms bordered by two verandahs, and I was about ten miles distant from any European. The first night I spent in my lonely mansion was dull enough. One of a large, cheery family, I began to wish that my lot had been cast nearer home. How well I could picture them all in Mauritius, and here I was far from every creature—as distant as could be. The lamp I had to brighten my solitude was manufactured by the bearer out of a brandy bottle cut in two, in which stood, stuck in half a potato, a wick of cotton wound round a thin piece of bamboo, it was not lively. I afterwards purchased a pair of plated candlesticks with glass shades, and when these figured on the table *vice* the brandy bottle, I felt myself to be rather rising in the world, and a man of property! As I was very fond of riding, I soon found the means of routing the "blue devils." I kept what is called a "bobbery pack," and hunted jackals and foxes. My pack was composed of terriers, greyhounds, *tazies* (native greyhounds), and even pariah dogs, and gave me capital sport. Part of my duty was to ride over the indigo cultivation in the early morning, and, as I always had my dogs with me, if I started a fox or jackal off we went, and frequently ended in having a good scamper and a kill. My nearest neighbour out of the concern was W—— P—— at Poopree, for J—— S—— had left and gone to Bengal. Next to Poopree came Doomrah, where F—— H—— had taken the management. They came to see me now and then; and, when I could get leave, I returned their visits, and at Doomrah used to have great wolf-hunts. It was considered a great feat of horsemanship to ride these animals down, and I recollect one occasion on which we nearly succeeded.

We had gone out early in the morning, as it was in the hot season, and from the first grass we beat, out sprang a wolf which made straight away over the dry paddy-fields with us after him. We took it in turns to give him a spurt, keeping him at his top speed, while some of us made for coignes of vantage by short cuts which enabled us to rest our horses before starting again in direct pursuit. In this way we ran him for ten miles across the rice *chur*. The ground, baked by the sun, was as hard as iron, and told sadly on our horse's legs. I believe the wolf would have escaped in the end, if the inhabitants of a village we passed through had not caught sight of him, and despatched him with sticks before we got up to them. When we dismounted, we were so completely done, men and horses, that we leant up against one another to support us from falling on the ground. A short rest and a good breakfast put us men all to rights, but the poor animals did not get over the run as easily. Little "Opera Dancer," H—'s favourite riding nag, had her legs swollen as big as an elephant's and all the others walked very tender for days afterwards.

The great Sitamurhi Fair takes place annually near Doomrah, and during the time it lasts was always full of planters, who quartered themselves in the neighbourhood at the houses of friends, for the purpose of making purchases of bullocks, timber, and other necessaries for factory use. The fair is held in an extensive mango grove, and thousands of oxen are brought to it for sale. As well as being a fair, it is also the occasion of a Hindu festival, where offerings are made to the goddess "Sita," by women and children, who come in large numbers from long distances to worship, and show off their fine clothes and jewellery. If the weather is bad, the hardships these poor people endure is almost incredible; and the perils they run, in any case, at the fair ought to be enough to deter them, one would think, from returning. But, in spite of the cruel attacks of the professional thieves, who take advantage of the crowding or a row, to fall on their victims, and tear off their golden nose and earrings, leaving them in frightful pain, and terribly disfigured, they return undismayed the following year, arrayed with all the valuables that remain to them, again to be attacked and despoiled. The *fakirs*, or religious mendicants, are a great nuisance at this gathering, especially to the shopkeepers, from whom they extort blackmail, or rather, what they will, by playing on their fears of the professional thieves. If these beggars are refused what they ask for, they howl, and fight, and create a disturbance, which at once collects the thieves, who, in the confusion, often manage to make a clean sweep of everything in the shop. As a class, the *fakirs* are the biggest rascals in India, especially those who travel about. When thieves wish to escape from a district that has become too hot for them, they generally disguise themselves as pilgrims or mendicants. I am sure that if Government made a law treating these men as vagrants, it would do a great deal of good, and no Hindu would say a word against it. They are afraid of, and have no respect for, them, and would be thankful to escape from their extortions.

The price of bullocks has gone up very much since the year I first visited Sitamurhi Fair. In 1848 and 1849 you could have got a splendid pair for Rs. 80; you now pay for the same class of animal over Rs. 150. Timber, also, has much increased in price; a log that would have cost Rs. 8, is now Rs. 100—and this has not been the result of any scarcity of wood, but caused by the closing of the sale of it in the Nepal Terai forests by the Nepal Government.

My work at Sibnuggur as an Assistant Indigo Planter had not much to vary it, and might be described as monotonous; though, on the whole, I liked it. To rise before the sun, eat his *chota-hazri*, make sure that the factory ploughmen are ready to go to work, inspect horses and bullocks, and see that they are fed, mount his horse and go over all the indigo cultivation, is the daily employment of an Assistant. This may take him five hours or more; he returns *via* his factory zerats (home-cultivation), and gets under shelter from the sun by 11 A.M. After breakfast, he allows himself, in the hot season, a siesta till 3 P.M., takes a bath and a cup of tea to freshen him up, and goes to the office to look over the accounts, and settle any matter that may be in hand. It is nearly sunset before all this is accomplished, and time to remount his horse and ride round and inspect the work done since the morning. If there be blacksmiths and carpenters employed at the factory, he looks them up. This routine is closely followed out till November or December, by which time the ground for planting indigo has been properly tilled and made ready, when comes the measurement of the land to ascertain if there is the right quantity in cultivation. With a book and pen in his hand, accompanied by a boy holding a bottle of ink, the Assistant rides from field to field, while men with nine foot poles measure the length and breadth of them, calling out the number of poles in a sing-song voice: "*Now luggee, now!* (nine poles, nine!) when another takes it up: "*Dass, han, dass!*" (ten, yes, ten!) —or whatever the poles may be. I confess to having felt always much relieved when this part of my duty was completed. To get over it quickly, most men keep at it all day, and, as it is cold-weather occupation, the sun does not harm one.

Sowing the indigo comes next in order. First, all the drills have to be tested to see how much seed they average per acre. This done, and orders having been sent from the head-factory to begin to sow on a certain day, the drills are sent out in batches to different parts of the cultivation to be ready for use. Early on the appointed day the drill-shares are set to the proper depth and set going; and this is repeated daily till the whole cultivation is sown. At the beginning of May arrangements are entered into for the manufacture of the indigo, for advancing money for carts, pressmen, etc. Formerly it was more difficult to get beaters—the most essential of the men employed—than others, as only a certain caste of the natives would do the work, and they were hard to get, and troublesome to keep. Machinery, patented by A. Butler, now takes the place of these labourers, and makes matters easy. If rain has fallen at the propitious time—by the end of June—the plant is nearly ready to cut, and early in July the factory presents a very busy appearance. Carts arrive in hundreds, laden with indigo, which are backed, and the contents emptied into the vats, on each of which coolies are employed to carefully stack it. As soon as they have filled the vats and thatched them over with indigo, bamboos cut of appropriate lengths are forced in across them, under beams that hold them, for the purpose of keeping the plant immersed, and preventing it bursting up when fermentation sets in. Water is then let on till it shows above the plant when the flow is cut off, and the indigo is left to steep for about twelve hours. The liquid thus obtained is then run into the lower or beating vat, and the refuse that remains removed for manure or fuel. Operations are immediately begun in the lower vats, either by beaters or machinery till the fecula has been separated from the water and settled down. The water is then run off and the fecula pumped into boilers, which are gently fired. The fecula is again allowed to settle, and the water run off a second time; what is precipitated is once more slowly boiled, and, finally, poured on a large strainer called a table, where the indigo settles thickly, and the water runs off clear. On the following day it is put into press boxes—about three feet square—and thoroughly squeezed dry. The boxes are then taken into the cake-house, where the indigo is stamped and laid on shelves made of strips of bamboos till the process of drying is completed. It is then packed in chests and sent to Calcutta, where it is sold by either Messrs. W. Moran and Co., or Thomas and Co., or shipped to England.

Indigo is cultivated in two ways, by *zerat* and *ryotti* (or *assamiwar*). The first is homestead-cultivation by factory ploughs and labour the second, *ryotti* or *assamiwar*, is secured thus: A factory farms a village, and takes from each *ryot* an agreement to cultivate a portion of his holding for indigo. The *ryot* prepares the land and reaps the crop; the factory pays for the seed, sowing, and carting off to the vats. In 1847 the rates paid for *ryotti* indigo were very low—Rs. 6-8 per acre for good plant—and, as *ryots* often had to pay high rents, very little remained to the cultivator after paying this. The *ryots*, however, got this advantage, that the day the indigo agreement was written, the total of their indigo-account in full was placed to credit in their rent, which was finally adjusted at the end of the season.

Now indigo is well paid for, owing to a reform brought about by the Planters' Association, an institution set on foot under the auspices of Sir Ashley Eden, late Lieutenant-Governor of Bengal. The Association acts as an arbitrator in all questions relating to indigo, and as a buffer between overzealous officials and the planter.

There are two kinds of *ryotti* cultivation—that already named, and what is called *khoski*. This is cultivation given by *ryots* from lands in which the factory has no interest as a lessee. In olden times it was largely advanced for; but as rents went up, the ryots found it did not pay. As late as 1853-54, the Kurnoul and Dooriah concerns had very litter other than *khoski* indigo, and the difficulty was to keep the area of cultivation down; in fact it was looked on as a punishment by the *ryots* if you refused to enter into a contract with them to grow indigo. It was the custom at these places for the *ryots* to give a *salaami* of a cart-load of *bhoosah* (chaff) for every acre of indigo he got advances for. Oats also were to be bought cheap under advances—2 maunds (about 160lbs.), and two nets (about a cart-load) of *bhoosah* being given for every rupee advanced. If you get 40lbs. of oats now-a-days for a rupee, you may consider yourself lucky, and as to chaff (or *bhoosah*), you have to pay Rs. 2 or Rs. 3 for each cart-load. Though *khoski* indigo has somewhat declined in the district, there are still some villages that stick to the old system; the rates paid are, however, higher, and the *bhoosah* perquisite has been done away with.

The reason for the anxiety on the part of the *ryots* round Dooriah and Kurnoul to grow *khoski* indigo is found in the fact of the land there being low-rented; the *ryot* would take from the *zemindar* say, 20 acres of land, for which he would have to pay Rs. 2 per acre; he would at once proceed to the factory and enter into an agreement to cultivate ten acres *khoski* for indigo; he received an advance of Rs. 2 per acre; out of this Rs. 20, he paid Rs. 10 at once on account of rent to the *zemindar*, and kept the rest for his own expenses. As the season went on, other advances were paid. In this way he could always pay his rent, and have the produce of his remaining ten acres in crops for his own use.

Of late years, another kind of contract has come into vogue called *kurtuli*. By this the *ryot* makes over to the planter a certain number of acres out of his holdings; the factory pays the rent, and a sum as remuneration to the *ryot*, who himself cultivates the land, so that, though the planter is actually in possession of it as lessee, the *ryot*-occupant holds and cultivates under him. The zemindars have a great objection to this class of cultivation, as it places the *ryot* in too independent a position, and for this reason they do all they can to stop and oppose *khoski* also.

While on this subject, I will note my experiences and opinion as to the Rent Laws, past, present, and future—the essence of which, when I first put foot in Tirhoot, was this. A *ryot* might be called to appear at the village *katchary* (office) when wanted, when his account would be read to him and he would be required to pay up whatever balance might be found in it against him. This right was in some instances abused, but, as a rule, it worked well. It was withdrawn by a new Rent Act, and the consequences I consider have been disastrous to many *ryots*, for this simple reason, that it is against the nature of these people to pay until they are obliged. Should his rent not be demanded from him when it is due, he puts off the evil day, and uses the money for some other purpose, perhaps on the expenses of a wedding, or a feast. At last the *zemindar* pushes him for it, and finding that the wherewithal to pay up is gone, in a moment of exasperation, enters a suit against him, and "Jankee Gope" is served with a summons to answer for so many rupees. Every oriental loves a lawsuit, so, instead of going to his landlord and settling the claim, he sets out to the town where the *munsiff* (a subordinate judge) holds his court, and is introduced to a *muktear* (attorney) by some hungry "tout" for a small consideration. The *muktear*, generally a musty old gentleman in soiled raiment, wearing a huge pair of spectacles framed in brass, takes up the summons, and reads it aloud, he then asks what reply is to be made. The miserable *ryot* clasps his hands and begins to recite his side of the story. The *muktear* looks the picture of wisdom, but does not utter a word. At a hint from the clerk in attendance, "Jankee" wakens up to the fact that it is time to open his purse-strings, which from that moment do not close. The *muktear*, the clerk, and the pleader having each received his several fee, the attorney sets to work and writes out a reply to the *zemindar's* plaint. It is so brilliantly untruthful in its amazing statements that the *ryot* is beyond himself with delight, and finds it necessary to present "*muktearjee*" with an extra rupee. When the day for the hearing of the case comes on, "Jankee" appears in the witness-box and swears to all that has been stated for him in the written reply; but fails to give any proof, while the plaintiff proves his case fully. A decree is given in accordance for the zemindar, and the hapless "Jankee" has to pay, not only his rent claim in full, but interest as well, besides the costs of the suit. He turns on the *muktear*, and upbraids him, but meets with no sympathy, and returns to his native village a ruined man, to sell everything to pay up the decree, even to house and home.

Now, I am perfectly certain, had "Jankee" continued to live under the rent laws of 1847-48, he would not have fallen into this dire trouble. I have heard of *zemindars* who foster this propensity of their brethren for delaying the evil day of payment, and allow accounts to run on till just within limitation, and then enter a suit for, say, three years' rent. In this way they sometimes get rid of a troublesome *ryot*. Previous to the alteration in the legislation relative to the *ryots*, they and the *zemindars* lived happily together; now the rent courts are crowded, and where one *munsiff* did all the work, it takes at the present time half a dozen. The *patwari*, a man appointed by Government to keep the village rent-books and papers, is a constant thorn on the side of the *ryot*, and it is a pity he is not abolished, or the system improved in some way, for it works very badly. Should the *ryots* have the *patwari* on their side, they can defy the *zemindar*, and it is in the end a bad day for them if they come to loggerheads with *him*. If the *zemindar* falls out with the *patwari*, he may be led a dance he does not care to try a second time. This official's evidence is required in all rent-cases, and as papers are very easily manufactured to suit by the wily *kiasth*, he can, by a turn of his pen, alter the whole face of the question, and prove black to be white. To cheat these *betes noires*, I would suggest a law to enforce the giving and *taking* of leases in *writing*. The law at present obliges the *zemindar* to give a lease, if called on to do so, but does not oblige the *ryot* to take one from the *zemindar*. If every *ryot* held a written lease, he would be clear with his *zemindar*, and no longer in the hands of the *patwari*; his lease would state what he had to pay, and the area cultivated by him, and all payments of rent might be endorsed on it or given in forms to be supplied by the collector to the *zemindar*. A *ryot* with such a lease in his possession would be much stronger than he has ever been under the old, or will be under any new, Rent Act, while none of the rights or privileges claimed by the *zemindars* would be infringed. The old laws of the country were simple, and the people understood them. The Behar *ryot* is not a man of a very acute intellect—certainly far below his brethren of Bengal in that respect—and any change in the law is looked on by him with suspicion, even if it be for his benefit. A common remark of the peasantry when any improvement of an old system is attempted is, with a shake of the head: "*Mera bap dada kabbee aisa nehi dekka!*" (my father or my grandfather never saw things like this!) and their view is, like that of the late Lord Melbourne: "Can't you leave it alone."

Taking him all in all, the *ryot* is not a bad fellow if you treat him fairly, and do not bother him with improvements he neither wants nor asks for. See that he holds his land at a fair rent, getting a receipt for every pice he pays, and he will be a happy and contented man, and bless the "*Sircar Bahadur*."

CHAPTER IV.

MY VISIT TO TIWARRAH—I GO TO SUCKREE—A HAUNTED HOUSE AND GHOST STORIES—POOSAH: A GOVERNMENT STUD NURSERY—A FAUZDHARY.

Towards the end of 1848, I paid a visit to Mr. C—, who had asked me to come and see him when we parted after our tiger-shooting party. Tiwarrah, his factory, is about twelve miles from Kumtoul, and I rode over there in the morning. Here I met Mr. J— T—, who had been sent up to Tirhoot to look after the interests of the Oriental Bank in the many sugar factories that were under advances to it. I found him a very jolly and amusing fellow. Many tales are told of him and his eccentricities. One is about a fat Babu who owned villages that the factory farmed, and of which the rents were due. Having heard that a "*Burra Sahib*" (a great man) had come from Calcutta on business matters connected with the factory, the Babu set off at once to pay his respects to him, and see if he could not manage to get his money. On arrival he was admitted to the office where C— and T— were sitting. A chair was placed for him beside them, on which he squatted tailor-fashion. Having made a low bow, and inquired particularly after the health of the "*Burra Sahib*," he proceeded to state his grievances, and enlarge on the hardness of not getting his rents. T— who understood very little of Hindustani, took advantage of a pause to inquire what the "fat beggar" was talking about, and being told that he was asking for his money: "Tell him," said T—, "that money is very scarce at present, but as I should like to do him a good turn—." Here the Babu burst into exclamations of delight: "A prince indeed had visited the district! The essence of honour and justice had come among them!"—"I will pay him on a condition which must be strictly fulfilled." "Let my Lord speak the word, and his slave will obey," was the instant reply. T— got up, and solemnly taking a piece of chalk, which happened to be lying on the table beside him, carefully marked a line on the floor, then another about two feet off parallel to it. "Now," said he, "let the Babu toe the first line, and jump over the second, and he shall have a cheque for his rents." The unhappy man looked round to see if it was a joke, but finding both men quite serious, descended from his seat, toed the line, looked at the one to be jumped over with a despairing glance, seemed suddenly to feel his dignity hurt, and with a low *salaam*, marched majestically from the room. Later on he made another attempt to obtain what was due to him, with as little success. T—, on this occasion, was at the sugar works when the Babu came in search of him, mounted on his elephant, and was requested to descend and make his business known. The elephant had squatted, and the Babu's servant was in the act of putting on his master's shoes preparatory to his getting down, when T— suddenly eased off the steam safety-valve attached to the machinery. With a roar, out rushed the steam—at the same moment the terrified animal rose to its feet, and, with the nearly frantic Babu, hanging on like grim death, half unseated, sped away across the country as hard as he could go. It is needless to say that the Babu never tried again to see that "*Shaitan Sahib*" who had twice played him such tricks. F— G— was staying at Tiwarrah also. He had given up indigo, and was going to the Nepal frontier to trade with the Nepalese. For this purpose, he had brought up a lot of things to barter, amongst them some very old muskets, which T—declared he might show his confidence in by trying them himself, so having, as G— believed, loaded one of the pieces, T— seized our luckless friend, and holding him in front of himself as a buffer, put the butt to G—'s shoulder, G— all the time struggling to escape and shouting: "It may go off, I tell you, and kill us all." But though T— tugged with might and main at a string tied to the trigger, no powers would start the lock, so G— was released with the verdict: "That, though the weapons were undoubtedly of the dangerous order, the danger was greatly diminished by the fact that the guns would not go off."

In 1850-51, seeing no prospect of improving my position at Kumtoul, I applied to C— (who had gone to Dhoolie) for a vacant outwork under him, and receiving a reply in the affirmative, I started for Dhoolie, where I found C— and E— S—, and passed two or three pleasant days with them before going to my new home. During the two years of my stay at Sibnuggur, I had been able to gather together a few extra pieces of furniture and some pictures, with which I managed to make my little bungalow quite cheerful and nice. It was a much better house than the one I had left, well-placed above the edge of a lake, with a garden to the south, in which were several good mangoe trees. I had six rooms—drawing, dining, two bed-rooms, and an office—the sixth room was appropriated by the bearer for keeping lamps, etc., in. While dressing one morning, not many weeks after my arrival, my bearer informed me for my comfort that the place was haunted; that a man who had preceded me in it some years previously had committed suicide, when under the influence of love and liquor; and that his restless spirit was still seen to wander by the banks of the lake where he had destroyed himself. The story was this: In this life he had become enamoured of one of the fair young ladies then inhabiting the District, had laid his heart and hand at her feet, and been refused. Returning to the bungalow in a desperate frame of mind, he sought comfort and forgetfulness in drinking an unheard-of quantity of gin—a dozen squares!

—and having failed to find the peace of mind he sought, he prepared to die. Having planted a sword, point uppermost, securely in the muddy bank of the lake, he shot himself with a pistol, fell on the sword, and was taken up quite dead. It was a gruesome story, and my bearer capped it with another scarcely less disagreeable. There was another ghost, it seemed, which was given to playing pranks on my domain; who were cooking their food by the roadside, seizing what appeared, no one knew where. Shortly after his departure, the people about began to talk of a wild man who had on different occasions rushed out of the cane-field on travellers, who were cooking their food by the road side, seizing what was preparing on the fire, and disappearing with it whence he came. Every one was terrified. Shortly after these reports began to circulate, Walters' horse, on which he had been seen to ride frantically away, was found dead, and on search being made, Walters' body floating about in a deep *chur* (swamp) also came to light. It came out in evidence that the natives had seen a man galloping about the neighbourhood till at length the horse dropped dead from exhaustion, and the rider cast headlong, was drowned amongst the weeds of the morass. He was buried near the other poor fellow, but neither could rest in their graves, it was believed.

I was returning rather late from inspecting my indigo lands, not many days after the relation of these stories, when my bearer came to meet me, looking much disturbed: "Strange things have happened, sir, in your absence! Your slave went to eat his food, and coming back to the house not many minutes ago, found it in the state you will see!" Dismounting, I entered the bungalow, and found, as he had said, everything in extraordinary confusion—the pictures turned with their faces to the wall, the table upside down, chairs and tables in the same eccentric position! But one thing, I noticed, had defied the ghost, and thought it significant—the sideboard still occupied a dignified attitude on its castors, and my glass stood on it, as heretofore, unharmed. I was certainly rather puzzled. The bearer declared that he had heard a noise like the rushing wind through the house, and had been to see what was the matter, when just as I arrived, he found things as I have described. Thinking it over afterwards, I came to the conclusion that some friend passing through the factory, finding no one in, had perpetrated this little joke, and ridden off. Probably the bearer had gone off much further than he wished me to know after eating his food, and had not heard when, whoever it was who came, called for him. But to this hour, I have never been able to discover who played me this topsy-turvy trick.

I own I never felt happy on a dark evening here. One night I was sitting reading, after dinner, when looking up, startled by some sound, I saw, or thought I saw,—for I put it down to fancy,—a face peering in from the darkness through the window. It was a cold, wet night, the wind howling through the trees, which made things uncommonly creepy. I had almost satisfied myself that I was under an illusion, when again the face appeared. This time there could be no mistake! A cold shiver ran down my back, and my hair stood on end; but I put a bold face on it, and walked to the window. The face had again disappeared; but, on opening the door to investigate further,—and what a start I got! —crouching down on the ground, I saw a figure—a creature with dishevelled hair, teeth chattering with cold, and the few rags that covered it drenched with rain. Seeing that the thing was of flesh and blood, I addressed it, and calling to the bearer to bring a light, found the disturber of my peace to be a wretched idiot, who had taken shelter, from the storm, in the verandah, and moved, I suppose, by curiosity, had taken occasional peeps through the window, to the great detriment of my nerves. I felt much inclined to box his ears; however, having called the factory watchman, I made him over to his care, with orders that he should be fed and allowed to pass the night in the "*bhoosah* house."

My nearest neighbour was F— at Attur factory. I saw very little of him. He died soon after my arrival, and was succeeded by O— who left to go into the army, and was followed by G—. G— afterwards took up an appointment as road-engineer in Sarun, which berth he held for some time. During the mutiny he volunteered, with the force from Dinapore, to relieve Arrah. The force was beaten back; and he narrowly escaped with his life. A shot grazed his spine, and paralyzed his legs. Fortunately, one of Rattray's Sikhs—a big, tall fellow—who saw him fall, came to his assistance, and having got him, mounted on his back, half carried, half dragged him along to the river bank, when the fire of the mutineers having become too warm, the Sikh dropped him, and made for a boat. Fortunately, he was seen by Venour and Waller, of the 40th Native Infantry, who rescued poor G— for the moment by lifting him into one of the boats. They, however, had to leave him there to his fate, as Venour was shot through the leg while in the boat, and Waller and he jumped overboard and swam for their lives. It was here that Fraser McDonell crossed the river, and at the risk of his life rescued G— and many other badly wounded men. For this he got the Victoria Cross.

After G— left Attur, Y— from Dynamut factory, took charge, and many a wild day we had together. One of our exploits was a kind of steeple-chase. The Attur house being raised about 20 feet from the ground, you go up and down by a flight of steps which are rather steep and narrow. As we wanted the race to be a little more exciting, we agreed to start from the drawing-room and make the Suckree-house the winning post, a good five-mile course. Four of us started for this break-neck business. The horses were got up the steps with some difficulty, and into the drawing-room where we mounted. There were but two doors leading out into the verandah towards the steps. At the word "off," a rush had to be made to secure first exit. It was wonderful how we escaped; but we all reached Suckree without a scratch. The slightest mistake on the part of the horses, and we should have been killed or much injured.

On the low land to the north of Suckree, there is very good quail shooting ground, and many a brace of birds have I bagged when out shooting with Colonel Apperly, a son of the celebrated "Nimrod." He was in charge of the Government Horse Nursery at Poosah, and many a jolly day have I spent there. Poosah is a lovely place, with fine avenues of teak, and suckooah trees leading from one stable to another. The stables were neatly-thatched houses, well kept, with large embanked enclosures in front for young cattle to stretch their legs in. The garden was nicely kept, and full of rare fruits and plants. Poosah was originally intended for a Botanical Garden, and the Government Stud Nursery was established first at Hajipore. But they found the young horses did not thrive at the latter place, and sent them to Poosah. In about 1875, the Government leased this beautiful place to Messrs. Begg, Dunlop and Co., who wished to set up a tobacco factory.

The quail in the Suckree Chur remained till very late in the season, and we used to have good shooting in the early morning. I have often seen ninety brace shot, and on one occasion four guns shot three hundred brace—an enormous bag. During my residence at Suckree, we were visited by a tiger, who took up his abode in some big grass to the north of the factory; but he disappeared as quickly as he came.

At Suckree I had my first experience in *faudhary.*— The word is not easily translated, but it means a fray where a force of men is used.—The lease of a village not far from

Suckree, belonging to a neighbouring Rajah, was about to expire, and as we had advanced money, and got a written promise that the lease would be renewed, we went on preparing our *zerat* land. One day, however, we heard that the Rajah had ignored his written promise, and given a lease of the same village to a wealthy banker, to whom he owed money, and that the banker was going to send a force to take possession, and sow down the land we had had so much trouble to prepare for indigo. Finding the report to be true, and that the enemy was concentrating his forces, we at once called together a counter force, and by night had an army of about one thousand men ready. In the early morning the army was marshalled under the command of the factory jemadar or head cultivation servant. The drills and bullocks with cartloads of indigo seed started in advance. My work ended when they had all marched out of the factory, as I had been particularly ordered that I was on no account to go near the field of action. The *Jemadar* related to me afterwards the following account of the Battle of Tippery: "About half an hour after leaving the factory, we reached the Tippery village boundary, and putting our drills in order for sowing, sent them forward to the prepared factory *zerats*. No sooner were we on the land, than to the west, the Tippery army made its appearance, and advancing, the drills were obliged to retreat. Our men were then ordered to advance and meet the enemy. This they did with a rush and a shout; many of the young men in their excitement, jumping many feet into the air, as they tightened their *kammerbands* (waist-cloths) I thought victory certain; but our opponents were commanded by a very clever old man who had been in many a fight. Allowing the factory army to come on until it was about 20 yards off, the Tippery General performed a sort of 'up guards and at 'em' movement, for he ordered his men to take advantage of the west wind (which was then blowing half a gale), to stoop down and throw up the dust till they were almost hidden, then rush on, and suddenly, under cover of the dust, attack us.

"This manœuvre was promptly and well performed, a panic seized our men, and I had the mortification of seeing them come streaming back across country to tell the sad tale of our disaster."

The *jemadar* came up last with the wounded placed in carts. I found that three or four men who had gone a little more forward than they intended, had got some bad knocks, one man in particular had an uncommonly nasty crack on his head. The news of the defeat was not long in reaching the head factory, and the manager soon arrived to see what harm had been done. The wounded men were plastered up and notice sent to the police; as the manager had to return through the Tippery village, I volunteered to return with him in case we might be attacked, so we mounted our nags, each of us carrying a good stick, and riding on the side of the road close to the hedges for fear of an ambush. However, we saw no one. In a grog-shop near the river a few of the enemies (wounded) were lying on the floor, but whether their position was owing to blows or liquor, we did not inquire. Next morning C— and I returned, and passing through the village, found the banker's people busy sowing the lands we had prepared before. It was amusing to hear the ploughmen squealing to their bullocks to go on fast, and to see the small army sent to protect them from attack, hopping about, and jumping into the air in a kind of dance of triumph as we passed. I did feel so inclined to put spurs to my horse and charge them, but on suggesting such a proceeding, I was told not to be so foolish! This was my first experience of a *fauzdhary;* and, though I had to act in a similar way on one or two occasions, I am glad to say that rows of this kind are now seldom heard of: planters and *zemindars* fight their battles in civil courts. A row of this kind was a great windfall to the police. The *darogah* (now called head inspector) arriving on the spot, both sides make arrangements that the best of food and every comfort should be available for this great man (for the time being); and the side he honoured with his company was looked upon as the winning one. His head clerk, or *mohurrir*, had also to be suitably provided for, and after him the *burkandazes*, now called constables, made *koosh* (pleased). Then came the game of "What will ye tak', or what will ye gie?" both sides being powerful and wealthy. The *darogah sahib* wrote out his report, and having been well tipped by both sides, contented himself with announcing, that both were equally guilty, and sending up for trial before the Magistrate two or three of the smaller fry of each side. In due course they appeared before the *Huzoor*,* who, following up the cue set by the police, punished men of both sides by a short imprisonment. We, after consultation, made up our minds to let possession slip through our hands, and try the civil court. A very amusing incident occurred some years ago in connection with the police. The *Burra Sahib* of the police was to come to Sonepore, his camp having preceded him; the district police were consequently fussing about getting everything ready, so that he and his officials might have every comfort. The great man arrived with a number of guests, and all retired to rest after the fatigues of the day. At about 4 o'clock in the morning there was an alarm of thieves. A good deal of shouting, and noise followed; and, after a time, it became known to the people in the camp, that the big man's camp had been robbed—he and his guests having been relieved of a quantity of jewellery. The *darogah* was at once summoned.

---

* *Huzoor* = Presence,—a term of respect used to officials.

Hearing what had happened, his distress was great, and he forthwith went to arrange for the capture of the thieves. By sunset he had caught them, and secured all the stolen property. The head of the police, a C.S. of long standing, immediately seeing in this *darogah* a clever, energetic, and intelligent policeman, ordered his promotion, and that a sword of honour should be given to him. The "outer world" will tell you how it was all done; the *darogah* paid some *domes* (men of the lowest caste), to go and commit the burglary—they would get a few months' jail, but they did not mind that, being accustomed to it. The stolen property was to be kept handy, and made over to the *darogah*. This was all carried out: the *domes* getting their reward in cash, went to jail, and the *darogah* got promotion, and a sword of honour.

CHAPTER V

RIDE OVER TO DOORIAH FOR CHRISTMAS—"DULCINEA DEL TOLBOSO"—RETURN TO WORK.

CHRISTMAS in India, as in England, is a great time for feasting and making merry—large parties being given. In December 1851, I was invited to a gathering at Dooriah by C— G—; and as his Christmas parties were noted for grand shooting and hunting, as also for open-handed hospitality, I started on the morning of the 24th December to ride some forty miles. I had previously sent off my horses to the different stages on the journey, driving my two buggy-horses ten miles, as five miles is considered a fair stage for a horse in harness over *katcha* roads. The remaining thirty miles I was to ride, and having only two riding-horses, was compelled to borrow a third. Ten miles is a long stage for a riding-horse, the usual distance given being only eight, but as it was in the cold weather, a little extra distance did no harm. Leaving my own place at about 10 A.M., I got over my first ten miles in a little over an hour, and mounting my country-bred mare "Dulcinea del Tolboso," I was not long in clearing the next ten miles.—My good old mare was destined to make herself a name in the very stirring times of the mutiny, for I sold her in 1854 to one Paddy Dunn from Mirzapore, who rode her all through the thick of it in company with the gallant Venables. Mr. Dunn received a handsome property for his plucky behaviour, and I hope "Dulcinea del Tolboso" was placed, after the heat and burden of the day, in a comfortable paddock to eat, and dream away her uneventful life in peace and happiness. —My next stage was performed on a borrowed horse, and remembering the saying anent "a friend's horse, and your own spurs," we skimmed along the road at a brisk pace. Winter days are short in India, and as I had halted for some time at the club in Mozufferpore, I found "the shades of night were falling fast" before I reached my last stage, where my sturdy little "tat," "Peter," commonly called "The Pig" (from his likeness to a good-sized porker), stood ready saddled. It was quite dark before I reached Dooriah, tired, dusty, and hungry, where I met with a hearty welcome from my host and his party. After dinner, when the table was cleared and our cigars were lit, we discussed the programme of the morrow.

It was arranged that we should hunt in the early morning, after which we should mount our elephants which our worthy host had provided, and shoot over the lowlands on the banks of the big Gunduk, where hare, partridges, quail, and wild pig abounded.

Long before daylight we were astir, and having fortified the inner man, we soon made a start. The dogs had been sent on in a covered cart to the grasses we proposed to beat. There were terriers, greyhounds, and one or two *nondescripts* that gave tongue, and ran on scent. The greyhounds were put in slips, and posted at different corners of the grasses. When all was ready, the horsemen formed line, whilst the terriers and other dogs hunted about. We had not long to wait for our first scamper. A jackal broke away, and a pair of heavy kangaroo hounds were slipped at him with a ringing "Tally-ho." Off we all went in pursuit, over ditches, into roads, through grass fields, the jackal trying all he could to dodge the dogs. At last, in a weak moment, he took to the open, the dogs at his brush. The pace grew fast and furious, the excited huntsmen hullooing encouragement at the top of their voices, the terriers behind yelping furiously. The jackal strained every nerve to reach a patch of the jungle not fifty yards off, where he would be safe, but the leading dog having seen this, put on a last spurt and, just as Mr. *Geedhur** was almost safe, seized him, and the two rolled over together. The other dogs soon ran in, and finished him. One by one the horsemen came up; some having made acquaintance with mother earth—the consequence of trying to negotiate big ditches objected to by their horses,—but most of us had not been so unfortunate.

After the hard work our horses and dogs had undergone, we thought it as well to proceed to the shooting ground, where outside a fine mango grove we found our elephants in readiness, and what was still better to the eye of the hungry sportsmen a *dejeuner a la fourchette*, spread under the cool and pleasant shade of the trees. We at once commenced operations, and for a long time nothing but the popping of corks, the clatter of knives and forks, and broken ejaculations were heard, such as, "More pie, please!"—"Just pass the beer, will you?"—"What a capital *moorghee!*"† evincing that ample justice was being done to the spread. There must be an end to all things, and so, alas! it was with our breakfast. Cigars were duly lit, the elephants called for, and guns and ammunition handed up to our servants, who had their seats behind us on the *howdahs*. About one hundred men were in waiting, each having a stick with which to beat the grass and jungle, and a pair of wooden clogs to protect his feet from thorns. Besides these beaters, there was a small detachment on our flank outside the heavy grass, carrying certain baskets provided with bottles, tumblers, etc., and we realized the fact that no man need thirst whilst he kept this little group within hail. It was not long before the game began to rise, and by evening we had a splendid bag of hare, partridge and quail, also—I blush to

* Jackal. † Fowl.

say it—of "pig;" but in those days pig-sticking was unknown in Tirhoot, and there was no disgrace attached to shooting a "porker." This part of the country was the only part of the country in which wild boar was found, but the ground was so bad that it was considered madness to attempt to ride and spear them. In 1863, pigs began to overrun the District. Whence they came none knew; but the natives said that the *Doosads* (swine-herds) had been told by one of their priests, that a curse would fall on the heads of those who kept pigs, and, in consequence, they at once let their herds of swine loose, which took to the jungles and big grasses, and in time became wild. In these days one can have pig-sticking almost anywhere in Tirhoot, Chumparun, or Sarun. J— S—, of whom I have mentioned as living at Poopri, is said to have been the first man to stick a boar in Tirhoot. He did it off a little Arab, which had been lent him,—as gallant a little nag as ever stepped. It had been left with him by a young man who had commenced life as an indigo-planter, but afterwards, getting a commission in the East India Company's service, left Tirhoot to join his regiment, leaving his trusty little steed to follow when he had settled down; however, they never met again, as the poor little Arab caught cold and died. We lost sight of his master during the mutiny; but some years afterwards at Lucknow, whilst looking over the graves of friends who lay beside him "*who tried to do his duty*,"* my eye caught the name of my old friend. He, too, "had done his duty." We spent a very jolly week at Dooriah, hunting, shooting, and billiards being much enjoyed. On 31st December we sat up to "watch the new year in." On New Year's Day we all set off for Mozufferpore, where we spent the day—the party dispersing to their homes next morning.

---

* Epitaph on Sir H. Lawrence's tombstone: "Here lies Henry Lawrence, who tried to do his duty."

Returning to work again was very dull, but after a few days I soon got back into the old routine. K— McL—, who superintended Attur factory, often came from Chupra, where he lived, to look round, and I was generally invited to meet him, thus spending many happy evenings in his society. He was a fair performer on the violin, and sang some good songs "Maggie Lauder," among them. Who will forget "Ho Maggie, hey Maggie, hi Maggie Lauder!" sung in chorus, by a dozen voices to the accompaniment of old Mac.'s fiddle? Young (his Assistant Manager) could give you a lively ditty with violin accompaniment, when the good old song of "Duncan MacCallaghan's Ride" was warbled forth with true Scotch accent. I almost fancy I can hear "'De'il tak the hindmost!' says Duncan MacCallaghan, laird o' Talli Ben Jo," chorused forth by the company in mirthful harmony. Poor Young died on his way to England, where he had been ordered by his doctors. Mac., too, has passed away.

CHAPTER VI.

GO TO KURNOUL—FATTENED GHAINEES:—"MANY A SLIP 'TWIXT CUP AND LIP"—HOW CATTLE ARE TREATED—BRAHMINI BULLS—NARROW ESCAPE OF J. S.——FALSE CASE.

In November 1852, I was offered the sub-managership of Kurnoul, and as the pay was Rs. 280 per month, I gladly accepted it, and on 1st November took over charge from D—. Kurnoul was a very good concern.

The dwelling-house was prettily situated on the banks of a small stream, and the undulating ground round about it greatly added to the *coup d'oeil*. The land near the house was dotted with fine large trees and clumps of bamboos. The stables and coach-house were substantially built and nicely situated. The garden was some distance from the house, and had been well cared for—grapes, mangoes, and plantains being plentiful; and as winter was just coming on, I found a splendid supply of vegetables ready for my use.

My predecessor had got into trouble with the surrounding *zemindars*, through having undertaken the management of a beef club. He had purchased a number of dwarf bullocks, called *Ghainees*, noted for the fine beef they make, had taken great care of them, and fattened them well up, ready for killing. A few days before the first bullock was to become beef, one of the *zemindars*, having business in the factory, paid his respects to D—. As they were sitting in the verandah, the *zemindar* remarked the *Ghainees*, which were grazing in front of the bungalow, and asked what was the use of keeping the dwarf cattle. D—, without thinking, replied that they were to be killed for food. The *zemindar* was of high caste, consequently this announcement was very offensive to him, so he got up, made his bow, and went away.

Next day a petition was sent, asking that the cattle might be spared, but D— took no notice of it. About noon of the day on which the first *Ghainee* was to die, whilst all the factory servants were away at their homes, having their meals, a force of over a thousand men appeared and drove off all D—'s fattened bullocks; consequently the club lost their money, for only one was eventually recovered. They were driven right off to the Gorrukpore jungles, and then let loose to become most likely the prey of some hungry tiger.

The whole matter was put into the hands of the police, and eventually a few *zemindars* were imprisoned.

Hindus have strange ideas about the treatment of cows, Brahminy bulls, and bullocks. They will not allow any of them to be killed; yet the way they ill-treat them is dreadful. If a cow is ill, they will not give her medicine, for if she died, the donor would lose caste. The wretched bullocks working in carts and ploughs have nearly every joint in their tails dislocated, and their necks are very often badly galled.

The Brahminy bull fares best; but if he is caught trespassing in a field, he is well pelted with clods, and if he is not savage, beaten with sticks over the head and ribs. Yet if a bullock die with his head under the yoke, the driver is outcasted; the same happens if a cow, or bullock die while tied up, the person who tied them having to do penance, and feed the Brahmins before they are readmitted to caste.

Brahminy bulls are very destructive, and where Europeans and Moslems prevail, they are quietly caught and used in carts or killed for beef—the Hindus shutting their eyes to this, as they prefer their crops to the sacred bull.

Brahminy bulls are let loose much as scapegoats were in olden times. A man's grandmother dies, the grandson takes a small calf and brands him with the *tirsool,* "the emblem of Trinity used by the Hindu God Khristna," and drives it out of the village. The calf having the run of the crops soon becomes a fine big bull.

At Benares they are an intolerable nuisance to the *bunnias* (shop-keepers); there they roam about the bazaars, putting their noses into the baskets of grain placed at the window for sale, and thus they fatten on the best of food. If the *bunnias* only dared, they would make short work of these impudent cattle.

My nearest neighbour, when at Kurnoul, was J— S—, who had been many years in the country; he was only some five miles off, so we used to visit each other very often. He had, some years before I met him, a narrow escape from being murdered by a fanatic Hindu. If he had not been very cool, and shown great presence of mind, he would have been killed.

He was one day sitting at dinner about 4 P.M.—for J— S—, like many old planters, kept early hours—when suddenly a native rushed into the room with a drawn-sword and held it over S—'s head ready to cut him down. S—, glancing up at the man, caught sight of a large gathering of ruffians outside, and at once seeing resistance was useless, quietly asked the man what was the matter. He replied, "I have been sent by Ram to *loot* and slay, and this," pointing to the upraised weapon, "is his sword." I don't want to kill you at once; if you will give me money to feed my army that are waiting outside, I will spare your life for a time." S— replied: "I will, of course, give you whatever money you want, but I must send for it to my banker, and if you will allow me, I will send now for it by a man on horseback." This was agreed to, and a trusty Mahomedan syce departed with an order on his banker, but also with instructions to see the Magistrate and give notice of what was going on. Another man was sent to Kurnoul to put J— H—, who was then at that factory, on his guard, as the man in charge of Ram's sword had made known his intention of paying a visit there after he had replenished his coffers at Raujpoor. The gentleman of the sword seated himself in the verandah, awaiting the return of the messenger with the cash. Before long, members of the fanatical army began to disperse, and suddenly the man of the sword took himself off, for rumours of the Police and Magistrate being astir, must have reached them and their commander. Not long after their exit, the Magistrate arrived, followed by a number of policemen and village watchmen, who started in pursuit, S— having joined the party. He of the sword of Ram, was traced to a house standing within an enclosure, entered by a door which had been fastened and barricaded. The Magistrate called on the inmates to open and surrender, but as no response was made to repeated calls, the Magistrate, a good horseman and well-mounted, put his horse at the mud-wall, which he cleared at a bound, but landing on the slippery ground inside, the horse's legs went from under him and he rolled off. In a moment the fanatic, who had hidden himself in the house, was out with his drawn-sword, and had not a village watchman, who had climbed over the wall after the Magistrate, knocked him over, it would have been all up with the C.S. The fanatical leader was secured with several of his followers found hidden in the house. They were all sent up to the sessions, and imprisoned for long periods. S— had come to India when "John Company" ruled supreme, and no non-official European could remain in the country without a permit,—and this right he forfeited if he did anything that was displeasing to the eyes of the powers existing.

He told me how a native, whom he did not get on with, tried to have him turned out of the country by getting up a false case against him. A charge was sworn to before the Magistrate that S— had lost his temper with a *ryot* of one of the neighbouring villages and had had him tied with a rope and dragged by bullocks over a field, from the effects of which the man died; and that his body had been thrown into the river, etc. S— was put on his defence. He was quite astounded at the charge, for it was utterly false, yet the evidence brought forward against him was not to be shaken and things began to look ugly, when one of S—'s factory servants, who was standing near him, whispered into his ear: "Why, there is the supposed murdered man sitting in court listening to the case." S— noted this on a slip of paper, and handed it up to the Magistrate. The man was arrested, and the whole thing came out. So jealous, however, were the officials in those days of what was called "interloping" influence, that though the case was shown to be a vile conspiracy, S— had to leave the District, and it was only after he had arrived in Calcutta that he managed to get the order rescinded.

CHAPTER VII.

JOURNEY DOWN THE RIVER IN CHARGE OF THE INDIGO—SONEPORE FAIR AND SONEPORE RACE MEET.

Not long after I had joined Kurnoul, I was ordered to proceed as far as the place where the Big Gunduk River runs into the Ganges, in charge of the Dooriah and Kurnoul indigo on its way to Calcutta. The navigation was very dangerous down the river, and one of the senior assistants always had to see the Indigo safely past this particular spot. As the great Sonepore Fair was in full swing about this time of the year, the indigo once off safe, the man in charge was able to amuse himself for a few days at this most enjoyable of gatherings. Leaving Dooriah at night, I drove down to the river, where my boats lay in waiting. I was soon on board and asleep. When I awoke I found we had gone several miles on our way. The air on the river was, however, very cold, and I found it necessary to wrap myself up well till the sun was high above the horizon. It was slow and tedious work, travelling in a native boat, but I managed to pass away the time shooting. The Big Gunduk is the boundary between Tirhoot and Sarun; it is a broad, shallow river, except in the rains when it is deep and very rapid. In November it was dotted here and there with sandbanks, and on these were all kinds of aquatic birds, including wild geese and ducks, and basking in the sun numbers of alligators; so, with all these to fire at I managed to keep myself amused. In the evening we had to fasten the boats to a sand bank; and then by the light of a very dim oil lamp, I managed to read till I fell asleep.

On the third day I had got my boats safely through the dangerous part of the river and into the Ganges, and as my responsibility was over, I made my way up to the Sonepore Camp.

Sonepore stands on a point of land where the Ganges and Gunduk meet. The natives call the fair "Hurrier Chutter." But the village in which stands the splendid mango-grove, covering some hundred acres, is called Sonepore.

The juncion of any two streams is held sacred by the Hindus, but when these streams are the mother Ganges and Gunduk, their power is great, especially at a certain age of the moon, generally falling at the end of October or beginning of November. At an hour ascertained from the *Pundits*, thousands of men, women, and children rush into the water. Those who reach the water, exactly at the second calculated, are supposed to be at once cleansed of all sin. Offerings of flowers and kids, also money, are made to the river, and it is distressing to see a wretched little kid floating down the river, bleating for help to save it from drowning, while at another place, two strong men of the lower caste may be seen fighting for another, nearly tearing its legs off in their struggles for its possession. For days after, the poorer classes search in the muddy bottom of the river near the bank, for the small copper coins that have been thrown in as offerings at the bathing time. On the day before the bathing-day the roads leading to Sonepore are crowded with pedestrians of both sexes, also conveyances of every denomination. Women of all classes, dressed in the brightest of colours with all the jewellery they have, sparkling on their ears, wrists, ankles, and noses—some travelling on foot carrying the youngest of their family astride on their hips, others, better off, riding in bullock carts with a covering to protect them from the sun and cold as well as the public gaze. The ladies of the "upper ten" travel in palanquins covered over generally, with a red cloth, in which is cut a little hole on each side to admit air, or to be used as a peep-hole, from whence they can see and not be seen.

After the bathing-day the fair begins to clear, and very soon is almost empty. The mango-grove, where the European encampment is pitched, is near the race-course. The canvas-town that rises into existence as if by magic ss, in a very short time, full of life and gaiety. The large camps with their streets of tents, are neatly and regularly pitched, the *shamianahs* handsomely carpeted and furnished; while at the back the dining tents, down the centre of which are placed long tables, indicate that a luxurious and comfortable style of hospitality will soon be dispensed.

There are generally several large camps to which a number subscribe, and ask their friends; there are also a few private and smaller camps. The routine of Sonepore camp-life generally commences with races, usually fixed for a Thursday. The day before, all are assembled in camp, and at about 9 P.M., the bugle for the Ordinary sounds, and such as are of a sporting mind, go there and join in the lotteries on the races to be run in the morning. At daylight next morning, a cannon is fired from the race-course, which rouses the camp, and shortly after, the band of the regiment from Dinapore marches down from the race-stand to the end of the encampment and back again, to the lively strain of a regimental quick march. After these two hints to turn out, the camp is soon alive, and shortly after carriages, dog-carts, and conveyances of all kinds, and pedestrians are to be seen making their way to the race-stand. By 8 A.M. all have arrived, and soon after, the saddling bugle goes. The grand-stand is the verandah of the ball-room; couches and chairs are ranged all along the front towards the racecourse, leaving plenty of space behind for those who wish to warm themselves by a smart walk, or constitutional, to promenade up and down. At one end of the verandah, coffee, tea, and biscuits are provided; during the interval between each race the band plays, while the ladies, not to be outdone by the sterner sex, make their bets for gloves, or join in rupee-lotteries on the next race. By 11 A.M. the races are over, and all hasten home to breakfast, and spend the afternoon in calling, etc. All Sonepore puts in an appearance at the evening drive round the course; this presents a very gay appearance. In the centre of the circle formed by the racecourse, troopers belonging to the Irregular Cavalry from Segowlie entertain the public by competing at tent-pegging and other feats of horsemanship. This, however, has now given way to polo, and a struggle for superiority between a Trans-Gangetic and a Tirhoot team is always viewed with great interest by the fair lookers on, who behold the contest from the top of four-in-hand drags, seated on tandem carts, or carriages of all kinds.

Being the ball-night, the drive comes to an earlier conclusion than usual, and at 9 P.M., the bugler sounds his horn, giving all notice that in half an hour dancing will commence. At this signal all is bustle and haste, those who had forgotten that time will fly, rush off to their tents to see that they look as charming as possible; the "mashers" take a self-admiring look at themselves in the glass, give their hair a touch up and their moustaches an extra twirl; then all start for the ball-room. Carriages arrive—young men rush down the steps of the ball-room to hand up Mrs.—, or help Miss— to alight. "I hope you have not forgotten No. 5!"—"Can you give me No. 14?"—"I can only give you one extra!" —"Thanks; shall we say the supper dance?"—while some naughty one suggests: "We had better sit out that dance" —and the band soon strikes up with a quadrille!

The ball-room is a most brilliant scene. The elegant dresses of the ladies and the varied and many-coloured uniforms of the military men, mixed with the sombre evening dress of the civilians, give the assemblage a gay and gaudy appearance. At midnight the band strikes up "The Roast Beef of old England," and at this signal there is a great rushing about of gentlemen in search of the ladies they are to take in to supper. To arrive at the supper-room you go into the verandah, and turn sharp half-right, walk down through a passage, which connects the ball with the supper-room—passing into the verandah you find the doors of the supper-room open to receive you. The happy couples find themselves in a long room. The supper stands on a table running up the centre of the room which is tastefully decorated with flowers that have been sent over from Bankipore,—for, if some of the gentlemen attend to the racing requirements, a number of the ladies take a great deal of trouble in embellishing the ball and supper-room. The ladies all take seats, while the gentlemen wait on them. The champagne corks soon begin to pop, and the knives and forks to rattle—gradually the din becomes less, and the crack of a bonbon cossaque followed by a little scream tells that the "dear bewitchers" have done supper, and are now about to go in for a little light amusement. The crackers having come to an end, the ladies and their partners make for the ball-room, leaving the supper-room in possession of the "wall flowers." Some of the elder gentlemen look forward to this repast with a good deal of pleasure. Many will remember an old General from Dinapore who had to *chaperone* some young ladies, and how he used to make himself comfortable soon after arrival and go off to sleep; but, as punctually as clock-work he would awake at ten minutes to twelve, and with a benign smile inform his nearest neighbour that in ten minutes "The Roast Beef of old England" would sound.

After supper people began to leave, and by 2 A.M. most of the ladies had left. Then the young men went in for second supper. By 4 A.M. the camp is still. The only noise heard is the howl of a hungry jackal, inviting his mates to join him in a feed off some well-picked bones he has just discovered. I have also heard at early dawn, the voice of some youth, under the influence of love and second supper, warbling in most melancholy tones, "Green leaves come again," as he tries to distinguish his own tent from the many others round him. The next or bye-day is passed playing lawn-tennis, and at large luncheon parties; in the afternoon, again, all go driving or riding,—as there is no ball on this evening, the band plays on the course near the race-stand; in the evening, dinner parties; and at half-past 9 P.M., the lottery bugle sounds, and all those interested in the races bid their hosts good-night and take themselves off to the Ordinary, which is held in the supper-room. There is a ball every race-day, namely, on Tuesday, Thursday, and Saturday; and the lotteries on Monday, Wednesday, and Friday. On the Sunday Divine Service is held in one of the large *shamianahs*, the chaplain from Patna officiating. The racing is generally very good, and horses from all parts of India come to compete. The purses are paid from funds subscribed by the visitors; they are collected thus: On entering the weighing-yard, which is also the lounge between the events, one of the stewards told off for the purpose places before you a subscription book, when you are expected to enter your name for as much as you can afford. Of course, no lady pays. The different Rajahs about give purses—Durbhungah and Bettiah, give a handsome cup—to be run for, so that, at a full Sonepore, the prizes are valuable. Alas! Sonepore as a place for races and gaiety is fast fading away. The large camps at which hospitable residents from Bankipore entertain their friends are also things of the past. Who can forget the long lines of tents attached to M—'s camp, the hearty greeting to all old friends as they arrived at Sonepore, all the fun that went on and the trouble their ever kind host and hostess took to make all happy?

The scream of the locomotive, as it rushes past on its way to the North-West, warns us that Sonepore is doomed and the end is at hand. The charm of Sonepore was the large picnic it represented; that gone, a visit to Sonepore resolves itself into a matter of business to purchase horses or other cattle.

CHAPTER VIII.

LORD MAYO AND JUNG BAHADOOR AT SONEPORE—BARGAINING "A LA ORIENTAL"—GERMAN MISSIONARIES.

THE year in which Lord Mayo met Sir Jung Bahadoor of Nepal, and some years after when Lord Northbrook passed through on his way up-country, were two of the most successful race meets Sonepore has on record.

Jung Bahadoor came down in great state, with a bodyguard of about three hundred men. He and his followers had a large piece of ground under the shade of mango trees portioned off to them. On the arrival of the Prince of Nepal he was met at the river Gunduk by an A.-D.-C. in the Viceregal carriage, and conveyed to his camp. A battery of royal artillery saluting him as he entered his encampment, where he was received by his own bodyguard who presented arms.

Jung Bahadoor's many wives had insisted on accompanying him to see and witness the sights and the fun, and bathe in the sacred Ganges. There were over thirty of these partners of his weal and woes, and as each had a retinue of women-servants there was a goodly number in all. Next day I went and called on Sir Jung, and found him looking at Lord Mayo's jewellery and comparing it with his own. Lord Mayo's were beautifully set, and snone forth with dazzling resplendency, while Sir Jung's, representing enormous value, were dully set and badly cut. Jung Bahadoor was very affable, and conversed freely in Hindustani, which he spoke well; he was a little man with a sharp, restless, and cruel eye. The face was clever but cunning; and you might hope in vain for mercy if once in his power.

The morning after his arrival, he and his suite arrived at the race-stand on their state elephants. These animals were magnificently caparisoned with cloths of gold and golden *howdahs*. A Durbar or reception was held at midday, and all Europeans, as well as native gentry, invited to attend. It was held in a large *shamianah*, at one end of which was a raised platform with two steps up to it. There were three chairs of gold on the dais; chairs in rows down each side of the *shamianah* were placed, the front row to one side for the members of Sir Jung's staff, and, behind them the native gentry. On the opposite side, chairs were placed for the Europeans, while up the centre was a carpeted walk leading to the dais. Before midday all the chairs were filled, and shortly after Lord Mayo (in court-dress, wearing his star and band of the Order of the Garter) walked in. All rose in token of respect, and His Lordship bowing to each side took his seat in the centre chair on the dais; as he did so, a royal salute vollied forth, and the band of the European regiment played "God save the Queen." A few minutes after the Viceroy had taken his seat, a commotion outside announced the arrival of Sir Jung and suite; again the guns boomed, the guard of honor saluted, and Sir Jung Bahadoor entered, sparkling with jewels, wearing on his head a golden helmet studded with precious stones, and on top a ruby valued at three lacs of rupees, out of which dropped bird of paradise feathers. He was met by one of the Secretaries, while his son or brother was taken in hand by another. These Secretaries, taking them by the hand walked them half way up the passage where officials of higher standing met them and conducted them to the foot of the dais. Lord Mayo descending one step, offered Sir Jung his right, and the other his left hand, and seated them on either side of him. The other members of his suite had been placed meanwhile, by the junior secretaries, in the front row chairs kept for them. The Governor-General, after exchanging a few words with the Nepalese Magnate, desired to be introduced to the members of his suite; on this the Secretary handed them up one by one, another man calling out their names. Lord Mayo shook hands with some, bowed to others, and they passed on and reseated themselves. After this, Government-house servants, dressed in red and gold, appeared with large trays of *pan*, a leaf in which is inclosed spices, betelnut, and a mixture of lime and catechu. The *pan* was made up into little cocked-hat shapes, held together with a single clove, and beautified by a covering of silver paper. A Secretary went round with the attur-holder and sprinkled a little on each of the suite. Sir Jung and his brother had been specially served. After sitting the time required by Durbar etiquette, Sir Jung according to the custom of Orientals, asked to be allowed to take his departure, which being granted, he rose to leave, all the spectators rising at the same time. The Secretary again handed them down, one man going to a certain spot and making them over to Juniors, till they reached their conveyance, when the guard of honor again saluted. The big guns boomed and Sir Jung returned to his camp. Lord Mayo sat a short time after Sir Jung had retired, then rising, walked down the passage—the spectators rising. As soon as His Lordship was out of the *shamianah*, the audience dispersed. That afternoon the horse artillery from Dinapore were to exhibit their skill with their breech-loading Armstrong guns to the Nepalese Prince and Generals. There was, of course, a great crowd to see the performance in which Sir Jung took the greatest interest. The practice both with shot and shell, was very good. When the firing had stopped, Sir Jung examined and admired the light cannons; he then gave a general invitation to all, to come and witness a review of his troops, next day. That evening Sir Jung appeared with some of his staff at the ball; they were all most gorgeously dressed. Orientals do not understand ladies and gentlemen dancing together. They think it is a useless exercise. Their idea of the right thing is that the young lady should dance and the lords of creation admire. Several of the ladies went to call on the Ladies of Jung Bahadoor. They were ushered in by the husband, and were received by the principal and the youngest of the Ranees. One of the ladies who called, described them as cheerful, rather nice-looking women, with strong Mongolian features, and fair for Orientals.

The Ranees on parting with their visitors presented each with a piece of jewellery, the value being suited to the rank of the lady's husband.

Next afternoon the Nepalese troops were paraded. They were a fine body of little Goorkhas, with legs that no Highlander need be ashamed of. As they marched past, their band struck up "Should auld acquaintance." They had evidently learned their drill from some old French officer, for when they went at the double, they kept time to the *tap* of the drum which beat the *pas de charge*.

The last and most amusing evolution was the bayonet exercise, quick time. The band struck up "Pop Goes the Weasel," and the fixed bayonets worked up and down, here and there, in exact time to that well-known old tune. Not many of these gallant little fellows ever saw Nepal again; for cholera broke out in their camp next day, and though they were hurried off at once, the fatal disease never left them. One thing a Nepalese Goorkha fears greatly is a little soap and water, and to this aversion, I put down the attack of cholera that proved so fatal to the little force that visited us on this occasion. There were several fine elephants among those that came down with the Nepal retinue. While they were at Sonepore, one of the elephants brought to the fair for sale, went mad, and breaking loose, did great mischief, and people were in danger of their lives. Sir Jung hearing this, sent one of his hunting elephants after him; he came up to the savage beast on a sandbank near the river opposite, and at once charged. His Sonepore opponent put down his head, and rushed to meet him. With a terrible shock they met, both seemed to stagger for a minute, and then the mad one turned tail and bolted, pursued by the other. The chase was not a long one, for Sir Jung's tusker gained on the other fast, and as he was descending to a lower part of the bank, caught him in the rear with such force that he drove him head foremost into the sand, where the now very much-tamed elephant lay, receiving a dig in the ribs now and then from his stronger brother. The Sonepore elephant having hauled down his colours, his *mahout* or driver mounted on his neck, and off he marched, looking as sheepish and cowed as an elephant possibly could look. Lord Mayo's year will be long remembered by those who were present at Sonepore. The Viceroy's kind and affable manner to Europeans and natives of every class endeared him to all. I shall never forget the delight of a Hindu merchant from Cawnpore, who walked up to Lord Mayo as he was promenading the weighing enclosure, and made him a low *salaam;* His Lordship held out his hand to him, and, after shaking hands, inquired in English all about him. The man, understanding a little of what was said, replied by signs and a word or two. When he marched out of the enclosure, he was at least six inches taller; and one of the stewards taking advantage of his elated state presented the subscription book to him, and extracted a hundred rupees towards the race-fund. To this day the native merchant talks of the time when the *Burra Lat Sahib* (the big Lord Sahib) came to Sonepore. Lord Mayo was a good horseman, and delighted in a smart canter round the racecourse. After the races were over, he used to mount his big Irish hunter, and go at a rattling pace, his aide-de-camp flying after him. Our great sportsman and rider Mr. John, one morning gave His Lordship a specimen of good riding. He mounted a pony called *Bezique*, one of the most difficult animals imaginable to sit—to ride an eel, if you can fancy it, would have been easier. The little beast would dart forward, stop suddenly, letting her head conveniently bob down, so that there should be nothing to hold on to in case you were inclined to go over her head; to accelerate your departure she would give a nice little kick up behind; failing to dislodge her rider, she would suddenly spring to the right, then to the left. She seemed convulsed all over as if the saddle and rider tickled her into muscular contortions, but it was no use, Jimmy stuck to her like wax; suddenly a bright idea seemed to seize the little vixen, for she made a dart to where some branches of a mango tree came low down to the ground, and before her rider could evade them, a branch had caught him by the neck and swept him over her tail. Waving a parting farewell with her heels, which passed uncommonly near the rider's head, the young lady gracefully retired to her stable. It was not long after His Lordship's visit to Sonepore that, while at the Andaman Islands he was cruelly murdered by a fanatical prisoner. India, Native and European, rich and poor, mourned for this great and noble statesman. Somewhere about 1873, Lord Northbrook paid a visit to Sonepore, where he held a "Durbar." His visit, however, was only a casual one, and the durbar was not as grand as it should have been. His Lordship made up for it by giving a ball at the race-stand ball-room. Everything came from Calcutta by rail, and the whole thing was a most brilliant success. The supper was a *chef-d'oeuvre*. The long table in the supper-room was replaced by numerous small tables, on each of which was served a perfect *Petit Souper*. The "fiz" was good and all agreed in pronouncing His Excellency's ball the best and most enjoyable they had been to for many a day.

I will now take my reader round the Sonepore Fair. To do this efficiently you must secure some of the Government Commissariat elephants or borrow some steady ones from the Durbhangah or Beteah Rajah. Young elephants are half-trained and dangerous, and become quite excited by the noise and turmoil of the fair.

A very serious accident nearly took place on one occasion when some young ladies were proceeding on elephants to see the Native fair. The elephant on which one of the ladies was to mount was ordered to kneel down. The animal obeyed the order, but before the fair rider was settled on the pad, the timid monster jumped up, and the young lady was left for a time in mid air, for her cavalier who had mounted first held on to her manfully, but at last had to let go, and she fell at the feet of the lot of elephants that were waiting for the rest of the party. A gentleman, who was looking on, rushed in and dragged her out of danger.

Having mounted our steady old elephants, we start in Indian file down the main road, passing through the centre of the encampment. From our high position we can see the camp to great advantage. Each set of tents has a drive marked out among the trees, and on a board hung on a convenient branch, the name of the Host or Hostess—"Mrs. Feed-em-well's Camp," "Mr. Smoke-and-Peg's Camp," "The Tirhoot Busters," and so on. As you reach what may be called the east end, the camps get smaller and less pretentious. Passing these, you come to tents got up as shops, in which all kinds of European toys, groceries, brandy, beer, soda-water, etc., are sold; beyond, carpenters from Dinapore and Patna expose for sale chairs, beds, tables, and every article of furniture; while coach-builders offer dog-carts, carriages, and conveyances of all kinds and sizes to intending purchasers. Here the tents end, and the horse-fair begins; numbers of screaming, kicking ponies are being ridden up and down the broad road that leads you to the fair, the riders going as if their lives depended on the pace. Tethered under the trees on either side of the road, are the bigger horses of every class and denomination. Let us go and see what wonderful animal is picketted under that small *shamianah*. There stands a tall white horse with pink eyes and nose, and a wonderful mane and tail dyed all the colours of the rainbow.

He has a head-stall worked with gold thread, and on his legs gold bangles, while round his neck hangs a number of small lockets of silver containing charms and verses from the Koran. We inquire out of curiosity, what price is asked for this horse. The owner, an up-country man, with rather a swagger, informs us that the price is one lac of rupees, and that he is a horse meant for a Rajah to buy. Nothing daunted by the rebuff, we inquire what are the peculiarities in the animal to make him so valuable, and are told that he has all that is required by a native horse-fancier, that is, the hair on his forehead curls the proper way, and that behind the ears, has the proper twist. The beast is actually valueless to a European eye; his hocks are as big as your head, and he has splints and ring bones on his forelegs. Well reined up with a sharp bit, he will be considered magnificent by the natives, especially at a wedding procession. There he will be mounted by a native professional rider, who will send him along at a furious pace, then suddenly pull him up dead on his haunches, wheel about, and retire in the same way, then stop, and bridling the horse sharp up, make him perform a kind of *pas*, which would be called by a soldier "marking time." To this is sometimes added the firing off of match-locks and other Circus performances. With this kind of handling before many years are over, the poor brute has not a leg to stand on, and his mouth is as hard as iron. When he has reached this state, he reverts to the lowly position of a *teekah-gharrie* (hired carriage) horse, where he gets the most humble of fare and plenty of whip-cord, and finally dies broken-hearted.

As we strike the Chupprah road we turn to the left and pass to our right the Camel fair. At this point two roads cross, and the crowd is very great. Here you find the German Missionaries hard at their good work. Recognizing one of them, we inquire after his health and that of his wife, to which he replies. "I am well, good, Sir; but my wife, poor fellow, is very *sick.*" We express sorrow; and he goes on with his exhortation. The way these hard-working men have mastered the Hindustani language is wonderful. There are few Natives who have the facility of speech, or can speak what is called Urdu,—the language spoken in polite native society—as they do. These men are indefatigable in their work. They will stand for hours in the sun and dust, expounding the scriptures or arguing points of religion with some Moslem or Hindu. The Missionary always gets the best of the argument as he has studied the Koran and Shashtras thoroughly, and actually can quote passages from both, that the follower of the Prophet or the believer in Ram never heard of. It is difficult to understand how these most zealous workers manage to exist. They are all married and have families. The miserable pittance doled out to them with great irregularity by the Society in Germany barely pays for the most meagre food. Residents of the district about subscribe to the Mission; but this money is devoted to the feeding, clothing, and instructing of the converts. I fear that, after all, not much good is done. The converts, with one or two exceptions, turn out badly; and it would seem as if the story in the old Delhi Sketch Book had a great deal of truth in it. When the Protestant Missionary calls on a man to become a convert and join his church, the man replies: "Roman Catholic padri pay five-rupee piece for convert; what Massa give?" We must leave our old friend, the Missionary, to preach and proceed on our tour. As the camel fair is poor, and the animals neither beautiful to behold, nor pleasant to the nose, we leave them to themselves and make for the large clump of trees near the river. Here we find the elephant fair. Some of these animals are magnificent and stately specimens, while others are poor, under-fed, and under-sized brutes. There you see a dear little baby elephant little more than a day old. The old mother, rather grumpy at the crowd monopolizing so much of the youngster's attention, grunts and grumbles, giving an occasional little trumpet as if a warning of danger, when master elephant rushes under his mother for protection. Elephants are certainly curious animals, and most amusing to watch. You will see a little boy of five or six years old ordering about a huge monster who is as obedient as any schoolboy. In another place the *mahout*, being of a musical turn, amuses himself by singing, and at a certain part of the refrain the elephant joins in with a kind of squeak. I have seen elephants taught to dance and keep capital time. The *mahout* had a lot of small bells, like those used by dancing girls, on the elephant's feet; he then began to play on a small drum, singing at the same time, when the elephant commenced to hop about in the most ludicrous way. Passing through the trees, we come on the river Gunduk, where you see numbers of elephants having their morning bath. They look like great children being washed. Lying down in the water they first turn over on one side and are well scrubbed with a piece of hard brick; they then roll over to the other side. When thoroughly scrubbed and cleaned, the driver mounts on their neck, and they proceed to the sugarcane market, where a bundle is purchased. This the elephant raises to his *mahout*, who places it on the pad, and away they go home, when the elephant has a breakfast off the cane, which he seems to enjoy very much. The next place is the tent fair, this we pass quickly through, as there is not much to be seen. From this we make for the bird fair. To do so we have to pass through lanes of native eating and sweetmeat shops. I cannot say the dishes look tempting, while the smell of bad *ghee* makes you wish you had put a little extra eau-de-cologne on your handkerchief before you left your tent. However, Sonepore, like Christmas, only comes once a year, and many people see it but once in a lifetime. We soon reach the bird fair which is not much. There are birds of all kinds—Indian, foreign, and often performing ones. The din here, from the screeching of the different species, is overpowering, so we move on and make for the bazar, which will be found close to the temple where the people bring their offerings to the ruling Hindu god of the place. Passing on, you find yourself in a street with canvas shops on either side, where you can buy almost anything—goods from Manchester, Birmingham, Delhi, Cawnpore, the Punjab, Cashmere, or Afghanistan, and you can often pick up rather neat Indian-made curios at a reasonable price. The street turns to the right, and you again find a lot of sweetmeat shops. *Ghee* predominates here too; and a short visit is considered advisable. We proceed to the temple, of which, not much more than the outside walls of a rather clumsily-built mass of brick and mortar is to be seen. The door-way is crowded with religious mendicants of all kinds, some sitting, some erect, with one hand well raised above the head and a finger rigidly pointing heavenwards. The arm is withered, and the finger nails are more like the claws of a wild beast than that of a human being. Another is sitting cross-legged, and his bones and muscles have set and stiffened into the one position, out of which he has no power to move. Another is buried head downwards, up to the waist, two bamboo tubes are inserted into his nostrils through which he breathes. In fact, so many hideous sights meet the eye, that the *mahouts* are ordered to turn the elephants homewards, and, passing through another corner of the horse fair, we strike the Chupprah road near the big well that supplies most of the Sonepore visitors with water, then, turning to the left, up the road Maharaj Sing's encampment of Kabul horses comes in sight. This class of horse being cheap, strong, and hardy, is generally purchased for the use of Indigo Planters' Assistants. As I have been asked to purchase one or two for friends, I proceed to buy one. Taking a look along the two lines of Kabuls, I pick out a few that look like the kind wanted. Old Maharaj Sing, the horse-dealer, has been watching, as a cat does a rat, to see if he can make out by my face the one I particularly fancy, then throwing the rude reins (made of pieces of rope) over the head of the horse I pick out, he jumps on and away as hard as the beast can go; he then trots back, and afterwards walks the animal to allow of my judging if he is all right on his pins; I then examine him, and, as he seems to be all right, the important question: "What do you want for him?" is put. Perfectly amazed, the horse-dealer puts himself into a position of surprise: "What, sir, you who have bought hundreds of horses from me have to ask the price of that splendid horse, which is almost an Arab, up to great weight, goes like the wind, and for whom I refused Rs. 500 at Cawnpore!"

This last statement is like a hint. So my move is to walk away. Maharaj Sing follows and coming up inquires: "Don't you want the horse?" "Yes; but not at the price you name." "Well he has cost me a lot to feed; I was a fool not to sell him at Cawnpore, and I don't want to take him back. What will you give for him?" "Rs. 150," is the reply. "What! Rs. 150 for that horse? You're joking with me!" This kind of thing goes on for some time till

I see he is inclined to accept my price, when I slip a rupee as earnest-money into his hand, and the bargain is clinched. If, however, he does not give way, and I want the horse, I advance, say Rs. 25, and generally end in securing the animal.

Some of the old hands, and large buyers understand the way to bargain *a la oriental*, which is taking the dealer's hands in yours, a blanket is placed over them, then you begin operations. The joints of the different fingers represent so much money. The purchaser, say, presses the two first joints of the forefinger of the right hand, that means Rs. 200. The vendor in reply squeezes the same, but also pinches the first joint of the intending purchaser's next finger, meaning Rs. 250, and so on. A bargain is very quickly struck in this way, and as secrecy is considered the right thing, the dealer may sell much below what he asks, and no one but the purchaser be the wiser. We have now been all over the fair; so taking the racecourse where it skirts the camp as our way home, we reach it, feeling very much dislocated after some four hours on a rough elephant; however, once in a way it is well worth the trouble, and young people enjoy the fun and novelty of the thing. At last the end has come. The final dance has taken place, and all that remains to be done is to settle—the ladies, their *khansamahs'* bills—and the gentlemen, their lottery and race accounts. At mid-day the settling bugle sounds to give notice, and shortly after men, followed by their servants bearing bags of money, walk towards the supper-room where the settling comes off. At the head of the table, the Secretary sits with his books and lottery papers, this only of late years; for formerly every one had to make up and collect his own account which the Secretary now does, and deducts 5 per cent. from your winnings for the trouble, which does not benefit him, for his labour is that of love, and the 5 per cent. is credited to the

Race Fund. A Sonepore Race Secretary must be a perfect "Job." He has to attend to everything; and if anything is wanted from an elephant to a ten-penny nail, he must supply it, or meet the great displeasure of the claimant. Settling under the new system, is child's play to the old, and it is all over in ten minutes. Years ago, before the sepoys had turned *nemuk haram*, a lot of young subs, attached to one of the Native Infantry Regiments at Dinapore, put their savings together and came to Sonepore, determined to win a fortune. Their settling kept them at work from early morn till sunset, and when, after paying out and receiving several thousand rupees, they balanced their accounts, they found one rupee to the profit side, which they divided as their winnings among them. As you leave the settling-room, you notice that tents are fast falling and carriages and dog-carts, full of passengers, are leaving: as they pass you give them a farewell cheer.

The unfortunate ones who have to remain behind on that day could express their feelings in Moore's words:

> "He feels like one who treads alone
> Some banquet hall deserted,
> Whose lights are fled, whose garlands dead,
> And all but he departed."

The place is soon a desert, strewn with straw, broken plates, pots, and dishes, and empty beer and champagne bottles, which always denote, in India, the place where the Briton has feasted.

CHAPTER IX.

MY CHRISTMAS PARTY AT KURNOUL—WILD BUFFALOES—SHOOTING AN ALLIGATOR—VISIT OF MY BROTHER—GET THE MANAGEMENT OF DOOMRAH—MY ASSISTANT KEEPS SNAKES AS PETS—REVIVAL OF THE MOZUFFERPORE RACE MEET.

As I now held the dignified position of Sub-manager of Kurnoul, and C. G— (whose Christmas party at Dooriah I have described) having gone to Calcutta on his way for a sea-trip, I determined to give a small Christmas party. Having issued my invitations and stated that we were to pass our time in shooting, I had to find out where sport could be got. So, summoning a couple of sharp men, I sent them off to seek. The evening before my guests were expected, one of the men came in and told me he had found a place simply swarming with game, and insisted on my going to judge for myself. As the shooting ground was not very distant, I ordered an elephant I had the loan of to be sent on ahead, and, in half an hour, followed in my dog-cart, and mounting the elephant, proceeded to look round. I found the report as to quantity of game in no way exaggerated; the hares were running about like rabbits in a warren, and quail and partridges seemed to swarm. I did not take out my gun, as I was afraid I might be tempted to fire, so I at once returned home quite pleased at the prospect of giving my friends such grand sport. They arrived at last, and, early on Christmas morning 1852, we started for the shooting ground. Here we found our elephants and beaters formed line and advanced. Our day's sport proved very successful as we shot forty-three hares, twelve brace of partridge, and several couple of quail, also a few pigs. As we were proceeding toward the spot where breakfast was spread, and when we least expected to see anything, what was our astonishment when up jumped a fine spotted deer and bounded away. Only one shot was fired at him; but it did not take effect. We were much disgusted at losing so fine a supply of venison.

Breakfast in the open air on a cool fine December day in India is always a cheerful meal. We were all hungry after our exercise, and every one seemed quite satisfied with himself and the world at large. The villagers flocked round us to look at the *sahibs* feeding, a piece of curiosity which we did not appreciate, so we asked them to move further away; this they did, but as soon as our attention was directed to our food, they again gradually drew nearer and nearer. The place where our breakfast was laid was a clear space, while all round was a kind of scrub jungle. There were footpaths leading to the cleared patch, by which our admiring on-lookers had come. One of our party hit on a capital plan to keep them back; he cut some cold beef, put it on as many plates as there were paths, then requested the crowd to retire. When they had reached a respectable distance, he placed a plate of beef on each path, and having informed the spectators of the contents, returned to finish his meal in peace. This plan was most successful, and the plates of beef were as good as sentries with fixed bayonets.

After breakfast we mounted again, and were just starting when a little boy, a cowherd, came running up to tell us that two wild buffaloes were in a big grass close by, and that they were very troublesome, coming out and attacking the tame ones grazing under his care. This was grand news; we all loaded with ball, and before long arrived at some very heavy grass. We were afraid it was too thick to beat through, but determined to try. Our perseverance was rewarded, for, as we neared the centre of the grass, it got thinner, and was not so high. Just then a shot fired to the right told us the game was afoot, and soon the banging became general. At last one of the buffaloes, badly wounded, tried to swim the river—the Big Gunduk—but before he had gone fifty yards, his heart failed him. He just managed to reach the bank when he turned over dead, and would have been carried away by the stream, had not one of the sportsmen, who was much excited, jumped from his elephant right into the water, and holding on by the dead animal's tail, dragged him triumphantly to shore. He proved to be a fine young bull, in capital condition, with a fair pair of horns. Having dragged him well away from the water, we started in pursuit of the other. He proved to be more savage, and if he had not speedily received his quietus, would have done mischief among the beaters. He also was a young bull. They had evidently been driven out of the wild herds to be found in the jungles above Bettiah, by some of their more powerful brethren. The low-caste coolies had a grand feast of buffalo meat. It was a case of "cut and come again," for it lasted several days. I had the hide carefully taken off and tanned, and found the leather made splendid traces. The two heads adorned the Kurnoul bungalow for many a day. Our sport on the day after Christmas was not so good; but we were rewarded for our patience by a big bag in the shape of a man-eating alligator. We were making towards our dog-carts and horses when an old Hindu woman came running out of a village very much excited, calling out that there was a big alligator on a sand bank near at hand, and that he had carried off several heads of cattle, and many men and children. We immediately dismounted, and taking our guns loaded with ball, advanced cautiously to the place indicated by the ancient dame. There lay a regular monster, basking in the evening sun. The order was whispered for all to take an aim, and at the word fire "to pull trigger together." This was carried out, and the guns went off as one shot. The monster seemed to struggle for a second, then striking the sand with his tail once or twice, glided into the water. We were much disappointed at seeing him disappear; however, the old woman told us that it was very shallow just there, so we called a boy we saw some distance off, and asked him to step into the water, and look if he could see anything. Thinking that we had shot some bird or small game, the youngster at once stepped into the pool, but had barely gone a couple of steps, when, with a yell of terror, he rushed out, calling out as natives generally do: *Bap, re, bap!* (father, oh, father!). When he had run some distance and stopped, we ascertained from him that the animal was lying at the bottom of the pool; but he could not say if he was dead or not. With some difficulty we procured a small boat, and crossed a stream that ran between us and our alligator. We then offered a reward to any one who would go into the water and find out. A plucky *gowalla* (cowherd) at once volunteered, marched into the water, seized the beast by the tail and began pulling at him. The minute the other natives, who had gathered round to look at what was going on, saw the alligator made no resistance, they all joined, and he was soon landed on the sand bank. He seemed quite dead, but to make sure, we thought we would put another bullet into him. Luckily all were told to stand clear, when the man who was to fire the final shot advanced. As behind the shoulder was considered the most deadly shot, he aimed there and fired. To every one's astonishment, the beast gave one tremendous lash with his tail, which would have broken any one's leg had they been in the way, and turned over on its back quite dead. It measured 19 feet in length, and it was as much as two bullock-carts could do to carry, and four bullocks to drag it, some five miles to the factory. The skull was a very good specimen and the teeth perfect. We found nothing of the men and children, reported to have been eaten, inside it, although often bangles and jewellery are to be found if an alligator has lately fed on a Hindu boy or girl, who have always some small ornament of value on them. This is the only man-eater I have ever shot, though many fish-eaters have fallen to my gun, one fully as long but not such a formidable looking beast, as the man-eater. They are known amongst Europeans as the "snubnosed" and "long-nosed." The natives called the former *boch* and the latter *go* or *gurrial*. What, with the two wild buffaloes and the big alligator my first Christmas party was a success. One of my guests was a Frenchman called Verpleough, he was up to all kinds of tricks, so some of the men determined to play off a trick on him. They got a pie-dish, and taking the pastry cover off, sent down to the river for a few frogs which they placed in the dish, covering it with the pastry top. The pie at dinner was set before "mossoo," who was full of life, chattering away. The pie no sooner placed before him, than he at once offered to help one of his neighbours. Cutting a big triangular piece he inserted the spoon, when out jumped the frogs right into his lap. With a yell of horror the Frenchman threw himself back, lost his balance and fell on the floor, carrying with him his righthand neighbour. It took some time for the gallant Gaul to recover his nerve, and during the rest of the dinner he eyed every covered dish with suspicion. Jokes of this kind were common in the district in those days; but men were more like schoolboys when they got out for a holiday, and the softening and polishing influence exercised over the rougher half of society had not had time to act. Though several ladies were to be found in the District, they were yet few and far between, and could be counted on your fingers. We all went on to Dooriah to spend New Year's day with A. H— who was the assistant there. We shot down the *daubs* (low lands) from Kurnoul to Dooriah, but did not make much of a bag. However, we spent a very enjoyable day; and on the morning of the 2nd of January, the party broke up.

I returned to Kurnoul where I had plenty to do, for I had to attend to the Dooriah work as well. I passed two very happy years at Kurnoul. My youngest brother from the Mauritius paid me a visit while I was there. He did not give me much notice, as I only received his letter to say he was coming two days before he himself arrived at my house, so I suppose the ship he came by carried both him and his letter. I had left him quite a little fellow, and, when something over six feet two inches uncoiled itself out of the *palkee*, I was quite taken aback. It was a great pleasure after so many years to see one's own kith and kin again, and we sat and talked of all the near and dear ones till nearly daybreak. He had had a dreadful journey of it. Men in Calcutta in those days knew very little as to how up-country districts were to be reached. The people, my brother was consigned to, had started him off in a *palkee*, by what is called a Government dak, that is, the postmaster arranges for a change of bearers every so many miles, and they carry you, by stages, to your destination. For this uncomfortable mode of transit, he had to pay Rs. 300, and buy a *palkee*, which cost him Rs. 50 more. If proper inquiry had been made, he could have come by horse-dak, that is, in a palanquin-carriage drawn by ponies, for Rs. 64. However, he was started off by this antediluvian style of travelling. All went well for the first two days and nights, but, on the evening of the 3rd, when he was hoping he was nearing the end of his journey, his bearers put down his *palkee* and bolted. Having heard of snakes and tigers, and the spot being a very jungly one, he drew his hunting-knife, the only weapon he possessed, and mounting on the top of his conveyance, determined to sell his life dearly. Not long seated thus, thinking how much more comfortable he would have been if he had remained at home in the Mauritius, he was awakened from his dream by a distant rumbling sound, and notes on a bugle came floating towards him on the breeze. He could not understand what it meant. The sounds came nearer and nearer, and he could make out a black lumbering object through the darkness. Determined to do or die, he jumped in to the middle of the road brandishing his *couteau de chasse*. A jaded pony half frightened by the *palkee* on the road, and the figure with up-stretched arms before it, stopped short. The driver in afright yelled out, and out of the *dak gharrie* jumped three young subs just out from England on their way to join their regiment. My brother quickly explained matters to them, when they insisted on his going on with them, and wished to put his *palkee* on top of their carriage. This the driver objected to, and, as they could not manage to lift it without his assistance, it had to be left behind. The conduct of the driver was talked over, and the youngsters coming to the conclusion that he must be leagued with robbers, arranged that they should take it turn about to sit on the box beside him with a cocked revolver pointed at his head, and to shoot him on the slightest provocation. The driver, trusting to fate, drove on; and, as he took them safely into Sherghatty by next morning, they formed a more favourable opinion of him, and took off the sentry. At Sherghatty, my brother left the light-hearted young subs, who proceeded on their journey. He was kindly and most hospitably treated by an old colonel residing at Sherghatty, who got him a fresh set of bearers and another *palkee*, and sent him on to Mozufferpore. Here he stopped at the club, which he took for an hotel, and very much offended the doctor (a pompous little man who lived at the club) by asking him for his bill. From Mozufferpore he came to Kurnoul.

From Kurnoul I was promoted to the charge of Poopree and Doomrah. I had had charge of the former for a short time before, and had to look after the work there, as well as at Kurnoul, and, as I got no extra pay, found it hard work. I was relieved of the charge of Kurnoul by my successor, A. Inglis, and went to Poopree in 1853-54. I had to superintend Doomrah, for which I got no pay; but received 5 per cent. commission on the profits. These profits were calculated in a peculiar manner; thus, the Indigo was priced at Rs. 120 per maund, then as many maunds were deducted from the total Indigo made at Rs. 120, as would cover the outlay, and on every maund over and above that you received Rs. 5 per maund. This was a very poor style of commission compared with how it is calculated now. I was very successful that season, making one thousand maunds at the two places on an outlay of Rs. 74,000 or thereabouts, and received the large sum of Rs. 1,800 as commission. At the end of 1854, the Tirhoot Indigo Association gave me the option of managing Poopree or Doomrah; and as the latter was the more cheerful of the two, I went there—J. C. Muir relieving me at Poopree. When I had charge of the two concerns, I had an Assistant at Bungong, an out-factory attached to Poopree, and another at Doomrah. The latter was a great man for training animals of all kinds. I gave him a young bear I had caught while out tiger-shooting about this time. In a few weeks he taught it to dance, wrestle with him, and if you pointed a stick at it, and made a noise imitating a gun, he would fall down and sham dead.

While quite young, he was tame enough; but got very savage as he grew older, and had to be given away to some performing Nutts (gipsies). My Assistant used also to amuse himself in catching snakes, and the most vicious cobra had no chance with him. These reptiles seemed to know he was their master, and would turn tail and bolt the minute he attacked them. His mode of procedure was this: As soon as they turned to go off, he seized the snake by the tail, and whirled it once or twice round his head, to stupefy it; then letting its head hang, he would impart a tremulous motion into the snake by shaking his arm as if he was suffering from ague. This seemed to have a paralyzing effect. He then let its head drop on the ground, and with a forked stick, pressed on the back of its neck. This made the snake open its mouth, when he inserted a piece of cork between the jaws, and with a bent needle extracted the poison bag. This done, the reptile was harmless; and he would keep them as pets. I must say I objected to them, with or without poison bags; and whenever I saw one of these objectionable pets, I knocked it on the head.

In January 1854, the Mozufferpore race meet was again set afoot. This had died a natural death. Some years before, partly on account of the heavy losses sustained by proprietors in sugar, and partly by a bad feeling that existed between the planting and civilian community. Lord Ulick Browne and A. R— who had been appointed as Magistrates to the district, were determined to try and remedy this unfortunate state of affairs, and notice was sent round that there would be sky races, and that the Station would give a ball to which all Planters, their wives and families were to be invited. Not to be outdone, some gay, young, bachelor Planters announced their determination to give a return ball to the Station, and this was followed up by a dance subscribed for by every one. It was one of the jolliest meets I have ever been at. The sky races were great fun; the horses entered being mostly our own riding and driving nags. In one case, a mare taken out of a dog-cart and then and there saddled, won a handsome silver tankard presented by F. D—, Magistrate, then at Buhaira. The pony race, where "Jack," "Junab-i-Ali," and "Kiss-me-Quick," vied for honours, and the grand finish for the Galloway Purse, where "Indigo," "Diamond," and "Chocolate," piloted by such cracks as

Simmy, Ulick B—, and Frank V—, are things of the far off past, though fresh in the memory of those who were but boys in those days. If the races were a success, our dances were even more so. The bachelors got a slight advantage; they discovered that a party of young ladies were passing through Mozufferpore on a visit to friends, so they at once sent them an invitation, and actually mustered eighteen ladies married and single.

The 13th Native Infantry kindly sent us their band, which put great life into the entertainment.

Before I left Poopree to come and live at Doomrah, we got permission from the Durbhangah Rajah to shoot in what had been his preserves at a place called Piprone. The late Rajah was not much of a sportsman, and the place had not been carefully preserved. We found, however, some spotted deer, peafowl, partridge, and a splendid wild boar. We bagged a deer or two, and some smaller game; but the boar escaped.

CHAPTER X.

ANOTHER SHOOTING EXPEDITION TO NEPAL—MUD-IMBEDDED ELEPHANT—A NEPALESE COLLECTOR.

Shortly after this, my old friends C. G— and J. C— wrote and asked me to arrange for a tiger-shooting expedition. This I did; and early in March we found ourselves again under canvas in the Nepal Terai. To have described one shooting party is to describe all, so I will confine myself to incidents that may interest my readers.

On the morning after our arrival and just before starting to shoot, a very dirty-looking Nepalese official asked for an interview, and demanded to see our permit to shoot. This was rather a stumper for us, though we had written to the Resident, and he had replied to say he was sending one, the piece of paper had not turned up. We informed the man in authority of this, and said, we expected it by that day's post when we would show it. He was rather unpleasant about the matter, but went away, so we started off shooting; but we observed that we could get no one to show us where game was to be found, and the Nepalese shikari, whom we had hired, did not look happy. On our return to camp in the evening, we opened our post letters in the hope of finding the required order; but no such thing had come. Again, next morning, the unpleasant official came, and this time told us we could not shoot, and must leave Nepal territory. This was a sad disappointment; and, as we had been to some expense, we determined to see what effect, as the Yankees say, "the almighty dollar" would have. The man was invited into my tent where we were all seated, and, to my disgust, the first thing he did was to half recline himself on my bed. First impulse pointed to summary ejectment, but that meant an end to our sport, so I said naught. J. C— opened the negotiations by insinuating that we would make him happy if he would only wink at the non-arrival of the permit. The man bit at once. He might get into trouble, and, of course, would expect to be rewarded according to the risk. We all felt that Rs. 50 each, at least, was about to be extracted. What was our astonishment, when his demand was placed before us, to find all he wanted was, that one of the deer we had shot should be given to him and sent with him, on an elephant, to his home! We presented him with two deer, and gave him some powder and shot; and off he started, having given orders that we were to receive every assistance from the villagers about.

The deer you get in the Nepal jungle is very dry, and European sportsmen hardly ever eat them, their servants feasting off venison and, where their caste will allow, wild pig. Of the game we bagged, partridge, hare, florican, pea and jungle fowl, were all that found their way to our table. A very young fawn cooked whole, with a stuffing of nuts, is not bad. Having got rid of our Nepalese friend, we started for the shooting grounds, and before long came on two young bears in some grass. Giving two "peons" a blanket each, we told them to get down, and throw the blankets over the young bears, and catch them. We, meanwhile, formed a semi-circle round the men to protect them from the angry mother in case she made her appearance. The men were plucky fellows, and at once rushed on the small bears, not bigger than good-sized pups, and rolling them up in the blankets, handed them up. They were put in the box of the *howdah* under the seat where provisions are generally kept. The little beasts kept up an incessant cry, night and day, while we were out. They, however, ate their food, and were not very vicious. One of these I presented to my Assistant afterwards, who taught him all kinds of tricks. Besides the bears, we bagged a leopard that day. He had been wounded; a bullet having passed through one of the joints of his tail. This made him very savage, and he charged like a tiger at my elephant, who at once turned and bolted; but as she turned round, I took a snap shot, and fancied I saw the leopard turn on his back. After a bone-breaking expedition on the runaway elephant of nearly half an hour's duration, she was persuaded to stop and return, and, sure enough, there lay a very handsome leopard dead. Our next day's bag consisted of another bear and two young ones, one of which was badly wounded, and had to be killed. We traced the old mother bear to a fallen tree, and, as the old lady objected to come out, we let off some fireworks in the different hollows of the tree. This had no effect, so the *shikari* said he would crawl in and see. The tree was on the ground,—a splendid one it must have been; but fire and age had hollowed it out thoroughly, and a middle-sized man could walk in if he stooped down. In started "Mooson," our *shikari*, but he was not long in making his exit. We all admired the clever way in which he evaded the bear; for, instead of rushing right away as he came out from the tree, he just turned and hopped on to the fallen trunk. The bear, with her two young ones, clinging to her hips, went straight ahead, and was immediately rolled over. The two little ones holding on to her like grim death. On this occasion we were out for over fifteen days, and though we got capital sport as far as small game went, we were not over-lucky with tigers, only getting one. He, however, showed fight. We disturbed him while he was having a good feed off a buffalo he had just killed, and was in no mood for a bolt. I was fortunate enough to see him first, and rolled him over like a rabbit. My *mahout* at once took my elephant towards the place where he fell, when, with a roar, he came at me. I gave him my right and left, but that did not stop him, and, in a moment, there he was, his hind legs holding on to the elephant's trunk, while his foreclaws were well dug into the poor animal's ears. I could, if I had felt so inclined, have stroked the head of the savage brute. He did look grand as he stared at me, his eyes starting out of his head, the hair on his neck and head standing on end, and as fine a set of teeth as one would wish to see, were most unpleasantly brought to notice. The elephant behaved very pluckily. She stood her ground well when the charge was made; but as soon as the tiger settled on her, she began to shake so violently to try and get rid of the tiger, that I was thrown down on to my seat, and could do nothing but hold on to my guns to prevent their being thrown out. My *howdah* had attained an angle of 45 degrees, and I could not now have held on much longer, when C. G— of our party, ranged up alongside, and shot the tiger from off my elephant's head. I had the greatest difficulty in getting out of my now very lopsided *howdah;* but, by making a man hang on to one side, I managed to scramble out of the other without pulling it on top of me. The tiger was a fine one, about 9 feet 10 inches in length. The next big thing that fell to my gun was a boa-constrictor. He was 17 feet long; and though I put a bullet right through his head, it was a long time before he was dead all over. We had great trouble to get him padded, as the natives are very much afraid of these reptiles. Our last adventure on this occasion was the sticking of one of our elephants in the mud, while crossing one of the small streams that run through the jungle. The beast was a weakly animal. It had been poorly fed, and made no attempts to help itself. It sunk deeper and deeper into the mire. We cut branches of trees, which we stuck into the mud at its sides; but to no effect. Most elephants when they stick in the mud in this way, will take advantage of every help that is put within reach of their trunk, and utilize the branches of trees thrown near them, by tucking them in under their side, then rolling over on to them, commence the operation on the other side again, and rolling over until a sufficient quantity of branches have been placed to support them, in this way they gradually work themselves out. Our miserable beast would do nothing, and gradually sank; a few minutes more and only his trunk would have remained above ground. One of the *mahouts* suggested making the other elephants pull him out bodily. He said, there were two elephants who had been used to drag the dead elephants away for interment, and that he thought they would be able to rescue this one. Fortunately, we had a spare *howdah*-rope, and this, with some trouble and no little danger, the *mahout* had to pass underneath the mud-imbedded elephant; for there was always the fear that he might take it into his head to help himself by tucking things under him and commence with the *mahout!* They kept, however, well away from his forequarters. The rope having been fastened, and then secured round the neck and chest of two other elephants, the order to pull was given. The two elephants at once set to tugging, and the wretched one in the mud was suddenly hauled on to his back, where he lay resisting, and kicking with his heels in the air like a naughty baby. The two elephants, being strong and well-conditioned, gave another long and strong pull, which brought the refractory one out of the mud, with a flop as loud as the explosion of a good-sized bombshell. It was a relief when we got him out; for if he had died, it would have added very much to the cost of our shooting party. We had been out for a fortnight, and it was time to return. Though we had not shot much, we had enjoyed ourselves thoroughly. The fortnight cost us Rs. 150 each. We had met and joined camp with the Soorsund Babu, so we had the use of his elephants to beat. These, with what we had, gave us a grand line of beating elephants. I think our total muster was seventy,—sixty of which we took out with us, the other ten remained behind to carry branches as fodder for the others. We were up, and in the saddle, early in the morning, having a long ride before we reached British territory. As we neared the boundary, villages became more numerous; and, not being quite sure if we were on the right road, we made for what looked like a village *kutcherry* (office). Here a very respectable and civil official came out and put us on the right way. Noticing several *ryots* in peculiar positions, some standing on one leg; others in the same position, but pedestalled on an inverted earthen pot surrounded by a thick bed of thorns, we asked why they were kept thus: "Oh," replied the official, "this is how we collect rent;" we inquired whether they found that the punishment had the desired effect. The reply was that these men would pay in an hour or so; but if the *saheb* would like to see some of the very refractory ones, the official would be glad to show them. Following him, he led us into a long, low-roofed house, and there we found about half-a-dozen men buried up to their necks in the ground. "These, sir, are great *budmashes* (scamps); but they will pay." We asked how long they were likely to be kept there, and the reply was: "By sunset they will have paid all rent due by them." On returning to the open air, the little Nepalese Collector with great glee explained to us the nature of the punishment of the one-leg torture. The man had to stand on one leg with the other foot resting on it, as well as to keep himself balanced on the inverted pot. Near him stood a man with a good long stick. At the slightest attempt, on the part of the prisoner under punishment, to put down the other leg, the earthen vessel was smashed at a blow, and the unfortunate ryot would fall sprawling on his hands and knees among the thorns strewn to receive him.

As we mounted our horses to go on, the little official, with a grin on his face, remarked that he hoped we had noticed everything, and that when we returned to our country, we would try his plan with our ryots, and find it succeed. It is a strange fact that the Tirhoot ryots are constantly bolting into the Nepal Terai, showing that there they are treated in a way which they understand, and where they are not harassed by new laws, which are changed every few years, and where no "Ilbert" may intrude his little bill. Justice in Nepal is very summary. Sir Jung Bahadoor, when he came to Sonepore, had a living instance of it in his suite. This was a treasurer who had made free with the coin under his charge. The offender's right hand was ordered to be cut off, which was forthwith done. He was not dismissed from his place; the punishment had condoned the offence, and, as Sir Jung remarked with a knowing twinkle of his little eye, "he is not likely to steal again." The treasurer rode a beautiful Arab, and managed him most skilfully notwithstanding his handless arm.

A sharp canter brought us to our dog-carts, where we separated, and each proceeded to his own home. On reaching Doomrah, I found a letter from my Assistant, asking for leave to go with a party to shoot in the Rajah's preserves at Peeprone, and, as I would be delayed a day or two at Doomrah, I sent a reply by express with the required sanction. The party shot some deer and peafowl, and returned after a couple of days' shooting.

CHAPTER XI.

I TAKE CHARGE OF SHAHPORE-MIRCHA—JOURNEY, AND VISIT TO CALCUTTA—OUTBREAK OF THE MUTINY.

In 1856 I was offered charge of Shahpore-Mircha, which I accepted. As the manager who was to relieve me at Doomrah was away on leave, I found myself in charge of that place also. I had, therefore, Doomrah, Shahpore, and Chitwarrah on my hands, and, as my Assistant at Chitwarrah was on the sick list, I had plenty to do. The head native servant or *moonshi*, one Kali Prasad at Shahpore, was supposed to have the factory under his thumb. He certainly had acquired a lot of property, and had a great deal of power; but I found him a very good man, and he took great interest in the place.

He told me he began life as a writer on small pay in the concern; that the proprietor of the factory finding him sharp, gradually promoted him till he became the head native servant. He then, by doing a little banking, gradually amassed money, and purchased landed property. His father before him had already some *zemindaris.* I may mention that he eventually became a shareholder in the factory, and that his son, or rather his widow—for poor old Kali died some years ago—is now proprietor of the whole concern.

About this time I had occasion to go to Calcutta, and, as two other friends were going also, we arranged to travel together. We drove to Bankipore, and there found our *dak gharrie* or *palkee* carriage, waiting. We had taken supplies for the road; and, as our first day would be Christmas Day, a turkey and a couple of bottles of "fiz" formed part of our store. We went out of Bankipore with a flourish, as the trap was horsed; but, after going some fifteen miles, we came to the end of the macadamised route, and were then propelled by coolies. This was very slow work, and it was well after 10 P.M. before we reached the Jehanabad *dak bungalow* (rest-house) very hungry and sleepy. The old *khansamah* was not long in getting out the bumpers, and by the time we had eaten a few slices of turkey and finished our two bottles of champagne, we felt quite lively again. We had no time to lose, the things were packed, and we were soon *en route* again. When we awoke in the morning, after rather an uncomfortable rest, for a *dak gharrie* is not meant to carry three, especially all good sized men, we found ourselves close to Gyah. As it was very cold, we stopped and brewed some coffee, and found a cup of strong coffee a great "pick-me-up." By 10 A.M. we were comfortably seated in the Gyah *dak bungalow* at breakfast. The verandah was crowded with men offering for sale images of elephants, sacred bulls, etc., carved out of Gyah stone. Gyah is to the Hindoo a very sacred city, and the Hindoo priests, who have possession of the different temples, make a very good thing out of it. They actually, during the pilgrimage season, send out "touts," who go miles out on the different roads to persuade pilgrims to come to certain temples, and there are often most serious riots between the employees of the proprietors of the different temples. Gyah is made extra sacred, as it is one of the places where Vishnoo put his foot on earth. He seems to have been going on one foot with a kind of hop before he took the next step, as the "Vishn Pud," or footprints of Vishnoo, seem all to be in one convenient corner where all the temples stand. The supposed footprints are cut out of stone. This represents the impression of a foot of gigantic dimensions. When a wealthy pilgrim goes to any of these shrines, he is supposed to fill the footprint with gold or silver coin. This is, of course, taken by the "Gyewalls," as the proprietors of the temples are called. Gyah is a very dry place, the bare hills in the warm weather throw out great heat. The fields are surrounded by low embankments to catch any rain that may fall, and when the soil is moistened, it becomes a sticky red clay. Beware of Gyah mosquitoes: they are the most vicious little insects ever met with. There is a story told of a Scotchman, who lately arrived from his native heath, and who had heard of mosquitoes (most likely Gyah ones) from some of his travelled friends, inquired on seeing an elephant if it was a mosquito.

From Gyah we were propelled by coolies to the Grand Trunk Road. There is nothing to see but large sun-burnt plains on which a few herds of graceful antelope were feeding on the little grass they can pick up. They are very wild, and if you attempt to get near them, off they go bounding high into the air before they settle down to a steady pace. Reaching the Grand Trunk Road, we changed our coolies for horses, and away we went at a more cheerful pace. The scenery, as you pass the noted Dunwah Pass is grand, and, as you have ascended to a higher level, the cold is intense. The road is naturally very much uphill, and to warm ourselves and ease the horse, we got out to have a brisk walk, but when not very far from the top of the hill, the driver told us we would be safer in than out of the trap, as tigers very often jumped out of the jungle and carried away men. We took the hint and got in. After sunset, we spied the twinkle of a *dak bungalow* light, and ordered our Jehu to pull up; our provisions were soon unpacked, and the *khansamah* added a few potatoes to our supplies. We made a good dinner, and lighting up our pipes, started on our way rejoicing. Next morning we found ourselves in a grand climate somewhere among the Santal Hills, where our conveyance pulled up to change horses, and we were surrounded by an admiring crowd of very lightly clad children. We were much amused by the ingenious way in which they kept themselves warm; each carried an earthen *kuttiah* (a kind of earthen pot) in which were some live embers. This when they squatted down, they popped under the little clothing they had, and thus kept themselves warm. It took three days and two nights to reach Calcutta, but the journey had to be timed so as to arrive at Rauigunge early enough to catch the train to Calcutta, which then only ran as far as that place. By 9 A.M. we found ourselves at Howrah, the East Indian Railway terminus. We had to gather our goods together, and employ a few coolies to take them to the steamer at the railway pier, where the ferry-steamer lay, and she took us across the Hooghly. Now this river is crossed by a fine bridge standing on floating pontoons.

I had not visited Calcutta since my arrival in the country, but found very little change in it. One or two fine buildings were in course of erection, but a man from up-country soon tires of the constant sameness. The one pleasant thing is the evening drive on the Strand by the river's bank. Here you enjoy the cool sea-breeze that begins to blow about sunset. The number of really stylish equipages briskly driving up and down the watered way, and the number of well mounted horsemen and women puts much life into the scene. The Eden Gardens existed in a small way in those days, but under another name. There, now, with the band playing, is found a most delightful lounge for the weary denizens of the City of Palaces. While in Calcutta, I went to see the Indigo sales at the Mart. On arrival there, I was asked if I would not have some lunch, and walking into a long apartment something like an empty store-room, I saw a table round which were men all busy at lunch. Thomas and Co. and W. Moran and Co. are famous for their cold beef, salad, and draft beer tiffins, and I can say I enjoyed mine. As the clock strikes two the sale begins. One of the partners mounts the first chest of Indigo to be sold. These are generally sold by tens; they are assorted by the brokers, so that the colours may run as evenly as possible. To sell ten chests does not take two minutes; the bidding is so brisk, the great object of intending purchasers being to catch the auctioneer's ear first with the final bid; this is shouted out by half-a-dozen men at the same time, for they know to a rupee what the batch will go for, and when it comes to the final bid, the scream for precedence is bewildering. Indigo sells now from about Rs. 225 to Rs. 280 per maund. After the failures of 1847 Indigo fell to very low prices, but gradually rose again, varying with the demand. If the crop be poor, and the demand good, prices range very high.

We were not sorry when the time came for us to leave Calcutta, which we did towards the end of January, 1857, returning as we came. It would be useless to describe our trip back. We passed many sepoy regiments encamped by the road, for this was the marching season, and we were overtaken by General Anson, the Commander-in-Chief, who had been to Calcutta to see his family off to England. We have often thought how lucky it was the mutiny did not break out while we were on our journey as, if it had, we could not have escaped. Poor General Anson did not live long after we saw him; he died before Delhi worn out by the cares and anxieties of that siege. In due course of time we reached home, and were glad to get back again. In May, 1857, we heard unpleasant rumours of mutiny among the sepoys, first from Barrackpore, then an outbreak at Meerut. These soon spread like wild fire over the country. To show that the natives had some idea of what was going on, a *khansamah*, an old servant who had accompanied his master on a visit to Calcutta, one evening as he was helping him to undress, said: "*Saheb*, is it true that all natives are to be made Christians?". To which his master answered jokingly, "yes." "Then," replied the domestic, "I would not give much for the cold meat, etc., it will all be stolen!" A native who is in caste is barred from eating anything that has been at a European's table on the plea of its being to them unclean. But the day a native becomes an outcaste, he calls himself a "Kistian," *i.e.*, Christian, and, as Baboo Keshub Chunder Sen said in a lecture at Mozufferpore, at once adopted all the vices of the European, but none of his virtues. The cold viands and master's liquor were bound to go once the conversion took place. The conversion of Moslems and Hindoo, by ruse or force, if necessary, by the English, was the red rag flaunted by those who wished to fan the fire of rebellion, and the report of bullock's and pig's fat being used in the lubricating composition for the cartridges was all to this end. The Commander-in-Chief published a General Order denying the report, but to allay any fear, as to losing caste by biting the cartridges, new drill was set on foot, whereby the cartridges were to be torn, not bitten. When the regiments mutinied, they thought nothing of using these very cartridges they so much objected to. While all this was going on, the startling reality was unpleasantly brought home to us by a letter from the Magistrate, summoning us into the station (Mozufferpore), to assist to protect it and ourselves. As the summons seemed urgent, I at once sent out horses to the different stages, and in a few hours after, started, armed to the teeth with one double-barrelled gun in the splash board, another put up behind the buggy, and a revolver in its case at my feet. In this way we, my wife, and I, for I was now a married man, journeyed some fifteen miles, feeling anything but happy at the look of things. Our little daughter, we had put into her small basket cradle at our feet. Arrived at Mozufferpore, we went to Secunderpore, where the Magistrate and Collector lived, and to whose house we had received an invitation. We found a number of planters and their families already gathered there. Leaving my wife and child there, I started off round the station to find out what was wrong, and gathered that trouble was expected from the "Nujeebs," a provincial battalion who supplied men as guards for the treasury, etc. One of the officials, a good linguist, had disguised himself, and loitering about the Nujeeb barracks, had overheard some treasonable talk. The Magistrate had, therefore, considered it right to call in all Europeans for mutual help in case of need.

Meeting several planters, we talked over the state of affairs, and determined to call on the officials to meet us, and say why they had called us in, and what they wanted done. A letter was accordingly drafted and sent, asking all the officials to meet us at noon the following day. At that hour we assembled, and were told by the Magistrate we were wanted to mount guard as sentries over the treasury, as the *Nujeebs* could not be trusted. This we objected to do; but suggested that we were ready to disarm those suspected, and thus get rid of the threatened danger, and, if necessary, send the treasure to Patna in our factory-carts under a planter escort. This did not meet the views of the Collector, and we did not see the force of leaving our wives and families to take care of themselves, while we took care of the Government treasury.

The meeting ended, therefore, in nothing being done. The planters from the far-off districts began to arrive, and soon there were over three hundred men, women, and children in Mozufferpore.

CHAPTER XII.

WE FORTIFY THE DOCTOR'S HOUSE—THE "VIEILLE GUARDE"—TAKING A PRISONER—FALSE ALARM—MURDER OF MAJOR AND MRS. HOLMES—MUTINY OF THE NATIVE INFANTRY AT DINAPORE—DEFENCE OF ARRAH—THE MUTINY OVER—HOMEWARD BOUND.

THE Magistrate could not entertain all, and it would not do for us to be scattered over the place, so the doctor and Mr. Weston offered their houses and grounds, and we formed two camps and messes. The houses were 500 yards apart, but stood almost in the same grounds. We all moved into our new quarters; the ladies and children occupying the houses, while the gentlemen slept in tents formed into small camps, one at each flank of the houses, and one in the front, as an advanced guard. Each of the camps supplied two sentries, and we all had to do our two hours' watch every night. At a meeting, one of our number was appointed commandant of the garrison, and he again named his subordinates, placing one man in command of each small camp. Besides these camps, there was a portico guard composed of old gentlemen, who kept watch till 11 at night. The reason for establishing this "Vieille Guarde" was, that the ladies would not see that there was any danger, and insisted on enjoying themselves. The young men were quite of the same opinion, and the commandant was at his wits' end how to keep the sentries to their duty. At last the bright idea of a guard, to consist of non-dancing men, who were to act till 11 o'clock, suggested itself, and the arrangement was carried out. A General Order was issued to the effect that at 11 o'clock all lights were to be put out, and dancing, etc., stopped. We had just got things into working order, when the Magistrate asked for a few men to go out and seize a *darogah* (head inspector of police), who was reported to be up to mischief. Three men and the Assistant Magistrate were chosen. One of the planters had his house near where the police station stood, and sending out word, that he was coming with some friends to shoot, they started in the evening. Early next morning they drove straight to the police station, not a minute too soon, for they found the *darogah* writing a letter to the rebels, inviting them over to loot the treasury, his horse ready saddled for a bolt, in case of need. He was very much astonished when he was arrested and placed in charge of the three gentlemen of the Blues, who marched him out. While arrangements were being made for having his papers examined, one of his guards noticed the *darogah* eyeing the revolver, which one of them was holding very carelessly, and paying more attention to what others were doing than to his prisoner. The inspector suddenly made a grab at the revolver, but the man who had been watching him, caught him a smart blow over the fingers, which made him leave it alone. He was now put on to the back seat of the dog-cart pinioned, and tied to the back railing of the trap. His guards then jumped up, and they drove off to Mozufferpore. Here a tent had been erected as guard-room, and two men were placed as sentries over him. The wretched man evidently saw that things were not all right for him. He was a Moslem, so he began at once counting his beads and praying. At night, a guard of Irregular Cavalry, part of the 12th Irregular Cavalry, commanded by Holmes at Segowlie, took charge of the prisoner; and next morning he was placed in an *ekah*, and sent off to Segowlie under an Irregular Cavalry escort to be dealt with by Major Holmes. On the evening of the next day, we were surprised to see the escort and prisoner return; and a private communication from Holmes, to say that his men were much averse to having the peeler hanged at Segowlie, he being a Moslem; so he had sent him back, and advised his being sent to Patna, to the Commissioner there, who seemed to have no fear of consequences, and had already strung up one or two mutineers. Giving the unhappy man a night's rest, we packed him off to Patna under the same escort. He was not long kept waiting, for he was hanged that evening, martial law having been proclaimed, and justice was quick and sure. "Warris Ali," for that was the rebel's name, died, calling on all Mahomedans to inform the King of Delhi that he had been true to him to the last. The seizing of a rebel, and his passing a prisoner to and from our camp, caused some little excitement; but we were destined to have another little shock, rather unpleasant while it lasted. One night, one of our sentries to the front, observed a long line of lights suddenly advancing towards the house, and, as he was consulting with his brother sentry whether he should turn out the different guards, two or three natives rushed in through the gate, calling out "Bagho Sahib!" "Run away, Sir!" Meanwhile, the garrison at the next house had been alarmed, and the men were turning out, when one of them not quite awake from his slumbers, accidentally discharged his gun. The report of danger had been conveyed to the ladies of this house, and they were in great alarm, but when the gun went off, there was a regular panic. Fortunately, the report had frightened more than the garrison; for, as soon as they heard it, the advancing line stopped, and in a second, every light was thrown to the ground. Just then our mounted patrol (for we patrolled the town also to see that order was kept) arrived. One of the men, a fiery Scot, drew his sword, and explaining that he would like to try the temper of his blade, was about to set spurs to his horse, when a sentry held him back, and told him not to be foolish, for what could he do one against hundreds. The Scot drew out a pistol, cocked it, and presenting it at the man, called out, "just you let go," which he did at once, and the horseman at a bound disappeared in the dark. He was followed by the rest of the patrol, and we expected to hear shots every minute, but in about half-an-hour they returned. They reported they could see or find nothing but the smouldering torches, and, though they scoured the country, not a sign of a living being could be found. This sudden appearance and disappearance has always been a mystery. Some thought it might have been a wedding procession, but knowing we were in camp, and looking out for an enemy, I doubt if a wedding procession would have come there; besides this, wedding processions do not march silently. My idea is that it was a *ruse* to try us, and see if we were really on the alert. The shot accidentally fired; they at once took as a signal for attack, and knowing that the sudden extinguishing of the torches would facilitate their retreat, they threw them down, and dispersed over the country. The men we suspected were the Nujeebs; if they could have got rid of us, over ten lakhs of rupees were in their hands. On Sundays prayers were read in the open air under the shade of the house. A guard overlooked from the top of the house in case of a sudden attack. We had stored numbers of bags of rice and *dhal* (a kind of split pea), and hundreds of earthen pots of drinking water on the top of our residence. The verandahs were protected by sand bags. Things, however, soon quieted down again after this alarm. The rains set in, and it began to pour; this rather damped the ardour of the gallant Blues who had to sleep in tents; and as a report, which afterwards proved false, of the fall of Delhi, and defeat of the mutineers, was received, we made up our minds to return to our homes and await the turn of events. The whole thing had, after all, been a very pleasant meeting, and we were rather sorry when the time came to part. I forgot to mention that we took another prisoner, a small "zemindar" (landholder), living near Doulatpore factory, who took advantage of the absence of the manager to proclaim himself king of those parts, and to collect blackmail on the river, stopping boats, and making them pay toll. This coming to the Magistrate's ear, an order was given for his arrest, and two men, one of them the manager of the factory, started off to drive about fifty miles and carry out the order. The thing was most successfully done, and the man caught in the act of issuing orders for certain illegal proceedings. The manager, W. C. B— , as soon as he reached Doulatpore factory, started off for the village where this man lived, and, entering the enclosure in which his house stood, found him, sitting in State with the members of his council round him. B— holding out the warrant to him, called on him to surrender, at the same time pointing his revolver at his head. The crowd of admiring courtiers were not long in making themselves scarce, and the unhappy "zemindar" was strapped to the back of the dog-cart. They at once started on their return journey, and by evening the zemindar was safely lodged in jail. He was tried and imprisoned for ten years. We were not to be left in peace at our homes long, for in about ten days or less, after our return, we received the news of the mutiny of the 12th Irregular Cavalry at Segowlie. They had murdered their Commanding Officer, Major Holmes, his wife, also the doctor of the regiment, and his wife. It was sad to think that a gallant officer who had been through many a campaign, leading these very men to victory, should be shot by them. His wife, too, had escaped from the Cabul massacre of the first Afghan War when her first husband, Captain Sturt, was killed. Mrs. Holmes was a daughter of Lady Sale, who was also one of the Afghan prisoners. The story told of the murder of Holmes and his wife by the natives is as follows:—

They were out for their usual evening drive, when Holmes saw a section of his men riding up to them. He immediately suspected villany, and called out to them: "I know what you want, it is my life; that you can have, but spare the lady;" the reply was a volley which killed both him and his wife. The mutineers decapitated poor Holmes, carrying away his head. The whole regiment then marched out of Segowlie, passing close by Lall Seryah Factory; they never stopped to do any harm, but continued on their road towards Lucknow and Delhi. The doctor and his wife at Segowlie refusing to come out of their house, it was fired, and they being driven out by the flames were shot; their bodies were never discovered, the fire having consumed them, house and everything. The news of this sad tragedy reached D— (who lived some nine miles away) in the afternoon, and he determined to make an attempt to recover, and bury Holmes and his wife. This he did, and had them buried at Motihary, the chief town of Chumparun. The only European saved from Segowlie was a little child of the doctor's, who was out with her nurse for a walk. The *ayah* (nurse), hearing what was happening, hid her little charge in a native woman's house, and as soon as the Irregular Cavalry left, took the child to the nearest European, who sent her on to her relations. The day we heard of the mutiny of the cavalry at Segowlie, the news of the mutiny of the three Native Infantry Regiments at Dinapore arrived. All hope of escaping seemed to us to be at an end, and the Commissioner of Patna, being much of this opinion, sent an order to the officials under his orders, to at once muster at Patna, and to call in all the residents of their districts, and bring them with them. This order was acted on, notice being sent to all residents in the district to go to Patna; and after dinner all officials, non-officials, and others started off for a moonlight journey to Patna. Before continuing what took place in Tirhoot, I will state to my readers how the regiments mutinied at Dinapore. There were three regiments there, the 40th, 7th, and 8th Native Infantry. Public opinion was very strong on the disarming of these regiments, but some of the officers objected to it. The Commanding Officer and Adjutants had great confidence in their men, so the evil day was put off. At last, as a detachment of the 37th Queen's happened to be at Dinapore with the 10th Queen's, it was determined, at any rate, to remove the ammunition, consisting of so many rounds per man, in possession of the regiments, so ammunition waggons were sent off to effect this. The carts were sent to the magazines of the two furthest off regiments; at first the men did not understand what was being done, and the ammunition carts had removed the caps and cartridges of one regiment, and were on their way to the next, when the men turned out and forming, made a rush for the cart.

Meanwhile, all the European officers had joined their men and tried to keep them quiet, but to no effect; they rushed down after the carts, which by this time had come on to the parade ground of the next regiment. Why or, wherefore, no one seems to know; the regiment, on whose ground the other had trespassed, fixed bayonets, and drove the trespassers off, so that the officers of that regiment felt convinced of their loyalty. Meanwhile, notice had been sent to the European regiments and artillery to move up from their lines about a mile distant, and the minute the Native Infantry heard the tread of the Queen's regiments and the rumble of artillery, a panic seemed to seize them, the evil-disposed firing at their officers (some of whom in their enthusiasm were going about trying to stop the men from leaving), while a few loyal sepoys walked about knocking up the muskets of those who were trying to shoot down their officers. Seeing the firing commence, the invalid soldiers of the European regiment (who had been armed and placed on the top of an hospital overlooking the parade ground), began to fire, and this settled the matter, for the Native Infantry Regiments at once went off; some men of the 7th and 8th remained, and about one hundred of the 40th Native Infantry. The guns arriving late, limbered up, and sent a few round shot after the mutineers who were far away in the distance by this time. The mutinied regiments made their way to Arrah, where they found the residents had fortified the station billiard room, into which the Magistrate and Collector had taken all the Government treasure. The latter soon found themselves besieged. The defence of the Arrah house has become a matter of history. There were besides the residents, some of Rattray's Sikhs, now the 45th Native Infantry, in the house, and they helped most materially in the defence. A well had to be dug in the ground floor, as they were short of water, this the Sikhs did at once. The alacrity shown by them in seizing some sheep that had been allowed to stray near the house was much admired.

The mutineers, without a leader, showed very little pluck; they had got a small cannon which they fired from the roof of an overlooking house, but the artillery men hid behind the chimney stack, pushing the gun out and firing at random. A leader well primed with *bhang* (hemp) having been obtained, one or two attempts at a rush were made, but, fortunately, there were in the Arrah house some crack shots who picked the leaders off, when the main body at once turned and bolted. The mutineers once tried to smoke out the little band. Piling up dry grass, with quantities of chillies mixed with it, they set it on fire. Fortunately, the wind changed just then, and the besiegers got the worst of it. The officer commanding at Dinapore, as soon as practicable after the mutiny of the sepoys, had sent off a force to relieve Arrah, but they were unfortunately caught in an ambush, and so cut up that they had to return to Dinapore. When the remnants of the force arrived, they were met by the women of the regiment, and their lamentations were loud for those who had not returned. From grief, their emotions turned to fury, and they surrounded the General's quarters, calling on him to come out; if he had, they would have pulled him to pieces, for they considered his not disarming the sepoys to be the cause of their sorrow. The men of the Native Infantry who had been true, were placed in tents behind the officers' mess-house. A report had gained ground among the European soldiers that their remaining was merely a *ruse*, and that those who had gone off would return by boat at night, and, assisted by those who pretended loyalty, would murder all. The effect of this was, that just after the officers had dined one evening, a great uproar was heard; and rushing out to see what was wrong, the officers found that the native soldiers had been killed as they lay asleep. The assembly was sounded, and the arms of the Europeans examined; but though every one knew who had done this, things were in too critical a state to take notice of it. The Arrah garrison were getting sadly pressed when Sir Vincent Eyre, with a party of the 5th Fusiliers and two guns, marched on Arrah from Buxar, and defeating the mutineers, relieved the place. Stories of the mutiny have been written from every part of India. I will confine myself to what happened in our district. The day after all the officials and residents had been summoned to Patna, I got an express from my neighbour J. C— telling me that all officials had left the district, and, advising me to go over to him, thence to Poosah, and from there by river to Jeetwarpore, which place he proposed we should fortify and remain at until obliged to move on. We were not long in answering this summons, and reaching Dhoolie, found J. C— ready for a start. We arrived at

Poosah at mid-day, where a boat was all ready. We were joined here by several young men from the neighbouring factories, and the officer in charge of the Poosah Stud. Dropping down the river, we reached Jeetwarpore next morning When at Poosah, we heard that the detachment of Holmes Irregular Cavalry (then at Mozufferpore), hearing the main body had mutinied, at once began to loot. Captain B— and his nephew had a narrow escape; they arrived at Mozufferpore after the officials had left, and rode up to the Magistrate's house where they found an old servant only to receive them, who begged of them to go on, as the troopers had already sent once to see if any "Sahibs" were still there. Fortunately they started at once, for not ten minutes after they had left, the troop of cavalry galloped up and surrounded the house, then entered, and helped themselves to everything that might be useful. They then went to the stable and took all horses that had been left behind. We were some three days at Jeetwarpore, and not a letter or paper had we received; we were therefore perfectly ignorant of what was going on elsewhere. I had sent an old *syce* (groom) to see what had become of the post; late at night, on Thursday, he arrived with a regular bundle of letters and papers. He then told us what had happened at Mozufferpore. The Sowars, after looting the Magistrate's house, rode down to the Treasury, and called on the Nujeebs to divide the treasure with them (The Nujeebs had been well fed by the bankers of the city, who knew once things got into a state of anarchy that they would be the first to suffer.) This they refused to do, saying, that as they had charge of it, they would keep it. Some unpleasant words then passed, and the Nujeebs fired on the cavalry, who took to their heels. Those bankers who live on the main road which passes through the town had invited a body of Nujeebs to guard their premises; and, as the troopers rode down the street, a parting volley was fired. My washerman had been with the *syce*, and he remarked, "a lot of powder and shot was expended;" but when I asked for an idea of the number of slain, I found that there was only one wounded, and that, an elderly woman one of the troopers was carrying off. The poor thing had her thigh broken by a bullet. Hearing that Mozufferpore was left without an European head, volunteers were called for from among our small party, and some five or six men decided to go in the next morning. The *syce* explained the non-arrival of our post; he said, the Sowars had kept the Bengalee Postmaster locked up for fear he should send notice to Dinapore, and they might be interrupted. The next day our men drove to within five miles of Mozufferpore, and then mounting their horses, and taking their guns and swords, rode on. As they got into the heart of the town, the men and women met them, and threw themselves down before them, beating their breasts; they were delighted to see white faces back again, as they knew that they were now safe from being looted. The police had already given one or two of them a screw up. The post office being central, the horsemen made for the place, dismounted, and held council as to what was to be done now they were in possession. As they were talking, they heard the distant noise as of a big mob approaching, and seizing their double barrels prepared to do or die.

What was their delight to see their old friend, the Magistrate, accompanied by the Government Schoolmaster (who had volunteered to return with him) ride up, followed by half of the population of the place. The Magistrate's first act was to interview the Nujeebs, and express to them how satisfied he personally and the Government were with their behaviour and ordered a handsome reward in cash to be given to each man. The Magistrate and all the Europeans returned that night to Dhoolie, and next day those of our party returned to Jeetwarpore, while the Magistrate and the Schoolmaster joined the other officers who had been ordered to return to Mozufferpore. Shortly after a detachment of Sikhs, under Lieutenant Waller, was sent to Mozufferpore, the doctor's house was properly fortified, loop-holed, and christened by some wag "Fort Pill Box." It was well stored with rice, *dhal*, etc., but, fortunately, its services were never required. We had many alarms after this, but things gradually settled down. We had regiments of Goorkhas from Nepal quartered in Mozufferpore for a time to interrupt mutinous regiments supposed to be trying to make their way to Delhi; also the Yeomanry Cavalry which did such good services in Goruckpore. This was a corps raised in Calcutta and armed with old arms, which some said were those used at the Battle of Plassey one hundred years before. Be that as it may, they did good service with them. Our plans in retreating to Jeetwarpore were, in case of necessity, that we should retire on Doulatpore factory, further down the river, where a garrison had formed; and there the house had been well protected with iron sheeting, while long rakes with their teeth sharpened and turned point upwards, formed a very good *chevaux de frise* in case of sudden attack. The top of the house was provisioned, and a stair led through a hole in the roof in case a retreat there was considered necessary. If we had been driven out of this, we would have retired down the river, and reached the Ganges. We were, however, never in any danger from a rising in our own district, the people being purely agricultural; a very few men having enlisted as sepoys, and most of these knowing what was to happen, I fancy, took leave, and came to their homes where they remained till all was quiet again. With the fall of Delhi, and relief of Lucknow, British rule again asserted itself, and the disturbing reports that used to keep us in such an unhappy state of uncertainty began to cease, and matters gradually to run in their old groove.

As I had now been out in India over eleven years, I thought a change home, after all the excitement of the last few months, necessary; so about the beginning of December, 1858, we started by steamer for Calcutta, the road being still dangerous from bands of rebels. After a trip of eight days we reached Calcutta, and in a few days after steamed out of the City of Palaces in the good ship *John Bell*, once more bound for old England.

TIRHOOT

AND ITS

INHABITANTS OF THE PAST.

JAMES SLADE.

One may call spirits from the mighty deep, but will they come? No! There is nothing, however, to prevent my recalling the past and placing before the present the deeds and doings of many jolly fellows who were white-headed when I first came to India, and whose sons and grandsons in many cases represent the immediate present. I will begin taking them in order of seniority as far as my memory serves me. Good old Jemmy Slade!—how few are there now in the district or out who remember him? He came out to his uncle, Mr. Ball, who now reposes under a mass of masonry in the Raujpore Indigo Factory garden. The days when Slade arrived in the district were wild days, and I remember his telling me how his uncle and a gentleman called Woods, who managed Seeraha Factory, insisted on his drinking on his immediate arrival, threatened to whip him if he did not, and when he did and became the worse for liquor, they whipped him because he got drunk. This happened in the middle of the day, but all windows and doors were shut to make it appear night. Slade was in India during the days when interlopers, as they were called, were viewed with suspicion, and a man who did not hold a license from John Company was liable to be turned out of the country should anyone trump up a false charge against him. Slade had suffered from these unfriendly attacks and I will mention one of the charges made up against him, which was proved to be false and Jemmy so got off. Here is the case some of his native friends dished up. They made a representation to the police that Slade had a spite against a man and had ordered him to be tied by the legs and neck to two pairs of bullocks and made what the cultivators in Tirhoot call a *hingah* of, used to rub down and smooth the land after ploughing. It was represented that the man while undergoing this treatment died, and was thrown into the river. Well, Slade was brought up for preliminary trial before the Magistrate, the case proved up to the hilt, and things were looking very black for him when his Munshi, who was in court, whispered to his master: "The man you are accused of killing is in court." So Jemmy wrote a line to the Magistrate who was presiding, and he immediately ordered all the doors of the court to be closed and no one allowed to go out,—when the dead man was found very much alive. It turned out they were so sure of getting the prisoner punished that the guilty one could not resist the pleasure of hearing sentence passed, and was caught.

Old Slade also passed through another unpleasant experience, and that was when a man who said he held the sword of "Ram" suddenly appeared behind his chair while he was sitting at dinner. The holder of "Ram's tulwar," with the sword drawn, called on him to provide his "army" with food and money. Slade did not lose his presence of mind. He replied that he had no money in the factory, but would send for some to the nearest station, where his banker lived. This was agreed to, and a syce was sent off on horseback to bring out money, but also with a note to the Magistrate calling for help. A few hours after the "army" began to get uneasy and desert. Evidently news of coming help was in the air. At last the holder of Ram's sword got unpleasant news and he and his immediate staff cleared. A few minutes after, the Magistrate appeared with a posse of "chowkidhars." Slade joined the Magistrate and off they went in pursuit and traced the marauders into an enclosure. The Magistrate being young and active put his Arab at the wall. The game little horse cleared it, but the flooring on the inside of the enclosure had been smoothed down with mud and water and the Arab's feet slipped from under him when the Maistrate found himself on his back, and the gentleman of the sword, who was hidden in a house within the walls, on top of him. Fortunately one of the village chokidhars had followed the Magistrate, and he gave the holder of the sword of Ram a tap on the head which rolled him over. The man of the sword was pinioned and taken off to do ten years' hard labour. Several others were caught and got lesser punishments. Jemmy Slade was a good old fellow but his mind had been much narrowed by so long a residence in this country. He dearly loved to hear his own voice and lay down the law. He looked on everyone as a grif and used to begin his theories with "Mark my words, no one but a grif," etc. Eventually old Jim had to throw up the sponge and go. He retired to Bath. I met my old friend several years before his death; he was comfortably housed, but he was not what he was accustomed to be—"King of Raujpore."

CAPTAIN HENRY BECHER.

There are few still remaining who remember that good old salt, Captain Henry Becher. He began life in the East as an officer in the East India Company's navy, and used to delight in fighting some of his battles over again after dinner. The tumblers, wine-glasses, and plates represent the enemy or lee-shore, wind, ships, etc., and the old gentleman having placed each in position began to move about ships, elements, etc. The tumblers were generally filled with beer, representing the wind. A wag one day thought he would *non plus* the Captain; he emptied the tumbler full of beer which represented the wind, when the old man cried out "Steady there, steady! you'll have the fleet on a lee-shore if you use up all the wind." Captain Becher had an old East India Navy list where his name was mentioned as Lieutenant Henry Becher, *deceased*, opposite which in big scrawly letters were written "*Not yet, thank God,—H.B.*" I cannot say in what year he came up-country, but it must have been in the early thirties. He started as an indigo planter at a factory to the north-east of Tirhoot called Beerpur. He was very fond of carpenter work, and employed some fifty carpenters. On one occasion these men had finished what they had been set to do and the English writer wrote to Becher, who was away on a visit to a friend, to ask what they were to do, now they had finished the work they had to do. The old Captain was not much of a linguist, so he asked his friend to reply. "What am I to say?" asked the friend. "Tell them to hold on by the slack till I return." How this was translated into Hindustani has never yet transpired.

Old Becher was a bit of a fire-eater, and though I never heard of his having fired or been fired at, he had a pair of brass-barrelled pistols that were the terror and amusement of the district. There are many yarns told about them. One evening after dinner the Captain thought he had been insulted by one of the many planters at the Club. He was just about to start for his home, but meeting in the verandah the man who was supposed to have insulted him, he addressed him: "My name, sir, is Henry Becher. You know where I am to be found when wanted." With that he made for his trap. There his old syce Byro (as much a character as his master, and who was always on the lookout in case the old Captain was a sheet in the wind) was waiting. The Captain immediately gave him the news.—*Byro, Byro; burra laraye hoga* (Byro, Byro; there will be a great fight). To this Byro replied with a slight sneer: *Ap karwagt laraye karta. Gali dejeige: laraye mat.* (You are always wanting to fight; abuse, but don't fight.) Another time having had a difference of opinion at a party with one of the guests and called him out, he started for home, and immediately set to work to cast bullets. As the quarrel had been rather a serious one and might have ended in bloodshed, one of the party gave notice to the Magistrate, who started off to bind our old fire-eater down to keep the peace, and caught him red-handed, having cast no less than fifty bullets to do for the "black and blue gentleman" whom he had fallen out with. Another yarn about Captain Becher, and one of his old syce's wise sayings is told. Becher had been dining at Khanti Factory, and as it was New Year's Eve had been pretty free with what he called the *Kiki de Vini.* I suppose he thought this name had a French smack about it, and that it meant liquor. Bidding his host good-night he climbed into his buggy (he lived about half a mile away), and off he started. After some half hour or so the old chap began to think he should have arrived and addressed old Byro, who was sound asleep wrapt up in his blanket behind the buggy. Byro awoke shuddering. *Kya sahib?* (What is it?) he exclaimed, to which in reply the following query came from his master—"Byro, Byro *khub poncheyga?*" Byro sagely replied and retired forthwith into the depth of his blanket,—"If you go on driving round and round the *Nogole* (circular front by the house) I don't suppose we will ever get home!"

"Another story about the old Captain and I will end. He had been on a visit at Hatowri Factory when Bob Taylor ruled that concern. He (R.T.) had had some difference with the ryots in a certain village Captain Becher had to pass through. He had given the old sea dog a trap to this place, where Becher was to be met by his own. Arriving there he, to his surprise, found his buggy, horse, and syce surrounded by a lot of shouting natives flourishing sticks. The old gentleman, though unarmed, marched into the midst of the howling mob and harangued the meeting thus:—"*Buggy Captain Becher ghora Captain Becher ham Captain Becher and hamara bat tamasook hie,*" which he translated as: "This buggy belongs to Captain Becher; the horse is Captain Becher's; I am Captain Becher, and my word is as good as my bond." On hearing this, he said, they knew I was not Bob Taylor, and I passed on unmolested.

After leaving the E. I. Co.'s Navy, the Captain, as I said above, tried his hand at indigo planting, but as his ideas of calculations and those of the agents differed, he gave up that industry. He borrowed an outlay of Rs. 50,000 and sent to his Calcutta agents Rs. 5,000 worth of indigo, and when they expressed themselves surprised at the small return the old gentleman was very indignant, as he said—"Confound them; I have given them 10 per cent. on their money." At the age of about seventy-nine the Captain went to Calcutta, and while there passed away peacefully. He went to bed apparently quite well, and was found dead in his bed in the morning. Thus died the poor old Captain, jolly old companion, the essence of kindness, and a perfect Lord Chesterfield as to politeness.

JOHN MACKENZIE.

John Mackenzie was one of the most genial and kindest hearted of men, beloved by all who knew him. He was born in 1803 at Galston Parish of Barvas in the Island of Lewis. He was educated at the Marischall (Aberdeen) College under Professor Jack. He was a finished scholar and elegant writer, and was, therefore, looked up to by all the planters of his day as a man of first class education and one who could put what was required down in a few well-expressed words and well to the point. Mr. Mackenzie had seen a good deal of life in his younger days. In 1823 he had a very narrow escape of being drowned, being the only one saved out of 150 passengers. It may be interesting to detail the circumstances of his escape. He was on his way to India, and was then a tall young man and very powerful. In 1823 there were no steamers or any regular conveyance between Stornaway, the capital of the Island of Lewis and the south. As Mr. Mackenzie was bound for India he took passage in a Stornaway vessel that was going to Ireland, and thence to Liverpool, on board a packet called "The Alert." The ship by bad navigation struck on a rock not far from Holyhead. The captain and crew deserted the ship and passengers,—going off at once with the only boat and leaving the 150 passengers to perish. Mr. Mackenzie was a good swimmer, but had great difficulty in getting clear of the drowning passengers. Once he was dragged down, but managed to struggle to the surface. Then he and two others swam to an object they saw some distance off which proved to be an egg crate, and to this they clung. One dropped off and the other who was lashed to the crate died of exhaustion. Mackenzie was eventually picked up insensible and carried by the boat that rescued him to Holyhead where means were used to restore him to life. He had kicked off all his clothes but his shirt, and suffered terribly from the cold. He was taken in by the officers at a military outpost who were most kind to him and supplied him with clothes and money as he had lost all his own. His money he had tied round his waist, but as it was all gold the weight was so great he had to let it all go to save his life.

Shortly after Mackenzie sailed for India, his only friend there being Mr. Murdo Mackenzie a cousin. Murdo Mackenzie founded, if I mistake not, the Calcutta Exchange (Mackenzie Lyall and Co.) He also made the acquaintance of John Colvin, who eventually became a fast friend, and through his influence got John Mackenzie a berth as an assistant at Attur Factory under Mr. Sterndale, whose daughter afterwards married Sir Cecil Beadon, late Lieutenant-Governor of Bengal. The year young Mackenzie made his *debut* as an indigo planter proved a very propitious year: the factory made a very big season, namely, 1,000 maunds which sold at an average of Rs. 300 per maund, giving an enormous profit which must have gladdened the heart of Macadam Stewart, who was one of the proprietory firm of Gillanders Arbuthnot and Co. In 1833 Mr. Mackenzie had a severe illness and took a trip home intending to return to India in a year after. Great reports, however, about this time were spread of the fortunes to be made in Canada, and Mr. Mackenzie determined to give it a trial; especially as his mother to whom he was much attached did not care that he should return to India. (She unfortunately died on the voyage out.) On arrival in Canada they found things were not what they had been painted, and they much regretted they had ever left the Lewis. For a time Mackenzie acted as Agent for the Canadian Land Company and edited a paper in that Company's interests. He also acted as a Volunteer during the Mackenzie riots in Canada, and was given a commission as a Captain in a battalion of the County Sherbrook in Canada. (Strange to say some years after when managing Meerpur Indigo Factory in Champarun, a Magistrate, who was said to be not quite *compos mentis*, had Mr. Mackenzie arrested as the rebel Mackenzie because he heard he came from Canada!) This commission is dated 28th April, 1835. The appointment was made by Lord Aylmer, Captain-General-in-Chief, Provinces of Lower Canada. In 1838 he had 100 men who hailed from the Lewis placed under him as Volunteers. Before this he had a roving commission from the British American Land Company. I now quote to show how highly his services were estimated, a letter from the Commissioner written in Sir Alexander Galt's handwriting—"We, the Commissioners in Canada of the B. M. L. Co., considering that it is desirable for the Company as well as important to emigrants that the value of their operations and the value of their territory be more generally known, considering also your experience in the country, your general intelligence, your kind philanthropic disposition, your intimate knowledge of the operations and objects of the Company, and having confidence in your wise discretion for fulfilling with faithfulness and zeal a mission on their behalf, we do now request you to proceed with the least possible delay on a tour or journey through Maine, New Brunswick, etc., etc., or as much thereof as you can attain, especially where there are British settlers desirous to obtain richer soil and more productive climate, etc., etc., etc. (Sd.) JOHN FRASER and A. C. WEBSTER. Commissioners."

In about 1847, Lord Elphinstone, who was making a tour through India, met Mr. Mackenzie, and was so taken with the charm of his manner and refined mind that he offered him the management of all his Ceylon estates, which unfortunately he did not accept. In 1848, Mr. Mackenzie purchased, in partnership with Mr. John Beckwith, the Jeelwarpur Indigo Concern and took a trip home with his family, some years after, returning again in 1855. In January 1857, just before the Mutiny broke out, he again went home, and thence to Canada. The long winters were too much for him, and in 1862 he and his family found themsleves again in Tirhoot. Thence they went to Naini Tal, where a house was built, but after a time as all his daughters were married or about to be, he made up his mind to leave India for good, and eventually retired to Island Bank, Inverness, where he died in 1868. He was buried in the pretty little cemetery of Tumnahurich where a handsome tombstone marks the spot where lies one of the finest and best of men. Such a leader to guide young heads in our indigo troubles at the present moment would be, indeed, a blessing. Mr. Mackenzie had a younger brother who was an assistant under him, but he died young and reposes under a bamboo tope at the Buchour Indigo Factory, now the property of the Maharaja of Durbhanga.

JOHN GALE.

John Gale, I first met in the early part of January, 1848. He was known by his intimate friends as John Cherry Gale, as he used to sing a song called "Cherry ripe," and any peculiarity of this kind was quite enough to be the cause of a nick-name which often stuck to a man for life. John Gale was, if I mistake not, son of Captain Gale, an officer in the E. I. Co.'s service. He started life as an indigo planter, but when sugar became a mania in Tirhoot, John Gale at once dropped indigo and went in for cane and expensive machinery. This sugar craze was introduced by one Mr. Robinson, who came up from the Mauritius. He was certain large fortunes were to be made in sugar, especially in Tirhoot, where land and labour were cheap, and he managed to talk over a great many. It was a good spec for Mr. Robinson, as he was also a manufacturer of steam engines, and had brought out a speciality in engines adapted for cane crushing. Our local poet thus wrote of Mr. Robinson and sugar:—

"The Lion King stretched out his hand,
"Talked of the cheapness of Labour and richness of the land,

"Of twenty maunds a Begaha,—
"Take the cypher from the aught, divide the ten by two,
"The result will be the product exceeded but by few.
"Then things went on right jolly,
"Till the district was dotted o'er with monuments of folly."

The above is all I can remember of this effusion, but it went on for many stanzas. It was written by George Williamson, if I remember right a relation of Mr. Williamson of the firm of Williamson Magor of Calcutta. He had been in the West Indies as a sugar planter, and got an appointment from the Tirhoot Association of London. He did not get on with the Superintendent, and so relieved his feelings by launching into verse. There is a great deal of truth in the few lines I have quoted, for on the sandy banks of the rivers to the north of Tirhoot immense masses of machinery are to be found strewn about, and high chimney stacks are the monuments of folly which represent the ruin of many a good man, and the spot where large amounts of capital were sunk.

Sugar, which was started with a tremendous flourish of trumpets, gradually died a natural death—where the return from an acre of sugarcane began with ten maunds, it really dwindled down till it at last fell to a couple of maunds. That was as much as the impoverished land would yield, and the expensive machinery that had to be purchased gradually ruined most of those who had put their trust in sugar. John Gale was a man of great moral courage and determination, and he made up his mind to work with the strictest economy, and by gradually doing away with sugarcane and bringing back indigo, try to reduce his debit balance, and bring his head above water. This he set to work to do, and after very many years of steady work he was able to retire very fairly well off. John Gale had a nervous peculiarity, and if you did not know of it, you would be apt to get a bit of a start. When coming into a room, if he was excited or in an absent mood, he would start off with a hop, step and a jump, rub the fist of one hand into the palm of the other, at the same time making a bubbling noise with his mouth; rush up towards you, stop dead opposite you with an absent smile on his face. A stranger's first idea must have been to turn and fly, but the smile was generally very reassuring. Another of his weaknesses was a little *jeu de mot* he liked to indulge in, and youngsters were always laying a trap for it. If John Gale was about at the Tirhoot Planters' Club, just as he entered the breakfast room one of the boys would call out "Confound it the eggs are all hard boiled." John then wonld out with it "*Harder where there's none*," and with a hop, skip, jump, rub of his fist and burr-r-r with his mouth, fly out of the room.

Pundoul Concern had several outworks, but only at one, namely, Buchour, was there an assistant, whose name was Hubbard, a very amusing fellow. Hubbard left the district in about 1849, and went to China, where I heard he did well, but I do not know if he is in the land of the living or not. Pundoul was noted for its garden, for John Gale was very fond of gardening, and it was a well known fact that he often fed his pigs on pineapples, for Pundoul boasted of a Pork Club, and was noted for its hams and bacon, and good they were or should have been considering how daintily these animals were fed. There was rather a good story told in connection with this Pork Club. One of the members of the Club suspected the man who apportioned the meat of keeping back some of his portion. So he waited till his turn came round, and on arrival of his share took stock of it and convinced himself there was a deficiency. He then wrote to Gale to say that though he had received a pig's head as his share on several occasions, he had noticed that he never got a neck. I can fancy Gale's glee as he went with the usual "hooroosh" to his desk to write a long letter to say that "pigs had no necks."

John Gale eventually retired to Cheltenham, where he bought a house with a good garden attached. He passed his time looking after the fruit which he grew in great abundance. John Gale's first wife was a Miss Stalkartt, a relation of that kindly and well known old gentleman who lives at Goosery, near Calcutta. His second wife was a Miss Johnstone, whose brothers were in business in Calcutta. His sons, John and Marmaduke, followed their father's footsteps in the indigo line. They have now retired to England. The son by his second wife is an officer in the R. E's. If any of my readers go to Lordship Lane, Norwood, they will see Pundoul House there, and know that a Gale lives there. Tyroll trees were a great weakness of old John's, and Pundoul House was rather too much shut in with these, and though the place looked well when the trees were in full bloom, the mosquitoes of an evening were almost strong enough to lift one out of bed, and the man who saw an elephant on his first arrival in or near Calcutta and asked if it was a mosquito, would not have been so far off the mark in his comparison if he had met with one of the Pundoul type. All the avenues round Pundoul were named, as well as the small sluggish stream that flowed past the back of the house, but I have forgotten the different names. Pundoul Concern has been rather dismembered of late. Buchour now belongs to the present Maharaja of Durbhanga, while Benepur, one of the principal outworks, has been bought by Mr. Percy Jones, son of that gallant old gentleman, Colonel Alfred Jones, who gained the V C. at Agra, during the Mutiny when a Lieutenant in the 9th Lancers, and where he was terribly wounded, his recovery being despaired of. Pundoul, the head factory, has also passed to other hands. John Gale died at Cheltenham, and I think sleeps alongside many of his old Tirhoot friends who ended their days there after or went before.

DR. BEGG.

Dr. Begg came out to India in about the end of the thirties. He came out to act as assistant to Dr. Charles Mackinnon, who was then Planters' Doctor. Shortly after his arrival Dr. Charles Mackinnon had to leave and Dr. Begg took up the work. He soon became very popular as he was most hospitable. The owners of big concerns made all their indigo seed orders through his agency, and this brought him a fair income over and above what he made as Planters' Doctor. With this money he in time bought a share in an indigo seed firm of Cawnpore—Christie and Co., which then became Begg, Christie and Co. During the Mutiny the members of the Christie family were all killed and Harry Brown, one of Dr. Begg's indigo factory managers, was sent up to look after things. He had a narrow escape shortly after his arrival, as he had to fly for his life into the Cawnpore entrenchment when Wyndham was beaten by the Gwalior contingent. Not long after this Harry Brown was recalled, and Dr. Begg's brother-in-law Donald Macfarlane, now Sir D. H. Macfarlane, M.P., was sent up to put things together. In 1853 or thereabout Dr. Begg purchased Kanti, Motepore, Belsund and Bekonpore factories, his chief and trusted manager being David Russel Crawford, who conducted the purchase and clinched the bargain. As often happens a hasty word destroys the friendship of years. David Crawford thought he should have a share in this purchase, and wrote to David Begg to this effect strongly. From that day the two friends became cuts and David Crawford left his comfortable berth at Kanti and purchased Futteteah

Factory. Many years after this I was walking in London with D. R. Crawford when I came upon Dr. Begg, and as I had to speak to him I dropped my friend and went on with him.

"Who's your friend?" asked David Begg.

"Don't you know?" I said. "Why old David Crawford."

"Is it indeed? poor old David!" and the good old doctor relapsed into silence as if thinking of the past.

After speaking to him of what I wanted I returned to David Crawford, who saluted me with; "Who was that grey-bearded old chap you went off to speak to?"

"Why," I said, "don't you recognise him? old Dr. Begg."

"No. Poor old David Begg!"

It was evident by the manner of both those men that a very deep-seated friendship had existed and was still there.

Dr. Begg had purchased Messrs. Bathgate and Co.'s business and in 1856 he sold out and set up Messrs. Begg, Dunlop and Co., taking young Dunlop, a very nice young fellow into partnership. Poor fellow he did not last long as he died shortly after I think of cholera. Dr. Begg was a right good friend to many a Tirhoot and Champarun man. He helped Joseph and James Hill in the failures of 1847-48 and to his old friend James Wilson of Kumtoul he was more than kind.

Jimmie had gone home, a grown-up man after an absence of about 28 years. He had left England a boy of twelve, and was determined to enjoy himself. The money flowed like water till one fine day the banker refused to cash his cheques. Then he found that he was well on the wrong side of his account. He managed to scrape enough together to pay for a passage out to India. On his arrival in Calcutta he went to his old friend Dr. Begg, and almost immediately got knocked over with severe illness when Dr. Begg took up the management of his affairs, and sent James off home with an allowance of £400 per annum till things bettered themselves. Poor Jimmie Wilson did not last long. He died shortly after getting home. There are many other such acts of friendship done by Dr. Begg I could relate. Before the Mutiny Dr. Begg returned home and resided in London. He lived at a fine place called Cannon's Park. Dr. Begg married while Planters' Doctor in Tirhoot Miss MacFarlane. They had no children. Mrs. Begg survived the old doctor several years.

There are few left now of Dr. Begg's contemporaries, or I am sure they would back me in what I say. The doctor had two brothers out here James and John. The latter got into bad health many years ago and went home and died. Poor Jim died not many days ago after a long and trying illness. One of his sons now represents his uncle of the past as Begg, Dunlop and Co. Another manages his father's tea garden in Assam. I wish I could have said more about Dr. Begg, but though I corresponded with him for many years in the most familiar and kindly terms, I only met him and his wife once, and this was when I had been invited to their house to receive one of the many acts of kindness he was always doing to anyone connected with Tirhoot.

KENNETH MACLEOD.

There are still a few, a very few, in Tirhoot, Saran or in Calcutta who remember that prince of good fellows, old Kenneth MacLeod. He was the son of the late Captain Niel MacLeod, of Gesto, in the Island of Skye. He left his native country at a very early age, sailing as an apprentice round the Cape for India, a way many youngsters in those days started in life. Arriving at Calcutta he was received by his cousin, Dr. Charles Mackinnon, who passed him on to one Bob Robertson, then manager of Belsund Factory.

Kenneth was a shrewd hard-working Highlander, and it was not long before he began to mount the ladder of life, for he soon became manager of Seryiah, one of the finest factories in Tirhoot, from the profits of which and Dholi both the estates of Dr. C. Mackinnon and E. Studd they built up the splendid fortunes they amassed. Seryiah now belongs to His Highness the Maharaja of Durbhanga and the late Mr. G. Llewellin. After a time MacLeod left Seryiah. He thought he saw his way to being practically his own master and make enough to keep him comfortably. He had many friends in Calcutta, and several in the indigo districts, among those Mr. John Mackenzie, who was a fellow Highlander from the neighbouring island of Lewis. It was a pleasure to see these two old friends meet with a hearty Gaelic greeting. Few understood the meaning of it, but the hearty way in which it was given made ample amends for that.

On leaving Seryiah MacLeod took up his abode at Telpa House, Chupra. There he had for a time to fight the fight of life. He told me that he at first found difficulty in putting enough money together to say his expenses to Calcutta by the Grand Trunk Road. However, it's a long lane that has no turning, and in times things got brighter, and the inhabitants of Chupra began to appreciate the value of Mac's advice and assistance. He was also able to do the old Bettia Raja a good turn, and they were fast friends ever after. MacLeod used to enjoy an occasional trip to Calcutta, and as several of the firms had indigo concerns that were not progressing well MacLeod was asked to superintend them. Among these was Dulsing Serai, a place Mr. W. Poe, of the firm of Abbott and Co., had purchased for a mere song, but finding it in a terrible state of confusion asked old Mac to take it in hand, which he did and put Tom Martin in charge, and the consequence was a record season such as has never been beaten before or since. Messrs. Gillanders, Arbuthnot and Co. then got Kenneth to superintend Attur. In those days Mr. D. McInlay was a partner in G., A. and Co. and as he was a Lewis man the two Highlanders were always great friends. Ferrier, nicknamed "Fagan," because he had a long beard and a Jewish nose, was put in to manage Attur, but after a time he was allowed to go, and Ogilvie came in his place. After a while O's friends bought him a Commission in the army and he left, and Garstin was put in. He, however, bettered himself, eventually getting the engineering of the roads in Chupra. During the Mutiny he volunteered, and went to the relief of Arrah, but was wounded when the relieving force was beaten back. Garstin was followed by Young, a hard-working chap, very simple and the essence of good nature. He unfortunately always did the wrong thing at the wrong time. So his friends called him "Pudding Head" and the name stuck to him to the last. Old MacLeod used to enjoy a little fun as much as any schoolboy, and I remember him at Attur on one of his inspection visits, having a grand time of it. After dinner he would send for his violin, and we would have "Maggie Lauder" with a good round chorus. Young was also musical, and he owned a violin, so he would strike up too and the fun would be fast and furious. Mac would jump up on to the table, and step it out to the "Devil among the tailors," played by Young. All this exercise was not gone through without a certain amount of thirst, and by the time we retired to bed we were all more than ready for sleep. After one of these nights poor Young, who did not understand that one might have too much of a good thing, wanted MacLeod to begin the last night's *tamasha* over again, when he was at once frowned down and snubbed. From that day he was dubbed "Pudding Head." Poor old "Pudding Head" worked well for MacLeod, for no man knew better how to get work out of his subordinates; he was a born leader of men. Gradually Kenneth MacLeod began to acquire shares in several indigo factories, and so well did he pick and choose his managers, and co-proprietors, men like Baddeley Cox and L. Cosserat that in a few years he and they had amassed large fortunes. Besides the factories in Tirhoot MacLeod had shares in many Chupra factories. He was very keen at a bargain, selling and buying, and many a deal he had with his old friend Kazi Ramzan Ali.

Let us just step across the big Gunduk to Sonepur, and there we will find MacLeod in his glory, managing the Planters' Mess. There are few if any now left of that jovial band. I can see the old chief at the head of the table, his face beaming with kindness and hospitality. Kenneth was a good judge of a horse, and had two or three race horses —two were Cape but one, a half English bred mare, was a special favourite. She was called Diana. I remember well the excitement in the Sonepur camp, the first year she ran. She was a mare of peculiar temperament, and was not to be driven. A man called Curran, a private in the old 1st European Bengal Fusiliers, had been got to look after her, and MacLeod finding the mare took to him kindly bought his discharge, and Curran was put up to ride this race where the N. W was represented by Sir Charles Oakley's Mercury and South Ganges by Mr. F. Vincent's Helen. Diana, being the pride of the Planter community, represented the Blues. At the ordinary the night before the race, the excitement was terrible. I heard an old gentleman who had never bet more than a 4-anna piece in his life offer to back Diana for a cool 500. Next morning we were all aroused, from our sleep by the Sonepur gun followed by the lively strains of the band which marched up and down to a quick march. We were not long in getting on our clothes and assembling at the grand stand. Presently all three horses appeared looking as handsome as paint and fit to run for their lives.

Diana showed a little temper. The band, 'twas said, had disturbed her last forty winks. However they came up to the post, and at the word off started Mercury leading, Diana next, but not moving kindly, and Helen last. At a corner where Diana had a weakness of running off the course Helen was made to rush past her, but Curran kept patting her and speaking to her. The mare seemed to remain sulky, for she would not improve her pace, and the other two sailed away, and we of the Blues gave up all as lost, when suddenly the little mare seemed to answer her jockey's coaxing and she started off. She did not gallop, she simply flew. Mercury was a good half mile ahead, with Helen not far behind. I suppose laughing in their sleeves at poor Diana, but when they heard the thunder of her hoofs as she picked them up, hand over hand, they thought they might try to put on a spurt, as the winning post was not far off, but it was no use. Helen was passed at the distance post. Mercury struggled on, but was collared half way up, and Diana won by a good neck. The shouts and hurrahs that followed this victory were deafening, and congratulations from all sides were showered on the Highland chief. As to Curran it was his ruin. He got innumerable presents in the shape of cash and riding whips, but what did for him was this, that during the whole of Sonepur he was never allowed to dine without quaffing of the glorious vintage of Champagne. Consequently he took to drink and he and his kind master had eventually to part. Diana ran for the first Governor-General's Cup in 1857, but broke down. Curran became a trooper in the Yeomanry Cavalry and did service in Gorrukpur in those stirring times. The last time I saw him was when going over Cook and Co's stable, with old MacLeod.

Should any of my readers ever find their way to a place called Dunach, near Oban, in the Highlands of Scotland, they will see there a picture of the Laird of Greshornish standing with one arm round the neck of his mare Diana. It is a fine picture. MacLeod was very good company, as he had a good idea of music and could tell a good and amusing story he was in his element among a goodly gathering of young men. His manner was genial and attractive. Children took to him at once, and it was a great day for them when they knew MacLeod Sahib was coming, for he always had some little amusing toy in his pocket, with which to captivate his young friends. After some 30 years in India MacLeod returned to his native home, *i.e.*, in 1858. He bought up several properties in the Island of Skye, and settled down at Greshornish, where he kept up his life-long reputation for hospitality. He had a grand music room at this place where every musical instrument under the sun could be found. He was a good landlord to his tenants. Poor Kenneth MacLeod breathed his last at Coulmore at the residence of his old friend and kinsman MacLeod of Coulmore; a fine old Highland gentleman very much of his own stamp. Our dear old friend forgot no one who had the slightest claim on him, for he left all his managers handsome legacies, endowed a hospital near Greshornish with money enough to pay all expenses and give a salary to a doctor. A printed note which was circulated among MacLeod's friends at his death says: "He will be remembered as one who achieved a great position with no adventitious aid and by no unworthy means, who turned it to good account during his life and earned the blessing of the poor, who never forgot a friend or one who had done him a good turn; and if he had any enemies had them only among those whose approbation was not a thing to be desired."

MacLeod was buried in the burrying place of the MacLeods of Gesto by the burnside of Bracadale, on the 22nd March, 1869. Kenneth never married. He left Greshornish to a nephew, Kenneth Robertson, who took the name of Mac-

Leod. Another nephew, Lauchlin MacDonald, came out to Tirhoot under MacLeod's auspices in 1861, and began life at Ottur under Young. The old chief always looked on him with an eye of great affection. He has followed his worthy uncle's footsteps and is now Laird of Skaebost, where he is greatly loved and respected by his tenants. He has also property in India where his ryots are treated in the same open-handed way as those of his native Island of Skye.

JUSTIN FINCH.

Justin Finch, of Shahpur Oundie Indigo Concern, was the fourth son of Joseph Finch. This gentleman (Joseph Finch) was a man of note, and was the first of this family who had come to India. Soon after his arrival out here he got attached to Sir Eyre Coote's staff, and was with him in the Carnatic during the war with Tippoo Saheb. Here he greatly distinguished himself. Hyder Ali's Standard bearer challenged anyone of the enemy to meet him in single combat, when Joseph Finch rode forth and attacked the man. After a most exciting set-to Joseph came off victorious, for he slew his man, cut off his head, and having possessed himself of the Standard presented it to Sir Eyre Coote. For this act of gallantry he received a gold medal with the following inscription: "Joseph Finch, Ob Res Fortiter Gestas Apud Sholeingurh, F.C., A.D. MDCCLXXXI." This brave deed was enacted in the presence of the contending armies just before the general action began. Anyone passing through Patna who has time to visit the Roman Catholic Cathedral there will find his grave, over which is placed a large slab with an inscription on it giving the history with full details of this remarkable man's career. I may mention that the medal is now in the possession of Justin Finch, eldest son of Joseph Finch and great grandson of our hero.

Joseph Finch left five sons—Jeffry, Simon, Joseph, Justin and Frederick. Jeffry Finch went to England in about 1848 with his sister Matilda. He was much respected by all who knew him, Europeans and natives. Both he and his sister are dead. I never met them myself, nor Mr. Simon Finch, who died, I believe, in the Gorrukhpur district. Joseph became proprietor of Bubnowlie, which was sold not long after his and his wife's death. He left sons, who are all dead except Simon Finch, who is a priest in France. Frederick for some time managed Shahpur Oundie. He left one son, Joseph, who is alive, in Tirhoot, and whose son Justin possesses the medal.

Justin, the fourth son, after Frederick went home, took charge of Shahpur. He was a right good fellow and a grand host, and treated his guests *en prince* when they visited him. There was splendid duck and snipe shooting near the factory, and many a good bag has been the result of a day on the *jhil*. Justin had every description of duck gun one could think of—the good old gun some six feet long with flint locks showing they were of ancient pedigree; breech-loaders of more modern construction, and a punt gun which I remember was brought up to Mozufferpur to be loaded with swan shot to keep off mutineers in the stirring days of 1857. All these guns required a good deal of skill in handling on a dug-out, and many a novice has been knocked overboard by the kick of these guns. Shahpur Factory could boast among other good things of a first rate Tealery which Justin looked after with tender care. The teal, pintail and other duck were so well fed that they were as fat as butter. Rather a good story is told of Finch and a civilian friend who dearly loved something good to eat. They were looking into the Tealery and admiring the birds feeding, when Justin, pointing with his finger at a fine big pintail duck, said: "Do you see that fine fellow there with the single long feather in his tail?

Well, when that fellow is well cooked with a good sauce—!" This was too much for the gourmet, who almost fainted at the idea, and gasping replied, "Ah don't, Justin, don't!" The prospect of the delicious morsel was too much for him.

At most of the race meets, at Mozufferpur and Sonepur, Finch, when he had a camp, did things in style. He had a lordly way of speaking and laying down the law. He once very nearly fell foul of Captain Becher's brass barrelled pistols, but the quarrel was made up. Old Justin, like his ancestor, was "all on" to fight, and as he was a very good shot the old Captain might have got the worst of it. Finch was a man of good solid proportion, and weighed a good round weight. I remember a bit of fuu on this subject that took place once when I was at Shahpur Oundie on a visit. We all went down to the indigo factory to be weighed—that is Justin his brother Joseph, Edward Studd, James Cox, and myself. On the way Joseph started a theory that the stoutest looking men did not always weigh the heaviest, as bones weighed more than fat, and he went on to say that though he did not show as much fat as his brother he was quite sure he weighed quite as much. (Joseph was not ever weighted either with fat or bone). However, they both mounted the scales one on each side. Meanwhile Studd, who was always a bit of a "farceur," slipped his walking stick down the inside of the leg of his trousers and pressed down the side of the scale on which Joe had mounted, and as he was the first to mount, the scale on his side rested on the ground. Studd, with the end of his stick resting thereon, stood gracefully as if he was leaning on his walking stick, and put all his weight in Joseph's favour. Justin was lost in amazement at the result, and Joseph with a cry of triumph called out "Bone must tell." At last, Justin perceived a wicked twinkle in Edward Studd's eye, and saw what was up. Gathering himself together in a most majestic way, he said to his brother,

"Joseph, they are making a fool of you," and descending from the scales walked away. Poor Joe was very crestfallen, and did not say much for the rest of the day, nor did we dare to allude to the little joke as Justin Finch had a particular objection to anyone playing a joke on him or at the expense of any of his relatives.

Shahpur Oundie, called also Patoree, is among the oldest of Tirhoot indigo factories. It was built in 1790, by Joseph Finch, the head of the family and the hero of the single combat. He, however, was not fortunate in his speculations, as one of his managers got possession of all the indigo made, and disposing of it, cleared out with the proceeds. This left the proprietor very much in debt, and the agents took over all his property except Shahpur Oundie.

Justin Finch died on his way back from Calcutta up the river on board a steamer, in 1861, I think. He was buried at Monghyr, but his body was afterwards taken to Patna to the burial place of his ancestor. After his death his brother Frederick came out from England to manage, bringing Charles Strachan with him, whom he left eventually in charge. Strachan himself did not remain long, and Mr. Lloyd was left in charge. He managed for many years the estate which had been put into Chancery. When at last the property got out of the hands of the Court William Finch, grandson of Joseph Finch, the follower of Sir Eyre Coote, was put in charge. He and his brother died a few years ago. William Finch left sons, but his brother died a bachelor. There are still living of the fourth generation seven male heirs, six in Tirhoot and one, the priest brother, in France.

DAVID CRAWFORD.

David Russell Crawford began life on the sea, and coming out as a young man to Calcutta, he was sent by his uncle, Mr. Stephen Crawford, then a merchant in Calcutta, to his brother, John Crawford, who managed an indigo factory in Bengal. In those days Bengal was in its prime, and many of the Bengal planters were small princes in their way. John Crawford himself had begun life at sea and was of a rough and ready class. The yarns I have heard told, of the wild doings of the owners and managers of these Bengal factories, were well worth remembering, but when I heard them I never for a moment thought I would be in the land of the living to write "Tirhoot and its inhabitants of the past." So many of them have been forgotten, however, I will as I go on try to recall some of the wild doings of these Bengal planters

One story that rather amused me was the gentle way in which an indigo factory was taken possession of in those times. A firm in Calcutta having bought an indigo concern had to get possession of it, for, as a rule, the planter proprieter did not see the fun of turning out in a meek and mild way because he had been sold up. The merchant, therefore, wrote to John Crawford, who was a friend and a well known wild young man, telling him that they had bought such and such a factory, and would he take possession for the firm? Nowadays a polite letter would have been sent to say, "Sorry, old chap, but I have orders to take overcharge from you. Will you come over to breakfast to-morrow," etc. This was not the good old style. The head fighting man was sent for, and a goodly number of fighting men called on to be ready next morning at a place convenient to the coveted factory. Meanwhile, the enemy having got notice that possession was to be asked for, had made arrangements for a reply. The attacking force in the early morning, having made an advance, were received with a volley, the bullets whistling about rather unpleasantly. This was a bit hot, so a council of war was called, and an old and knowing fighting man pointed out that the enemy were firing through the windows of the house. He suggested that he and another should make a detour and advance towards the house, keeping near the side wall, and as soon as they got near the point from whence the firing came, they should creep down near the ground (the house being of but one story), and as the guns were presented out of the window a good swinging blow with a stick was to be brought down, if possible, on the fingers of those firing, which would make them drop their weapons. On this the attacking force were to rush in and complete the capture. This was all cleverly carried out, and the native part of the defending force bolted, leaving the planter who was in command of the besieged and who was well saturated with gin. He was at once knocked over and secured. He very nearly caused an unpleasant accident, for while he was being tied up he managed to get out of one of his pockets a pistol which he was trying in a half drunken way to discharge. Jimroodin, one of John Crawford's fighting men, seeing what he was up to, caught him a crack on the fingers, when the pistol fell, exploding at the same time. This timely act on the part of Jimroodin saved the life of Andrew Crawford at whom the weapon was pointed and with whom the aggressor was at the time conversing in the most friendly manner. This was the way things were managed in those days, and if I recollect right, the ousted planter was taken back by the victors to their home and feasted to his heart's content.

As I have said before John Crawford was a very rough card. One of his favourite jokes was to make his assistants take off their shoes and run over a red-hot brick kiln. This was what Jack called giving them a taste of hell! Men of this peculiar turn of mind are not, I am glad to say, met with nowadays. However, this training certainly made a man of D. R. Crawford, for he was plucky to the backbone, and the very essence of good nature, and, as an old lady once remarked. "When Russell comes into the room it is like a ray of sunlight entering the house." In time David left

Bengal and became manager of Pupri Factory in North Tirhoot. Here he remained for several years. When there he had a strange adventure. His cousin, James Wilson, who was his assistant, having gone to bed one night, was awakened by hearing some one passing through his room into another leading to where David slept. Getting up on tip toes he followed the fleeting footsteps of the intruder, and just as he was passing into D. R. Crawford's bedroom, Jim, who was a very powerful lad, let him have one. This knocked the thief (for such he was) right into David's bed on top of him. David awoke in this sudden way let out too, and the wretched thief was pounded into a jelly. This was bad enough, but mark the sequel. A few nights after this Wilson was again awakened, as he thought, by sounds similar to that he had heard the time before. Getting up very quietly, off he went in pursuit. However, when he got to David's door nothing was visible. Meanwhile, David hearing footsteps on the other side of his door, jumped up, and they each opened the bedroom door at the same moment. They each saw some one in front of them, and went there first, and in a moment they were on the ground slogging one another. At last, one getting a nastier crack than he cared for, made use of strong language, and the other, recognising the voice, called out—"Is that you, Jim?" Then, breathless all, they both arose with noses bleeding and blackened eyes. They looked at each other and burst into roars of laughter. For they looked awful ruffians after the punishment each had received. For many years Crawford ruled at Pupri, but at last was promoted to the management of one of Noel and Co.'s indigo factories, and set himself up at Kanti Factory. Here he ruled for many years. He was looked upon as one of the best indigo planters the Tirhoot had ever seen. He was methodical to a degree, and having been brought up in his youth on ship board had been taught neatness, system, and method. Everything was in its place and the essence of neatness, and all work done and finished to the hour. David, though a good planter, had not much knowledge of horse flesh. There is a story of his going to a race meet. (This did not happen often for he was too tied up in his factory work and spare time for such a frivolity as horse racing.) However, he was introduced by some young friends to go to Mozufferpore races and after dinner to go to the ordinary. I suppose friend David had got a bit merry and so, hearing one of the racehorse's chances up for sale, he began to bid, and finally a horse with a very poor chance was knocked down to him for Rs. 150. "What a muff you were to bid for that brute," called out a friend. "Oh," replies David, "it does not signify. If he won't do for the saddle he'll do for the buggy," and, quite happy in the idea that he had bought the animal out and out, he went to bed —to be undeceived in the morning! After many years at Kanti David Crawford had a difference with his old friend, Dr. D. Begg, who had meantime become proprietor of Kanti, Motipur, Bekonpur, Belsund and Rajpund Factories, so he purchased Tatterreah and took overcharge of that place. Here he remained a short time and then went home to England, leaving his brother Andrew in charge. Poor Andrew died of cholera next year, and David had to return to India. He next put James Smith in charge, and again returned to England, and when some years after that gentleman left he sold the factory and retired for good. He died in Cheltenham at a good old age in the midst of many of his old contemporaries, who, again in their turn, have joined the majority. David Russell Crawford left two sons and two daughters. His eldest son now manages Bara, and is a worthy representative of his father. His younger brother, who is very many years his junior, is in England. Mrs. Crawford survived her husband but a short time.

In the first part of this paper I mentioned one Jimroodin, a favourite fighting man of John Crawford's. As his career is remarkable I will end this article with an epitome of the latter part of his life. As he had got into various troubles and scrapes in Bengal, the police were after him, and Jack Crawford had the greatest trouble in saving him from their hands. At last it got very hot for him, the police being almost at the door. So Jimroodin was called up and asked what he suggested should be done to save him. "Well," says he, "I don't see much chance of escaping, but perhaps if you had me killed and buried, I might be smuggled up to Tirhoot in the garb of a woman and escape." So Jimroodin's funeral was celebrated. He was duly buried, as far as all burial ceremonies went, while he in the flesh, representing a buxom young woman, was carried off in a *mohuffa* to Tirhoot, and made over to his old master's nephew, David, where he lived for many days in peace. He was true to his old master or any member of the family. During the Mutiny he watched over his old master's nephew, wife, and family, uninvited and unknown, and it was only when the storm was nearly over that he came to this gentleman, and, making a low salaam, said—"Sir, there is no danger now. Jimroodin had lost two fingers in the service of his old master, and would have given his head sooner than that his master should have received the slightest hurt." Alas! like many other good brave men Jimroodin has passed away. David Crawford was once called on to fight a duel. His opponent was John Becher, a nephew of old Captain Becher's. They had had some business row, and David, in course of conversation, spoke of Becher as an "unclean potato." This roused the ire of John, and he issued a challenge. The battle was to come off across the Nepal boundary. David, who was a heavy man and not much of a rider, drove out to Dynechuppra, a factory near the Nepal boundary, intending to pop over in the morning, while Becher, who was light and a good horseman, started before daylight from Mozufferpur and rode to the place of rendezvous. Just as David was leaving the house at Dynechuppra he was pounced upon by a couple of constables and carried back to Mozufferpore. Some one had given notice of what was about to happen, and the Magistrate had sent to stop this duel. John Becher, after kicking his heels about for some time, recrossed the boundary and returned to Mozufferpur, very cock a whoop. They never made up this quarrel, which really was a most stupid one.

JOHN STALKART.

John Stalkart, who was nicknamed by his intimate friends "Mad Jack" on account of his eccentricities, I first knew in 1848, when he was managing Pupri Factory. These were the days when everyone was expecting to make his fortune from sugar, but the illusion did not last, for soon the soil gave out, and the return per biggha became less and less till at last it became evident that sugar on a large scale would not pay, and managers and assistants got notice to look out for work elsewhere. At Pupri there were in those days no less than two assistants and one engineer, besides the manager—John Stalkart and Alfred Trife at Russoolp, C. Paterson at Bongong and Ferrier, the engineer, who lived in the chota bungalow at Pupri. Jack was always up to some dodge in the way of invention. He first started with buffalo carts. These were English carts dragged by a single buffalo. This was certainly a great saving, although in the very hot weather the buffaloes used to put John to great trouble by rushing into every puddle of water enjoying a good roll, and refusing to move until very extreme measures were used. The damage done to harness and shafts on these occasions were a great cause of grief to Stalkart. He had a great belief in the sagacity of buffaloes, and set to work to teach one of his most intelligent animals how to stand when snipe was flushed, so that he lying on its back, could have a shot without the unpleasantness of muddy boots and wet feet. He took one of these brutes in hand to train and soon taught it to stand when the nose string was pulled which was done the minute a snipe flushed. Having brought his buffalo to this state of perfection, he arrayed himself in light attire and, gun in hand, started off to the snipe ground, where he mounted and lay flat with the nose string in one hand and his gun in the other. The beast plodded on quietly till at last up went a snipe, the string was duly tugged, and Jack let fly. The explosion so close to its ears was too much for friend buffalo. With a grunt and a flourish of his tail, he sent Jack into the air and tail on end careered over the swamp very much alarmed, while Jack, after performing a perfect somersault, came down with a terrible squash into the sloppy mud, where he lay for some minutes with the wind fairly knocked out of him.

John had a remedy for most things, and a story is told of how he stopped sugarcane stealing. He caught a man walking off with a big bundle of sugarcane and had him brought up for judgment. He asked "Why did you steal this sugarcane you scamp?"

"Oh," replies the man, "because I was hungry." "Very good, if you were hungry, I do not mind, but of course, you intended to eat all you took away so let me see you do it. Sit down and eat it up."

So down the man sat, and ate and ate till at last he put his hands together and said he could eat no more.

"But you must," said Stalkart; "you said you were hungry."

The man made a fresh start but could not continue.

"Forgive me, Saheb, I cannot eat any more," said the guilty one.

"Very well, if I let you off will you promise never to steal sugarcane again?"

"Never, never, again," cried the gorged thief.

"Very good," said Stalkart, "if ever I catch you stealing again I will see that you eat every scrap."

The man cleared out at once and it was said he was a reclaimed character from that day.

Another of Jack's wise doings was the way in which he discomfited a madman who had been employed to oppose him in taking possession of some lands. Going to those fields Stalkart found a wild looking man confronting him.

"Who are you?" asked Jack.

"Oh," was the reply. "I am a madman, and I have been sent to fight for the land."

"All right," said John, "I'm a madman too. Here," he cries, tossing him an adze, "you take that and I'll take this one and let us fight it out."

Seizing his weapon Stalkart jumped on to his feet with a yell, but this was too much for the opposition madman, for he took to his heels and fled for his life, leaving our hero master of the position.

About the end of 1848, money became tight at Pupri and many of the sugar concerns were shut up or pay reduced, and Stalkart thought he must arrange some way to make both ends meet and save a little at the same time. So he took to practising with the pellet bow, trying to assist the commissariat by shooting minahs and doves. This not proving successful, as minähs were not so easily hit, and when knocked over were not found over dainty, he tried saving the ends of beer bottles and having the stuff distilled for vinegar and tried to save in this way. However, he found that the game was not worth the candle, so he had to drop it. Old Jack, however, was anything but a screw. He was always most hospitable, and anyone going to see him was invariably treated well, but he would always have a shy at something no one else would ever think of. Stalkart was a splendid horseman. He was the first man who ever rode and stuck a wild boar in Tirhoot. This was at Sohagpur jungle near Dooria Factory. The riding was very rough, the ground being seamed and open. He rode the pig on a very handsome little Arab, and was the only mounted man on the field. In those days wild pigs were not so common in Tirhoot as they are now.

Jack went to Dooria, and after that to Gooserie to his brother William. Thence he went to Darjeeling hills near Hopetown, where he studied agriculture and manures suited for tea. He also invented ploughs that were found very useful in Tirhoot. He was great on salt as a manure for tea, and many Darjeeling planters will remember the ingenious way in which he stopped the worthy Nepalese coolie from stealing this commodity off the lands.

Stalkart used in his latter days to ride a very vicious horse. He was a tall, powerful beast, and as Jack was a good heavy weight, and not very active, he had to climb on to his horse with the assistance of tea boxes and his syces. The animal knew him so well that he never moved till his master was on his back. There were not many of Stalkart's age and weight who would have dared to mount this animal, but the old pluck was there, and the horse knew he had a master hand on him. John Stalkart opened some three tea gardens. Ringtong, now the Ringtong Tea Company, a first rate garden, was one. Hopetown still belongs to his estate, and also one near Kalimpong. It was riding there to visit this garden that he met with a bad accident, getting a very severe fall from his horse, which injured his back and was eventually the cause of his death, for he was never in good health after.

John Stalkart married a lady from the Mauritius. He died not very long ago, leaving a widow and children. He was paralysed for some time before his death. He was a rare good fellow, and a capital companion. He had many fads, but he always had a good reason for what he set forth, and was so full of all his theories that it was difficult to get in a word once he started. Poor Jack was a great favourite as a young man, when I knew him first he was full of fun and kept everyone in roars with his amusing yarns.

Though I got to within easy distance of him in his latter days and we were both most anxious to meet, a meeting never came off. We should have had a grand "buck," especially as I had passed many days of my youth in the Mauritius, from where Mrs. Stalkart also came. But my old bones would not admit of my crawling so far up the Darjeeling hills, and poor old Jack was too frail to come down to see me.

TOM GIBBON.

Tom Gibbon was manager of Hatti Ousti Factory when I first met him. He had spent a good number of his younger days at sea. He found his way like a good many others up to Tirhoot to indigo, and had been lured into sugar—that golden dream that swamped so many good men in 1847-48. I was sent on my arrival to the district of Tirhoot to Hatti Ousti to manufacture some sugarcane belonging to the estate of David Brodie, who had died not long before. He had been tempted to try his luck, in sugar and had sown down some acres in cane. He died before the factory could be built, and old Tom Gibbon good-naturedly undertook to manufacture the cane with his machinery at his factory of Hatti for the benefit of the estate. Gibbon found that crushing cane and boiling the juice did not mean making sugar, for, as he wrote to one of Brodie's executors, he found he could make nothing but molassess. So as I was just out from Mauritius, where I had been on a sugar estate, I was at once sent to see if I could not do better.

I found the journey from Kuntoul to Hatti Ousti a good, long and very tiring one. I had to go through Ryam, Pundoul and Benepur Factories, and starting at early morning I arrived at Hatti, very tired, about evening. On arriving at the bungalow I found Gibbon was at the sugar house, which was some distance from the Big house, so I rode on and met my host at the sugar house door. He met me in a most kind and cordial manner, but as poor old Tom stuttered very badly I had some difficulty in making out what he said. However, we returned to the house, where a tub and a peg soon refreshed me. Gibbon introduced me to his daughter, who was very kind in ministering to all my wants, taking especial care that when I was at the Boiling house where I had to remain till late at night, a tray with what the Yankees call "creature comforts" always made its appearance about 8 P.M. containing cheroots, brandy, soda and sandwiches. Old Tom did not like the idea of me, a boy of seventeen, being sent to teach him how to boil sugar, as he had a very good idea of his own capability. However, as I stuck to the boiling, and Gibbon liked early hours he, after making many attempts to take me away from my work, telling me the native sugar boiler would do the thing just as well as I, at last gave in, and left me to carry out my work. Of this I was very glad as he would interfere.

I don't know what my success was, eventually, as I was recalled suddenly to Kuntoul, one of the blacksmiths in charge of the engine there having been smashed up. I had a very tiring ride back, and as I was wanted sharp had to put on pace. While at Hatti during off hours I had some grand wild duck shooting. I have seen a good deal of this kind of sport, but never so good as in those days at Hatti—small tanks surrounded by reeds that you could creep close up to and blaze away. Gibbon had a most amusing minah. This bird imitated him splendidly. He had a roughly made carriage which was drawn by two ponies, and whenever he wanted to go to the sugar house he called out for the trap, and the minah would immediately call *Gh-gh-gh-arrie Laoo.* The syce at once knew what was wanted, and brought the ghari. Sugar ruined poor old Gibbon like many others in those days. The amount of worry and trouble many men went through getting up heavy machinery which very often never reached its destination was a caution. I remember one man coming up by river from Calcutta with a big tubular boiler in two pieces, in one part of which he lived and in the other half, his servants and a tame bear—rather an unpleasant companion. The boiler was going up to Nurarh, a factory to the north-east of Tirhoot, but I cannot say if it ever reached its destination, though Kelly and the other bear did.

There is a story of how clever jackals at Nurarh are. Kelly and L. Cosserat had invited some friends over to that place and had ordered some beer from the station to provide for the feast. They were away from home themselves, and only returned with their guests just in time for lunch. Sitting down to the repast Kelly boldly called for beer. The bearer appeared with a most melancholy and rather dissipated face, and announced that the beer had arrived and been left on the verandah during the night and that jackals had come and broken all the bottles. This was, as Babu Unokool's biographer writes, "a pretty kettle of fish." A court of inquiry was called, and the evidence was going strongly in favour of the jackal theory, when one of the guests, more inquisitive than the rest, examined the bottles, and to everyone's astonishment found that the bottles, though broken, all had their corks carefully drawn! Then the cat was out of the bag. Not expecting the master back the bearer and a few choice friends had gone in for a spree, and arranged this little yarn which was very nearly believed. I need not say that due justice was administered to the offenders.

Before I end this I must tell a good story about old Tom Gibbon. He was very fond of talking about what he or his father or brothers had done, always going one better on anything put forward by others. At Bekonpur Factory one day there was a select gathering, among them Long Jimmy Cosserat, Tom Gibbon, old David Brown (nicknamed, the Gooroo, as he was looked upon as a very knowing old chap), and one or two others. After dinner, the wine cup having passed round pretty freely, Jimmy Cosserat started extolling the prowess of his father. Old Tom wished to come in with an account of what his father could do, but unfortunately the impediment in his speech which had become intensified by his excitement prevented his getting out what he wanted to say, while Jimmy went ahead. At last Gibbon, thoroughly exasperated managed to blurt out "D-D-Damn your father." This aroused Jimmy's ire. "What! you damn my father, sir?" he cried "Ye-Ye-Yes!!" replies Tom. "D-D-Damn your father, and your mother too, by Jove."

This was too much and nothing but blood could wipe out such an affront, so old Gooroo loaded (or pretended to do so) a pair of pistols, the seconds arranging that as it was night the affair should come off in an empty room then under repairs. So they were marched off by their respective seconds, and each posted up in the opposite corner of the room and a pistol handed to each. They could not well leave the corners as they were too top heavy, so old Gooroo, extinguishing the light, shut the door, and left the two antagonists in the dark. The remainder of the party then retired to bed. Next morning they went to see how things were, and to their alarm found the two men stretched on the floor with their pistols beside them. The first idea was that the joke had been carried too far, but a gentle snore from Tom quickly responded to by Jimmy showed that they were still asleep and working off the extra liquor they had imbibed. They had in their exhaustion each quietly subsided on the floor as he stood and gone off to sleep. The old Gooroo thought it would be advisable to clear out and get away from the combined wrath of Cosserat and Gibbon, which he did before they awoke. I never heard if there was ever any sequel to this yarn.

Tom Gibbon, after filling several berths in Champarun passed away, I forget in what year, but he had attained a good old age. He was a kind old gentleman, and those who still remember him will agree with me that he was an amusing and jolly old chap. His daughter, Miss Gibbon, married K. MacDonald, nicknamed the Yankee, because he hailed from Canada and sometimes "guessed." Tom Gibbon used to say he was the first to import minahs into the Mauritius, but that a Monsr. Martin forestalled him and took the credit of being the first importer of that bird to the Mauritius where it bears his name of "Martin." Gibbon had knocked about the world a good deal and had a goodly fund of amusing anecdotes of what he saw and heard during his wanderings.

"PADDY" COX.

James Cox, or "Paddy," as he was called by his intimate friends, came to India in the early thirties. He hailed from Kildare, where his father was a clergyman, and was consigned to an uncle (known as Paddy Medlicot) in India. James Cox's first berth was at Shawpur Mircha under Lewis Cook. The ryots at Shawpur were not the quiet, well behaved cultivators they are now, and as Lewis Cook was a "bit *zubberdust*" there was many a row, and Cox has often told me of the many escapes of a broken head he had on account of old Cook's quick temper. Paddy did not remain long at Shawpur Mircha. He was only personal assistant there except for a month or two when he went to Bhutowlea Factory, and here he found the Assamies even more warlike than at Shawpur, for they attacked him one day on the vats, leaving his sweeper for dead and walking off with a sword, a family relic which the sweeper had taken up to protect his master with.

From Bhutowlea Cox was offered an appointment at Coalporah, an outwork of Serjiah, on the large pay of Rs. 80 per month. However, things were cheap in these days, and men could manage to live on this small allowance with the several perquisites thrown in by the factory. Coalporah had the advantage of having a splendid duck jhil almost at the factory door, and Cox told me his expenses for powder and shot ran him into debt, for the first and last time while he was in the country, for he was always a most careful fellow. He was very fond of shooting, and it was a great temptation. From Coalporah Paddy went to Kurnoul as head assistant under John Howell, a jolly old gentleman and who was part owner of the place. He was a great *bon vivant*, and was a man of a good substantial weight. He was, however, an active man, and fond of riding, but it took something pretty strong to carry him. Cox seems to have had a very happy time at Kurnoul. After several years John Howell sold out; and Paddy became manager. He made one of the best seasons the factory had ever made up to that time. Cox was very fond of riding, and a good rider. He had two very smart ponies named The Captain and Paddy Whack. They were fast and good jumpers, and did well at the Mozufferpore Sky Races of those times. Cox was with John Howell at the time Rajpur was attacked by the "Ram-ka-talwar" man as described in my short biography of James Slade. As Mrs. Howell and her children were at Kurnoul at the time every arrangement for defence had to be made in case this maniac of the sword took it into his head to go to Kurnoul, which, however, he did not. They had an unpleasant time of it till they heard that the Magistrate had got this gentleman into custody.

Paddy had a good deal of fun in him, and was very much liked by the ryots. He had a queer way of punishing a ryot who was lazy at his work. At the measurement time, if the man was a Rajput he would enter him as a Doosad, a low caste man, and until he improved in his work his name remained as a pig driver, and it was wonderful what efforts these men would make to have these names changed to their right title. I remember one man when I took charge of Kurnoul, very many years after Cox had left, coming to me to have his title changed. As I had heard from Paddy all about this, I told the man I could not change what Cox Saheb had ordered unless his fields were very well prepared, and that I would go and see them two days after. When I went I found the lands well prepared, so I ordered his title to be changed from Doosad to Rajput and the man was quite happy. James Cox was a first class indigo planter, but he was lured into taking charge of Tewarrah as a sugar concern in 1847. The concern consisted of two factories—Tewarrah, or as called by the natives Burrerie, and Munkey, an outwork. Munkoulie, another outwork, was kept for indigo only. As everywhere else so at Tewarrah sugar soon brought the factory to a standstill. The Oriental Bank was some way mixed up with Tewarrah, and it sent up one Jack Tyndal to look after affairs, and pay up debts. As Cox had very little to do, and Tyndal was a capital fellow and a gentleman in every way, they had a very jolly time of it together, up to all kinds of larks, for Paddy was a regular Irishman. It was not often that Tyndal attended to business, but when in the humour he would have something to say to it for a spree. The yarn of how he promised a fat Babu if he would toe a line and jump a few inches over another he would pay him his back rents is recorded in "Reminiscences of Behar," as also other little lively jokes of his.

Jack had a jolly time of it up in Tirhoot hunting and tiger shooting. At last he was recalled to Calcutta but did not remain long there. He went down to Australia, where he married. He was fortunate in generally falling on his feet. He had several old relatives who generally died just in the nick of time, and left him enough to set him comfortably afloat again. Poor Jack died not very long ago. He had at last settled down in Ceylon, where he had charge of a big garden belonging to a company. One of his last jokes was played on an inspecting director who was not much liked. Tyndal invited a number of wild youngsters to meet the director. They had a rather noisy dinner, which became a bit rowdy as the evening got on. This the director did not appreciate, and was delighted when bed was at last voted for. He was not long in getting into his bed. The light in the room was dim, either on purpose, or from its being so late. The director got into bed, but with a howl of terror he jumped out, for he had come on something cold and uncanny which on examination was found to be the carcass of a pig that had been killed and prepared for use, and which Jack thought would be a pleasant companion for the director. I need not say that his anger was great, and that he left the garden before daylight. Whether the big man was afraid of being chaffed by his brethren in Committee, or that Jack had a strong interest in the Company, I know not, but the matter was not noticed. But I must stop and not forget that I am writing about Cox and not Tyndal.

Paddy, too, was what the Bengali Babu calls jockative. I remember two planters coming into Tewarrah who were in a great hurry to get on. They were themselves men who delighted in playing a joke on others. After making many excuses Cox said, "I can give you a horse, but you will have to be careful how you drive him, as he will only go his own pace. If you touch him with a whip he will kick your trap to pieces." "All right," said his friends, "we must get on even if we walk." So old "Shah Soojah" was brought up harnessed in the buggy, and Cox's friends started, the horse going at a mild trop as the road from the door led towards the stable; but as soon as the beast had passed his home he collapsed into a walk. Then the one driving gave him a gentle tap with the slack of the reins. This the Shah responded to by a whisk of his tail. "He does not seem to mind it," said one to the other. "Let's try the whip;" but alas! there was no whip. So the driver gave him an extra hard crack with the deins again. The response from the old horse was the same as before. Then the two men began to smell a rat. "By Jove! Paddy has sold us," they exclaimed, and getting out of the trap they dragged up a rahur plant by the roots, stripping off its branches and set to work to belabour the old horse, but there was no improvement in the pace, and after laying on till their arms were tired, they sat back in their buggy and let the horse have his own way —a slow two miles an hour. They vowed vengeance on Paddy for the trick he had played them.

From Tewarrah Cox went to Dholi as manager. This appointment had been offered him by Ed. Studd, who was then superintending Dr. Charles Mackinnon's (his brother-in-law's) affairs. It was during his management here that I got an appointment under him at Sukri, an outwork of Dholi, and I must say I spent the most happy days of my life with him. There was capital quail shooting at Sukri, and many a splendid day or morning's sport have I had there with Cox and Colonel Apperley, a grand sportsman who was then in charge of the Poosa Government Stud. He was a son of old Nimrod (that well known sportsman) and a right good companion as well. Paddy remained for many years at Dholi, and while there we on several occasions went out into the Nepal Terai after tigers and managed to bag a fair number of bears, leopards and tigers with other smaller game. It was while out at a tiger party that he suddenly got ill; either the sun or heat had affected him, and he had to be brought back at once to Tirhoot. As he had made sufficient to keep him going he made up his mind to go home to Ireland. He left Tirhoot in about March, 1861. Dholi under his rule flourished, and it was said that during the time Studd managed Seryiah and Cox Dholi, the two places cleared an average of a lakh of rupees a year each profit. Cox had bought shares in several indigo concerns, all of which did well. He also did a little speculation in horses, buying the undersized fillies from the Poosa Stud and selling them well.

Cox was a capital companion and a good friend. He was certainly one of the leading planters of his day. His factory work was carried on in the most systematic manner, and everything went on like clock-work, while the factory was managed with the utmost economy. Cox retired to his old county of Kildare at first. He afterwards bought a very nice house in Cheltenham. While in Kildare he married and shortly after came over to Cheltenham. He sold out most of his interest in indigo. He died on the 7th of August, 1892, in his seventy-second year, leaving a wife and children. His nephew, George Toomey, who had come out to him in 1856, and to whom he was very much attached, took over charge of Dholi and did well there. He afterwards left and went to Kanti, where he had a share and managed for his uncle. Poor George Toomey died in England a couple of months before his uncle. Cox is reported to have left property worth £80,000. George Toomey also left his family comfortably off. He, Toomey, was a shrewd, clever man, and very much liked by his brother planters. He was a worthy disciple of his uncle. Paddy Cox is buried in Cheltenham, where so many of the old friends and companions of his youth sleep. There are now two of Cox's nephews in the indigo districts of Behar, sons of Dr. Cox, Paddy's brother.

CHARLES GALE.

Charles Gale was a brother of John Gale, of whom I have already written in my paper No. 3. He on first coming out to India went to Dacca under Messrs. Wise and Glass, who carried on, among other work, a large sugar manufactory. From Dacca, after some years, he came up to Tirhoot, and through his brother's interest got employment in the Tirhoot Association, a wealthy company having their head office in London. He was appointed manager of Poopri Factory. By the death of William Howell (his brother-in-law) he was promoted to Dooriah, one of the big managements belonging to the Association,—Dooriah and Shahpur managers having as well the superintendence of all the Association's Factories. The pay was good for these days, namely, Rs. 500 per month. These two managements had the supervision over Poopri, Doomra, Amoih, Dynechuppra, and Kurnoul. They had the power to appoint and discharge managers and assistants where berths fell vacant subject to the sanction of the home directors. Gale joined Dooriah in the end of 1847. My acquaintance with him commenced shortly after. He was as nice and jolly a fellow as one would wish to know, a bit peppery if put out, but it never lasted.

I remember once his sister came to pay him a visit from

Calcutta. She brought up with her a swell Calcutta khansamah. Gale had got out his best crockery for the occasion, to do things in the very best form. Among this crockery there was a grand trifle bowl which Charlie cherished as the apple of his eye. This bowl stood on a crystal pedestal and was very handsome. Dinner went on all right, the trifle was introduced, and the contents duly served out by the host. The bowl was ordered to be removed to make room for the desert. The Calcutta khansamah, wishing to show with what dash he did things, and as if to show the up-country bumpkins how things should be done, seized the pedestal with a sweep. Alas! he was not aware the bowl and the pedestal were separate. Away flew the splended crystal bowl! With a howl Gale made a rush for it, and was fortunate enough to catch it before it reached the floor. Then with a face as red as a turkey cock he seized the dumfounded khansamah by the shoulders and kicked him out of the room. His sister was amazed, and all sat, not knowing what to say, the old gentleman looking very much ashamed of himself. However, he shortly got up and left the room. The chink of rupees was heard in the distance, and the khansamah was heard to declare that he would not mind undergoing the same operation daily at the same price. This was a sample of Charles Gale's temper. It was like a puff of gunpowder and all over in a minute, and then he was always ready to make amends.

There was no better host, and his Christmas parties were the crack ones of the district. The programme at these parties was generally as follows:—In the early morning start off hunting, and after several rattling good runs after jackals, lunch would be found ready under a nice cool mangoe grove. This feast would last till about 3 P.M. Then elephants with howdahs on their backs and our guns and ammunition all ready appeared on the scene, when we started off, shooting down the Gunduk daubs. There a goodly bag of partridge, hare and quail and sometimes other game was secured. We returned home well tired; but after a peg and a smoke we were ready to dress for dinner. This was always a grand feast, for Gale, while giving his guests of the best, always liked to have as good for himself, so he always had two turkeys roasted. First one came on, and from it his guests were helped. When that was finished No. 2 appeared, and from this our host had a liberal helping. After dinner some started singing and smoking, while others went into the billiard-room and knocked the balls about. On other evenings we used to be treated to fire-works. These jovial parties generally lasted four days, and we had a very happy time of it.

I remember one of these parties, however, nearly ending in a little unpleasantness. One of Gale's assistants had taken too much, and was a little rough with one of the guests. This Charlie rather resented, and he told the youngster if he could not behave himself he had better go to his bungalow. The young man, being a hot-headed Scotchman, at once took huff, and banged out of the door. We all thought he had gone off to bed; but no, about five minutes after a very shaky note was put into my hands to say that a pony was going for me and would I ride down to the little bungalow. Thinking that the youngster had been sobered by his ejection and wanted me to act as a peace-maker and put things right, I at once mounted the pony and rode down to the residence of my friend and dismounting entered. There was the rowdy one, sitting at a table with sheets of paper partly scribbled over before him, and by his side a glass of gin and water. He had a wicked look in his eyes as he turned to me and said, "Look here I have been horribly insulted. Will you take this letter to Mr. Gale and tell him that I am ready to meet him with pistols, swords or any other weapon whenever he likes." I remonstrated, and begged him to wait till morning when he would have had time to think over the matter, but on my saying this he jumped up and saying "Oh! you are one of the same gang!" made a rush for the corner where stood a big stick. Seeing this and considering discretion the better part of valour, I made my exit, the stick following me but with erratic aim. I jumped on the pony and soon got back to my friends.

Shortly after this we all retired to bed, and I had just got comfortably tucked in when Gale came into any room and showed me a letter from his assistant. This must have been a final effort after my speedy exit from the chota bungalow. The epistle called on Charlie to meet him in the early morning in the bamboo tope, and as he had no pistols, rifles would do, etc. Old Gale was plucky to the backbone, and would listen to nothing but fighting. I did my best to convince him that poor old Sam (for that was the assistant's Christian name) was so screwed that he was not answerable for his acts, and that he was not answerable for his acts, and that he should take no notice of what he had written. On this the old chap flared up. "What! what! Am I to be bullied by my own assistant?" Seeing he was in earnest I agreed to act as his second, and he at once wrote and sent off a letter to a friend for the loan of a pair of pistols. If these did not arrive I suppose there was to be a skirmish *a la* Yankee in which it was quite possible that I might be myself bagged, as after the night's fasting they were neither of them very steady. However, as I had promised I had to perform—*coute qu'il coute*—so I went to bed to dream of all kinds of queer things. I was just on the point of laying out my friend Sam (in my dreams), who had a big hole knocked through him, when my bearer awoke me suddenly. Jumping up with a cry of "What the dickens is the matter?" My servant informed me that the Chota Saheb wanted to see me. My first idea was that it was now a case of coffee and rifles, as the pistols had not turned up, and I really felt as bad as if

I was going to be one of the principals in the little business. However, gathering myself together, I arose, intending to go and turn Charlie out, but passing into the verandah I there saw Sam looking very seedy and dissipated. The first thing he said to me was "What the devil was I up to last evening? I find no end of letters strewn over my table and floor, some to you, and some to Gale. What was it all about, for I have no recollection?" I then told him all that had happened, and he seemed very much surprised. He asked me to go and explain things to Gale, and say how sorry he was; so I started to do so, saying I approved of what he was doing. Sam immediately flared up, saying "If you or he think I am afraid, let us have it out!" I told him not to be a fool, and went into Gale's bed-room and very soon made all right, for Charlie Gale, though peppery, never bore ill-will. I believe I was the best pleased of all three that the row had ended as it did. Poor old Sam died not many years after on his way home of abscess on the liver.

Charles Gale remained as manager of Dooria till the Indigo Association was about to break up and sell off their factories, when he made up his mind to retire. He went home and joined his brother John at Cheltenham. While in Tirhoot he had suffered from a sore tongue which made him rather nervous. The doctor out here assured him it was nothing, but alas! poor fellow, some time after reaching England, his tongue began to get worse, and after some time to develop cancer, of which terrible disease he eventually died. Gale, though he delighted in a rowdy party, was a good man at heart. He always went into Mozufferpore on a Saturday if he had to go in on business, so as to be there for Sunday and go to church. After he arrived in England he became very religious. "He married at home, and left a son who is in the army. Dear old Charlie Gale!" He was one of the kindest hearted men I ever knew, always ready for any fun, hospitable to a fault. The few years I served under him will always be remembered as the jolliest time of my life. He was very strict that work be properly done and attended to, and, like a good man, he was most particular in seeing to the factory cattle that they were well fed and attended to. He was up every morning at four and away down to the cattle troughs. Here he had a cup of coffee brought him, which he drank while he superintended the feeding of the cattle. A nephew of his had been sent out to learn his work, and Gale insisted on his getting up at this early hour to be present at the cattle feeding also. Now Master Arthur Howell (a son of John Howell of Kurnoul), loved sitting up late, and consequently was never in the humour to get up at the unearthly hour he was expected to. Every night as he went to bed, his bearer was warned to be sure to wake him up in good time. This operation was a most amusing one to an outsider while a very painful one to the servant. The latter would approach calling out "Saheb! Saheb!! The Burra Saheb has gone to the cattle." A loud snore would be the reply. In despair the bearer would approach and give his master's arm a shake. As sharp as lightning out would go the arm, and the servant have to retreat to get over the effects of a well put in whack on the side of the head. This kind of thing used to go on for fully an hour, when Arthur would take it into his head to wake up, and with a smile on his face ask the bearer why he had not awoke him in good time!

Charlie Gale was the subject of an article called "Tirhoot and its Inhabitants" which came out in the *Englishman* in 1851, or thereabouts. These articles were written by my old friend Archy Inglis and were considered most amusing papers. The article described Gale sitting down to a feast, his eyes sparkling behind his gold spectacles as he tucked his table napkin under his chin before beginning operations. Good old Charlie! It will be many years before Tirhoot sees the like of you again.

ARCHIBALD INGLIS.

Archibald Inglis came out to this country from Elgin. He was a *protege* of Dr. Charles Mackinnon, and started life at an outwork of Dholie Factory. His sojourn here was not of long duration, but while there he lived in a house built on the vats, for Thurma was not big enough to indulge in a bungalow. This luxury came later on, when the place had blossomed into a sugar factory. It had then become an outwork of an outwork called Sukri. In 1851 it was dismantled, and lay a kind of ruin for years, all the sugar machinery being brought to Sukri. However, as the price of indigo came round, Thurma was again started as an indigo factory. Inglis had long before this moved to Coalpoorah, an outwork of Seryiah, where he became an assistant under Edward Studd.

It was while here that my friend, who had a most amusing style of writing, started writing for the *Englishman* a set of letters called "Tirhoot and its Inhabitants." The authorship of these letters was kept very secret, Studd being the only one who knew who the author was. As Inglis's letter had to pass through Seryiah Factory he (Inglis) thought it better to let Studd into the secret. These letters, while amusing, were very inoffensive. Each succeeding week brought out a literary caricature of one of the many resident of the district. Curiosity was at its height. Guesses were made, but all wide of the mark. One man went so far as to draw the long bow, and swear he knew who it was, and has seen the manuscript of one of the letters, and when asked who it was he said he was bound to secrecy. Unfortunately he divulged the secret to a friend, who again passed it on to another, till it became common property. However, when at last Inglis disclosed himself, the man who said he had seen the manuscript had to confess he had drawn on his imagination. So great was the irritation at the non-discovery of the man who had written these papers that bloodshed was nearly caused. One man wrote to the *Englishman*, and said it was well known that the writer of "Tirhoot and its Inhabitants" was the gentleman who whistled "Norma" for broken victuals at the Planters' Club. This letter was signed with the writer's well known *nom de plume*. The musical whistler at once saw that this was aimed at him, for it was his wont to walk up and down the Planters' Club verandah whistling, while the members were at breakfast, till some one asked him to come in and partake. Bob Taylor, then at Hattowrie Factory, was asked by the whistler to call on the writer for an explanation and apology, which was refused. So a challenge was sent. Now the whistler was a first rate pistol shot, and could cut the ace of diamonds out at 20 paces every shot. So the writer of the letter, as the challenged, having the choice of weapons, chose broad swords, and as he was a very powerful man this was rather a stumper, and things looked nasty. However, just then Archy Inglis, hearing of all this, came forward and confessed himself as the writer. In the delight of the discovery of the author, the would-be combatants shook hands, much to the pleasure of the seconds, who did not see much fun in a broadsword duel.

Inglis from Coalpoorah went to Singiah Factory, and after a while left and took charge of other factories. He went home and married, and returned to manage Hursingpur Factory. Archy had a good Scotch twang, and was rather a nervous man, and it used to be the delight of anyone driving him to shake his nerves by driving very close to any deep rut in the road. Old Inglis would call out "*Tak care, man, there a hol in the rod!*" He was very fond of a joke himself at some one else's expense. I remember one Christmas he wrote Charlie Gale that he was sending him a basket of game. Shortly after a coolie arrived with a very big basket. "By Jove," says Gale, "Capital, capital. Just what I wanted—a grand lot of wild ducks!" The servants were then called to unpack. This they did with great diligence, and handful after handful of straw was pulled out of the basket; at last an uncommonly small quail was pulled out. This was all Archy Inglis's basket of game contained. Inglis was not much of a sportsman and a very bad shot. He, however, often joined shooting parties more for the conviviality of the thing than anything else. On one occasion, having purchased a new gun from Scotland, he went out duck shooting, and after many shots at last wounded a bird, which fell into the *jhil*. Following it up, he at last got a steady pot shot at the duck, which he rolled over. Turning round to his friend with a smile of exultation and delight he remarked, patting the butt of his gun: "Eh! man, isn't she a sweet little gun!"

Inglis managed many factories one after the other, and finally bought a share in Sudowah Concern in Sarun. He then retired home to Scotland. Finding his income from Indigo irregular, he sold out, and retired from Indigo. His two sons are in Indigo in this district. Poor Inglis was a splendid companion, full of fun and good nature, and to hear his chuckle as he discovered something funny about anyone was good for one's health. I do not know what Inglis died of, or where exactly, but it was a sad day for his many friends when the news came out to India. A friend writes me, anent Inglis:—"When my wife and I went to Elgin he and Mrs. Inglis were most kind to us and insisted on our staying with them at their beautiful house, South

College; and I need not say how pleasant they made our visit."

This was dear old Archy Inglis all over.

THOMAS MARTIN.

Thomas Martin, or Toby Martin as he used to be called by his immediate friends, hailed from the Emerald Isle. How or to whom he came out to this country I do not know, but I think he started as an indigo planter, either in the North-West Provinces or in Shahabad. The first I heard of him was as a protege of old Kenneth MacLeod's at Husna, a sugar factory to the north of Attur, which then belonged to or was carried on by Messrs. Gillanders, Arbuthnot and Co.; the ostensible proprietor being a M. Delasaire, a Frenchman who had been induced to invest money in sugar.

Tom was a clever, shrewd planter, and was up to anything. He made a name for himself by reclaiming Dulsing Serai Factory that had gone very much down below par. All this is recorded in my short biography of Kenneth MacLeod, so I will not go over the same ground again. Martin after managing Dulsing Serai for some years bought Bagwanpore Factory where he did well, and in 1857 taking advantage of the favourable exchange, *viz.*, 2s. 2d. per rupee cleared out of the country with a good round sum. He remained in Ireland some years, but returned to India and took up the position of Superintendent to Kenneth MacLeod's Chuppra and Tirhoot Factories, making Khanti in Tirhoot his head-quarters. Here he remained till he thought he had put by money enough to go home for good, when he returned to Ireland. Old Toby Martin was a capital fellow and a rare good companion and full of fun. He was very fond of practical jokes and if one was attempted on him he was always ready to accept such very good naturedly and give a *quid pro quo* if possible.

I remember once at Dholi Martin was starting on urgent business at night in a palanquin. Old Edward Studd, who was always up to jokes, was there, and when Martin had got into his palki, Studd tried to upset it. Martin called to him to desist but Studd persisted. "All right," cries Martin jumping out of the palki, "if you are up to jokes so am I." Seizing the *masal* (torch) from one of tht palki bearers he made for a fine stack of oats that stood near the house with evident intention of setting fire to it. This was too much for Studd, who called "peccavi," and Toby was allowed to get into his palki and go his way in peace.

Another yarn told of Toby Martin was that he found at one of the factories he managed a rather bumptious young man as assistant under him. Martin was of a rough and ready nature, and this young man's ways and ideas did not suit him. One day something happened that rather put the manager out, he used unparliamentary language to his assistant to which his assistant objected and he called on his manager fcr an apology. On his refusing to do so he called him out, and out they went. Pistols were loaded and they were placed opposite each other. The assistant on the signal fired. Martin dropped his pistol on the ground, and took up a cane he had brought out with him and gave the youngster a good caning saying: "You have had your shot at me and I am having mine at you now."

Between the years 1876 and 1883, Martin lived at a place called Priory Lodge, I think in Kildare. It was near his old friend and brother planter's house—The Priory. Two sisters and a niece lived with and kept house for him.

Martin was very fond of gardening and had a very original old chap as a gardner whom he taught. This gardener—a true Paddy—had a great contempt for anything Scotch, and particularly objected to growing *kale*—which he said took a power of grase (grease) to grase (grease) a whisp of it. I suppose he referred to the cooking of it. Tom among other little luxuries had set up a Turkish bath in his establishment. This he indulged in once a week and if any friends were with him he held a regular levee of "Companions of the Bath." Many of his friends put down the cause of his death to these Turkish baths, where the extremes of heat and cold must have undermined his system. He had not made many friends in Ireland, but any old Tirhoot friend was always welcomed with open arms and treated to the very best. He seldom moved from home, sometimes running up to Dublin, or now and then taking a sea trip in company with his niece. Sometimes he had to visit certain Spas and partake of the waters when troubled with gout.

Toby Martin never married. Gardening was his great delight, and he had a grand garden with all kinds of fruit and vegetable in it. His great forte was strawberries. He grew them all along the borders of his garden walks. At the end of these walks he had built two little houses in each of which resided a pet cat. These cats had collars round their necks to which were attached light chains, and the chains were again fastened to rings which ran on a light wire. running the whole length of the walk, so that the cats could promenade up and down the full length of these walks and so protect the strawberries from the depredation of mice and rats. Tom Martin was very fond of dumb animals and this was an original way of making use of his pet cats. Tom Martin died sometime about 1883, but I have not the exact date. He had one brother who was out in this country, Bob Martin. He had enlisted as a young man in that *corps d'elite* —the old Bengal Horse Artillery. His brother persuaded him to leave it and join him in indigo. He got into bad health after leaving the service, went to sea for his health, but died soon after his return from the Mauritius where he had gone for a change. Poor old Tom Martin was a good planter, a very shrewd man, a first rate companion and always full of fun. Though very strict with the natives they had such an opinion of his judgment and justice that they would travel many miles to place before him any difference that might have arisen, and abide cheerfully by his decision. There are not many left in the district now who remember Tom Martin.

WILLIAM C. BADDELEY.

William C. Baddeley was born, I believe, at Dhooli Factory, Tirhoot. He was a son of Colonel Baddeley, who commanded a regiment of Irregular Horse, a very quick-tempered man. It is said in Indian History that when riding at the head of his regiment advancing to the seige of Bhurtpur his horse suddenly fell into a dry well. On this Colonel Baddeley kicked up such a row that the enemy were alarmed and very nearly capitulated.

Baddeley started life at sea, I think first as a midshipman. This he gave up and came to live with his father, but the old gentleman was of such an irascible temper that he bolted and shipped as a seaman before the mast. Baddeley has often told me of his experiences during this period of his life. One in particular was that he and another friend had left a ship they had been on, as their time was up. They went on shore at New York, and had a gay time of it as long as their money lasted. At last getting short, they looked about for a ship. Men were scarce, and there was not much difficulty in getting work. They went to a grog shop, where they found a seemingly very nice young man, the captain of a ship who was looking out for men. He treated them to what Baddeley called Dog's Nose, a mixture of ginger beer and gin. When he had drenched them well with this he took them to a shipping office and they were duly booked. Next morning they went on board their ship and she set sail. Baddeley and his friend, with aching heads—the effect of the mixture, were loafing about the deck. The captain seeing them idle called to them to set about their work. Baddeley's friend immediately tried to crack a little joke with the captain as he had been doing the day before. Before the man knew where he was the Yankee captain took up an iron belaying pin and felled him to the deck, calling him a "d—d hog." Baddeley remarked that he took the hint and at once set to work, making up his mind to bolt on the first opportunity, as they had evidently caught a tartar.

After he had sown his wild oats he turned up as a planter in Tirhoot, and if I remember rightly started as an assistant at Rajkund Factory under Lewis Cook. Here he had a bad time, as Cook was a hard master. He used to be kept out all day, which in the hot weather was very trying. However, he managed to steal a march on Cook, for he used to go out, take his horse's saddle off and lie down under a tree and have a good snooze during the hottest part of the day. From Rajkund Baddeley went to an outwork of Pundoul, and thence as manager of Doomra and Dynechuppra, and from thence on old Sam Johnstone's death he took over charge of Shahpur Mircha, where he remained several years, and then went home, intending to go to New Zealand. However, at home he married, and being a good manager the Tirhoot Association whom he had worked for asked him to return to Shahpur Mircha Factory. So he returned to India. After a few years he bought a share in Doulutpur Factory in partnership with Kenneth MacLeod. He worked up this factory and in time made a good amount of money. When at Doulutpur during the Mutiny he with many others had to retire to Mozufferpore. While there he heard that some of the maliks at Doulutpore were trying to take possession of the factory as they thought our Raj had passed away. Baddeley got a warrant from the Magistrate, for martial law was on. He and John F. Mackenzie started for Doulutpore, some sixty miles off, in the early morning, came on the mutinous malik when he least expected them, walked up to him with a cocked pistol and called on him to surrender. The wretched man at once gave in, and the big gathering of his admirers sneaked away and the malik was bound and placed at the back of the dog-cart, and Mackenzie and Baddeley started on their return journey to Mozufferpore, where they arrived with their prisoner by that day evening. The man was duly tried, and got some ten years' imprisonment.

Some years after this Baddeley went home and settled down in Cornwall, where he bought property and built a big house. He came back to India after this once or twice.

In passing through Egypt he bought an Egyptian costume. This he wore the whole time he was in India to the amusement of many.

He was a great smoker, but this did not sooth his temper, which like his father's before him was very quick. On the way out from home some one made a remark about his "dirty little black pipe." Hearing this, Baddeley in a temper threw his pipe overboard, and swore he would never smoke again, and he kept his vow. The agents who looked after his affairs in Calcutta did not look forward to his periodical visit with any degree of pleasure as he generally led them a bit of a dance. Mr. W. C. Baddeley died in, I think, his 84th year, leaving several children. Mrs. Baddeley died not very long ago. Baddeley with all his quick temper was a very good fellow and a capital companion, especially when in a good humour. He was one of the most successful planters of his day. He understood the native character thoroughly, and from spending a good part of his life at sea and a good deal of it before the mast he had seen a lot of the world and its ups and downs.

EDWARD STUDD.

Edward Studd came up to Tirhoot under the auspices of his brother-in-law, Dr. Charles Mackinnon, who was planters' doctor in Tirhoot. Mackinnon was a great speculator and had had shares in many indigo concerns, as the mark "CMCK," still existing, as the mark on a number of indigo factory chests, indicates. Charles Mackinnon having, like many others, dabbled in sugar, paid the penalty and became greatly involved, so he made over his property to Messrs. Gisborne and Company, who gave him a small allowance to live on at home. Gisborne and Company placed the management and superintendence of Dr. Mackinnon's properties in E. Studd's hands. Studd took up his residence at Seryiah, Jack Smith being at Dholi. However, John Stace Smith and Studd fell out over some business matter. They had a great row, which nearly ended in powder being burned. On Smith's leaving, James Cox took over charge, and he and Studd managed, one at Dholi and the other at Seryiah. Their management proved very successful, and before many years they had pulled the places out of debt, and Dr. Charles Mackinnon was looked upon as a man of wealth.

Studd eventually purchased eight annas in the two concerns from Gisborne and Company. This eight annas had been made over to that firm as a kind of commission on their taking up the business and assisting him in his time of need. This was the beginning of Studd's wealth. He had made a little money by selling and buying horses, and was able to put down the lakh of rupees, the price of the eight annas shares. While Cox and Studd managed the two factories they did well, and it was said that they cleared on an average two lakhs of rupees yearly. In those days factories were managed more cheaply than now. Cox, at Dholi, got rupees four hundred a month and no commission, though after a time Studd allowed him commission; and when he first went to Dholi he had only one assistant on rupees one hundred, afterwards increased to a hundred and fifty. Studd was very fond of horses, and was a good strong rider. He had several good horses in his stable both for the flat and cross-country. He was also a very good judge of a horse. He was one of the few men in Tirhoot who ever rode down a wolf single-handed.

He noticed, while riding over his indigo lands, that a wolf he sometimes saw and pursued for a short distance always ran off taking the same route. So, making up his mind to have a try to spear this wolf, he arranged that a fresh horse should be posted some distance off, but close to the line of country the wolf was accustomed to travel. Taking with him a spear he started off, and, sending some coolies into a grass near where he had seen the wolf, they soon rattled him out, and Studd started after him, pressing him as hard as he could but gaining very little on him. At last, reaching the fresh horse, he quickly jumped on, and rode the wolf at a tearing pace. The wolf at last began to come back to him, and Studd very soon sent his spear through him. It was a good long run, nothing under twelve miles. I have only heard of one better feat than this, and that was when Maxwell, Smith and Forth rode a wolf from Illmarnugger Factory to Hattowri; the former on a Kabul horse called "Jack," a first class old horse, and the latter on a little country-bred mare. The wolf was ridden on to the Hattowri Factory Zerauts, where it was knocked on the head, clean done, by some coolies.

When Studd first retired to England, he leased Halerton Hall, but after a time he took Tedworth, which belonged to that well-known sportsman Assheton Smith. There he found ample stable room for his horses, as he went in for hunting and had a goodly number. He had also a very nice house in town near Hyde Park. His luck seems to have followed him home to England, for he bought a property through which a part of the Derby course ran. This brought him into conflict with the Turf Club. However, the matter was amicably settled and Studd came out of it very well; so much so that it is stated that he gave the Turf Club a certain amount of money to be run for. He was also fortunate with his horse Salamander, which won for him some £30,000 at one steeplechase.

Studd on quitting India left his brother-in-law, Henry Hudson, in charge of Seryiah. Studd lost his first wife out here, and went home very soon after her death. He, some time after this, while at home, married again. He had several children by his first and second marriages. The boys were alll of them active young men and good cricketers. It was his grandson who played so well for Harrow, in one of the last matches. Edward Studd was a man of very sober habits. He went to bed early and rose at most unearthly hours in the morning, and as it was too dark to do anything, he generally sought for some one to converse with. I remember when I was an assistant with Cox at Dholi, Studd paying him a visit, and at about 3 A.M. next morning he turned up in the bed-room where Cox and I were peacefully reposing. He went and sat down on the side of Paddy's bed, and started off talking about some piece of business that was on just then. I could see by Cox's movements in bed that he did not care for being disturbed, and out it came. Studd was pressing for an answer to an inquiry, when Cox in a very grumpy voice called out, "Go to—somewhere (it was not Jericho)." Studd, seeing no satisfaction could be got out of Cox, came to me, and started with "You lazy beggar, not up yet!" I, being but a humble assistant and in a way under him, had to wake up and talk, though I wished he had gone where Cox sent him to, instead of to me. Studd was a man very fond of practical jokes. He was a first rate billiard player. He had at one time at Seryiah two tiger cubs that were the terror of outside servants who came to the house. They were not vicious, but playful, and when we were playing at billiards, if we happened to have slippers on we sometimes got a nasty scratch, as they used to lie under the table and suddenly pounce on your poor feet as a kitten pounces on a ball of wool. They used to rove about the house night and day, and I remember on one occasion a bearer boy who was sleeping in the upper storey of the Seryiah house woke suddenly and saw one of the cubs standing near him. With a howl of fear he sprung up and tumbled over the parapet. Luckily there was a slanting roof just under on which he fell, and rolling down fell on the ground, only bruising himself slightly. These animals after a time began to get dangerous, and had to be shot.

Not long before his death Studd was very much taken with Moody and Sankey, and in time became a most enthusiastic follower of these men, subscribing most liberally to their mission. He wrote to old Tom Martin putting before him how proper it would be for him to come and listen to these good men, etc., but old Tom replied that he would prefer a tip as to the likely Derby winner from Studd. It was in hurrying to one of Moody and Sankey's prayer meetings, for which he was late, that I understand Studd ruptured a blood vessel. On this occasion he was cured, but not very long after he ruptured it again, and this caused his death. Studd died in 1876, aged 57. I may say that Studd was one of of the most fortunate men Tirhoot has ever known. All he touched seemed to prosper. He had a very shrewd adviser in his brother-in-law, Henry Hudson. I remember one of the last times I met Studd in London he was full of his praise as a shrewd and clever man of business. I should have mentioned that when the old Tirhoot Indigo Association of London sold off their factories, Edward Studd bought Dooria and Kurnoul Factory from them and gave a share of the management to L. MacDonald, a nephew of old Kenneth MacLeod. Here his usual luck followed him, for the first year's profit paid up the full price he paid for the places. At Studd's death L. MacDonald, according to agreement, purchased Studd's shares of these concerns. He retained Dooria and sold Kurnoul.

CHARLES SWAINE.

Charles Swaine was in 1848, when I first met him, manager of Doudpore under Mr. David R. Crawford, who had the superintendence of a group of factories then belonging to Messrs. Noel and Company. Charles Swaine was a Devonshire man. He came out to Mr. William Farley Lethbridge (whose daughter he eventually married). Mr. W. F. Lethbridge was then in Gaya at a place in the Rhotas hills. Swaine's first berth in Tirhoot was, I believe, Dinamutt, the outwork of Peepra in Champarun. Thence he went to Raghaie Factory, an outwork of Kanti; after that he was promoted to the sub-management of Doudpore, and finally to management of Kanti. In 1861 he had got into very bad health and was ordered away for a change by the doctor. He went up-country but died at Cawnpore, where he is buried. While managing Kanti he was also superintendent of all Dr. Begg's factories at Doudpore, Motipore, Belsund, and Bekonpore before taking over charge of Kanti. Charles Swaine left several sons and daughters. His eldest son, George, became manager and proprietor of Attur Factory and turned out a very smart and clever young man. It is not so many years now since he died. Charles Swaine was a man who was much respected and loved by all his brother planters. He was a very jolly chap and seemed to be always in good humour.

ROBERT EDINGTON RONALD.

Robert Edington Ronald was another son-in-law of Mr. William Farley Lethbridge. He hailed from near Glasgow, and was managing Doulutpore when I first met him. He was at first under the Landales at Lutteepore in the Bhagalpore Division. He not long after I met him left Doulutpore and got an appointment as a Deputy Commissioner in the Santhal Pergunnahs. He, poor fellow! lost his life at Deoghur, where he was killed by a mutineer. His body was rescued and buried by a faithful old bearer. Ronald had been warned that the regiment was going to mutiny and was advised to get away, but he stuck to the officer in command, his friend, and so lost his life. He left, I think, two sons and daughters. One son, who was a planter in this district, died a few years ago. Of the others I have lost sight. Name of officer murdered Lieutenant Cooper. He who escaped Lieutenant Rannie at Deoghur.

As it has been my object in writing "Tirhoot and its Inhabitants of the Past" to leave a record of those who have passed away in years gone by for the benefit of those now present, and as many of those now dead and gone were known to me, some by name only and others but slightly, I propose giving a short record of both these, giving the little I knew of each.

SAMUEL JOHNSON

Was in 1847 manager of Shahpur Mircha. I only met him once, and that was at a New Year's party at Kanti in

1848. He died very shortly after, and is buried in the garden at Shahpur Factory.

DAVID BROWN

Was nicknamed the "Gooroo," as he was considered a knowing old gentleman. He managed Belsund Factory in 1847-48 and after that Motipore. I think he retired to England and died there, after 1853, as I lost sight of him after that. Motipore was purchased by C. Oman, and David Brown left then.

R. CAHIL

When I first knew him, was managing Motipore. He was the son of Mr. Cahil who was a shareholder both in the Tirhoot Indigo Association of London and of Noel and Co., who were proprietors of a number of fine factories in Tirhoot and Champarun. R. Cahil retired from indigo in about 1849 or 1850, and went home to England, where he died.

JOHN ANDERSON

Began life in India as a planter in Bengal. He was nicknamed "Soojee" because he lived principally on this flour. He purchased Kumtoul Factory in 1856. He was there for many years. He was not a very successful planter, being too easy going. After some years Mr. James Forlong got him the management of the Durbhanga Raj. He was much loved by the young Maharaja and his brother. The late Maharaja eventually paid up a big debt due to Messrs. Begg, Dunlop and Co., and took over the factory and all landed property attached to the concern. The Maharaja also allowed Anderson a pension of Rs. 500 per annum. Old Soojee retired to Dundee, where he lived for many years, and died well on in years.

JOHN ANDERSON, No. 1

Had been manager and proprietor of Kumtoul many years before I came to the country. From there he bought and went to manage Hattowrie Factory, taking with him a favourite peon whom he had made jemadar. His name was Sunful Raie. At Hattowrie Anderson made money and went home once or twice. The last time he came out he did badly and had to give up Hattowrie. He, however, arranged to buy Nawadah Factory, and Sunful Raie was to help him with the money. However, at the last moment Sunful Raie failed his old master. It was a terrible blow for poor old Mr. Anderson, for he died soon after, people said, of a broken heart. His daughters married officers in the army. One was the wife of Captain Aitkin, who so gallantly defended the Baily Guard at Lucknow, while his wife was one of those locked up in the Residency. The other sister married Captain Williams, who also did good service during the Mutiny, and afterwards commanded the Moshee Serks Pioneers. I think Mr. Anderson had one son, who got a berth in the Revenue Survey under Messrs. Chapman and Wyatt in 1848. I met him while he was encamped in Durbhanga and afterwards up in the North-West. I think he was then in the Opium Department. Old Mr. John Anderson is burried at Nawadah Factory.

WILLIAM HOWELL

Was manager at Dooria, and died there in the end of 1847 or the beginning of 1848.

JOHN HOWELL

Was an elder brother of W. Howell. He was proprietor of Kurnoul, but sold this factory and bought Buchour, called Kemna by the natives. The spec. was a bad one as Buchour did not pay him. He sold out and went home, and died there, leaving three sons, Arthur, John, and William, who all came to this country and joined indigo. They all died young.

ALEXANDER BROWN

Began life in Champarun I believe. When I knew him first he was at Hattowrie. He had got the management of the place from Bob Taylor, who owned it, and Nawadah, where Tom Slade managed. They both had the promise of a four anna share to be paid for out of the profits. Bob Taylor died not very long after he had made this arrangement and the properties had to be sold. So Brown and Slade both got a handsome bonus in consideration of their giving up their claim to the shares in the factories under their management. Alexander Brown then with Slade bought Doulutpore Factory. He was not long there, for on his way to Peepra Factory, while resting at Mozufferpore, he was taken ill, and the doctor declaring he was suffering from Bright's disease told him he could not live long, and sure enough he died a day or two after. He was a right good fellow and a great favourite with everyone. He died in 1853 or thereabouts, and is buried at Mozufferpore.

ROBERT TAYLOR

Was proprietor and manager of Hattowrie Factory in 1848. I never met him. He was not much of a favourite though he had some friends. He died somewhere up-country of small-pox.

HARRY BROWN

Was a relation of old David Brown. He had been at several of the outworks of Motipore and eventually settled down as manager of Rajkund. Old Harry had bolted from home and enlisted as a gunner in the Shekawatti battalion. He was a most amusing old gentleman and always had some extraordinary yarn to tell. He was sent up by Dr. Begg to look after his seed business after the Christie family had all been killed at Cawnpore by the mutineers. Harry Brown was at Cawnpore when the disaster to the Queen's troops took place and had to take shelter within the entrenchments. Harry Brown contracted bad fever at Rajkund and eventually died at the Planters' Club, but I cannot remember the year.

SHEREMAN

Was proprietor of Jeetwarpur when I came out in 1847 The place had got very much involved, and in 1848 the factory was sold and bought by Messrs. John Mackenzie and Beckwith. The factory must have been built several years ago as Shereman owned it in partnership with Sir James Weir Hogg, as the mark on the indigo H. and S. indicates. Shereman left several sons. One was killed in the Cawnpore entrenchments, another died of fever and is buried at Jeetwarpore in the garden, another was in the Santhal Commission, I think, but I do not know where he died. There is one son left, Edward, who lives somewhere up near Joynuggur Factory.

JOHN STALKART

Generally known as Bekonpore Johnnie, was manager of Bekonpore Factory when I knew him. From thence he went to Japaha Factory, and after that got charge of a factory in the Bhagalpore sub-division. He was a nice little man, a very keen sportsman. After he left Tirhoot I seldom heard of him, but I believe he fell into very bad health and died. One son by his first wife is still alive and has an indigo factory in the North-Western Provinces.

GEORGE TOOMEY

Was a nephew of James Cox. He came out in 1856 to his uncle, who was then managing Dholi. George came out just before the troublous times of the Mutiny. He was one of those who, with others, started to retake Mozufferpore after the civilians and the rest of the residents had been ordered away by Mr. W. Taylor, Commissioner of Patna. In 1861, when his uncle left Dholi he took up the management and was most successful there. On his uncle purchasing Kanti and Motipur in partnership with Kenneth MacLeod he first went to manage at Motipore and thence to Kanti. Motipore they eventually sold to Mr. Thomas Fraser, and George Toomey and his uncle went on with Kanti. Toomey, however, gradually bought up all the shares except a four annas share held by the Hon'ble T. M. Gibbon. This share has now been purchased by Toomey's widow. George Toomey was a most successful planter and a worthy nephew of his uncle, who, I may say, was one of the best and most successful planters Tirhoot has ever seen. George was a capital host. He was a good and kind friend to several. He retired home to England, where he lived for many years. His death was sudden, and many mourn the loss of good old George as a good friend and companion.

JAMES SMITH

Began his indigo planting career in, I think, the North-West Provinces. He was born in this country, and was dark for a Eurasian. He was, however, educated in Scotland, and had a very strong Scotch accent. He first came to Tatereah under David Crawford (who had to return to India on his brother Andrew's death). After David Crawford gave up the management of Tatereah (which was his own property), James Smith managed for several years most successfully. However, on his uncle George Smith's death he was offered the management of Shahpore Mircha, where his uncle was managing for the old London Indigo Association. Here he remained as manager till the Association ceased, when he and the Munshi of Shahpore Mircha, old Kali Persaud, bought the factory. This place he managed for many years. He also managed a company got together to furnish carts and carry grain during the famine of 1873-74. This he managed so well that when the work was over, a matter of over ten lakhs was divided among the shareholders as profit There was no hitch in the working of this company. Everything went off smoothly, whereas in some of the other companies there was a good deal of heart-burning at settlement time. Smith after the famine went home for a time with his wife, whence he returned, and after remaining out for a short time longer he sold his share in the factory and went back to Scotland, where he died of heart complaint in 1881 or 1882. James Smith was a very strong business man, liberal, and a capital host. He had many friends in the district and in Calcutta.

JOHN MARTIN BECHER

Was a son of John Becher, who was a nephew of old Captain Becher. He was a Eurasian. Jack took his old grand-uncle as his pattern. He was the very quintessence of politeness. Becher began as a planter at a sugar factory outwork of Beconpore that stood near the banks of the Banmuttee river. This factory has been long closed. It was here Becher met with a nasty accident. He was attending to the working of the sugar-mill with lime water to prevent acidity, sitting with his foot resting on his piston-rod, whch kept moving to and fro horizontally, and getting interested in a book he moved his foot without thinking, and getting it between the key and the piston the key caught the sole of his foot and tore part away. Later on Becher became manager of Kumtoul, and when he left this factory purchased Joynaggur, Narharh, Nawada, Beerpore and Tewarrah. To carry on these he got an outlay of some three lakhs of rupees. Then the cash began to fly and precious little of it ever reached the factory. The consequence was that Becher came to grief. Just then Tom Slade took up the management of these factories for Becher and made a grand season, which enabled Becher to pay up what he owed. He would not, however, allow Slade to go on managing, as it did not suit Becher to be kept short of cash, so he again took up the management of his factories, and in a year's time he was again in difficulties. Becher was a man whom the natives had every confidence in, and they would trust him to any amount. What they said was that, though Becher did not always pay at once, when he did he paid up in full with interest added. Becher, or Jack, as he was generally called, was the essence of kindness and generosity. Any youngster fresh out from home was at once taken by the hand and shown the ropes. If a man came from up-country, and did not know where to lay his head, Jack took him in hand. The way he used to look after his old grand-uncle, Captain Becher, was a picture. He had a great admiration for the old gentleman, who was sometimes a little hard on him. For instance, Jack tried to raise a pair of moustaches, and on appearing before the Captain was met with "What do you mean by those d—d things? Go and take them off, and don't try to ape the Military."

Latterly he bought a factory called Dhurmpore, but this place he left very much involved. The place was much in debt to his old friend Nawab Syed Mahomed Taki Khan, who on Becher's death took over the factory. Jack Becher died at the Planters' Club of galloping consumption, and is buried at Mozufferpore.

WILLIAM BALDWIN

When I first knew him, was an assistant at Kanti under David Crawford. He was considered a very good assistant. He was a big, powerful fellow, and the natives held him in great respect. From Kanti he went as manager to Dowdpore, where he was for some years as an assistant manager. From thence he became manager of Jeetwarpore, but no sooner did he get into independent charge than he quite changed: did little or no work, and took to drink. He died in 1860, and was buried at Mozufferpore.

JAMES CULLEN MUIR

Was sent out from Glasgow to David Crawford as an assistant at Kanti. He did very well at first. He was rather a hard master with the natives. He was at Tatereah for a short time, and then got Chutwarrah, where he managed for some time. When there he built Dhurumpore to prevent people interloping. When the Tirhoot Indigo Company of London sold off their factories, Chatwarrah being one of them, Muir had to leave. He was for a short time at Poona. He then built an interloping factory called Kopee, in the Shapore Ouadie dehaut. He was at one time manager of Baghwanpore Factory, in the Monghyr district, where he was accused of having beaten a native and was found guilty and run in. Like many others, when misfortune came to him, he took to drink and died, but I cannot remember the year. He is, I think, buried at Kopee Factory. In his case a Munshi, who had done well under his master, Jimmy Muir, behaved differently to Sunful Raie, John Anderson's jemadar, for Muir's Munshi beggared himself in trying to help his master

---

CHRIS. STRACHAN

Was, I think, sent out by the London Indigo Association. When I first met him he was sub-manager of Chetwarrah Factory. He was nick-named the Count. He eventually, on Baddeley's going home to England, took charge of Shahpore Mircha, and on Baddeley's return he purchased Hursingpore, where he did very well. He was a very kind-hearted old chap. He had picked up a youngster who had been an apprentice in one of Green's ships, and taking a liking to the boy (his name was Evans) he gave him the run of his teeth and some small pay. Unfortunately Master Evans one day, while left alone at the factory, finding it dull, started shooting sparrows on the verandah roof. The consequence was that he set the place on fire, and Strachan had to pay for a new roof, and Evans was asked to go.

Strachan retired home to England, where he lived a wandering life. He left two sons, who are both dead. His daughters married, one at home, a solicitor, the other a major in the army, and the other a man in the Canal Department. Old Strachan left his children well off as he had shares in Dulsingserai, Hursingpore, and a tea garden Darjeeling way.

JOHN ANDERSON

Was sub-manager at Chetwarrah when I first knew him in 1847-48. He left indigo soon after and got a berth as

Deputy Magistrate and Collector, and was in that capacity in Mozufferpore. He was a man of good family, but a disappointed man. He died not many years after getting into the Uncovenanted Service, leaving a wife and one or two daughters. His brother, who was an officer in the artillery, and one who distinguished himself in the Lucknow Residency, was a bachelor, and on his brother's death supported his wife and daughters, leaving them at his own death well provided for.

JAMES AND JOSEPH HILL

Were sons of old Mr. Henry Hill, who was a partner of old Mr. W. Moran, whose son afterwards founded the late firm of W Moran and Co. They, James and Joseph Hill, became proprietors of Turcouleah, Seeraha and Bara. At the failure of the Union Bank of Calcutta in 1847, their father found himself heavily involved, and his property mortgaged and in the hands of an assignee. They, the two sons, went to Calcutta, where Dr. David Begg assisted them with money, and they settled up with the assignee, then a gentleman rejoicing in the name of Yankee Richards, if I remember rightly. Having cleared off the debt over the concerns, they found the matter of an outlay their next difficulty. They called in all their maliks, and arranged with them to wait till after sale of the season's indigo, and that they would be paid their rents, plus a good interest. The same arrangement was made with all the amlahs and workmen in the factory. The Hills had such a good reputation for integrity and honour that this arrangement was at once agreed to by all. James Hill retired to England some short time after, but Joseph Hill, a hard-working planter, managed Seeraha and Bara for a time without an assistant to help him, and was most successful. Turcouleah had remained closed, but was later on opened by Joseph Hill, and became one of the finest concerns in Champarun. After James Hill's death the factories were worked under Joseph Hill's orders. After Joseph Hill's death Seeraha and Bara concerns were sold, James Hill's sons, Dr. Hill and H. Hill, keeping Turcouleah as their own. They also have a share in that time fine concen, Motihadri. The indigo cakes and chests bear the mark still of M. and H.—Moran and Hill.

W M. STEWART

Came out to India to his relative Mr. Malloy, who was a solicitor in Calcutta in the 40's. He was sent up to Shahabad, and thence to his cousin, Tom Poe, at Dulsingserai, which place he eventually got the management of. In 1861 he started an interloping factory called Begum Serai. From Dulsingserai he purchased a share in Jeetwarpore from Mr. J. Beckwith, and a few years after came to manage at this factory. He was not a successful manager, and the failure of the Agra Bank in 1866 brought him to a standstill as his capital was all borrowed. He had to go through the Insolvent Court, in doing which he came in contact with Sir Barnes Peacock and Mr. Justice Phayre. He lost everything he had. Eventually through his wife's interest he got a berth under the Court of Wards over the Kunowlie Estate. During the famine of 1873, he became a partner in a carrying company to carry famine grain from the south of Mozufferpore to the sub-divisions to the north of Tirhoot. In this he cleared a large sum of rupees. He then bought a tea garden at Kotegarh near Simla, but this did not prove a good spec. Other investments that he made proved equally unfortunate, and he had to sell out of his tea garden. He again got work to manage a native's estates near Mirzapore, where he died from an attack of small-pox. It is said that if he had lived a few days longer he would have died Sir William M. Stewart. His second son (his eldest having died), is now the Baronet.

GOODENOUGH AND CURTIS

These two were living at Barhamporah; Goodenough in charge of the saltpetre works that belonged to Messrs. Mackillop, Stewart and Co., while Curtis was living with Goodenough as a friend. Goodenough was not long up in Tirhoot. He went down to Calcutta eventually to join the firm of Mackillop, Stewart and Co. Curtis eventually purchased Ramkollah Factory in Sarun, and after his first wife's death retired to England. He married again, and died a few years later. He was a big, good natured man, very fond of the good things of this world, and a capital host. In Scotland I heard that to be able to get over the moors when grouse shooting he invented a belt that went round him. This was fastened to a long rope attached to a pony, so that when hilly places had to be crossed the pony was hooked on and Bill Curtis hauled up gun in hand ready to shoot. As this exertion caused thirst, and Curtis loved his beer, he had a small corrugated barrel on wheels made, drawn by another small pony. This was filled with beer, and followed him about so as to be ready when he wanted it.

GEORGE PAULING

Was sent out by the old Tirhoot Indigo Company of London. He came originally to Doomreh and thence went to Amoih, and was then for many years under George Mitchell. From Amoih he came to Pupri, and while there he bought the Muzafferpore billiard room. This place he built on and made into a residential house, but he eventually sold it to Mr. E. Dacosta, who was a Subordinate Judge in those days at Muzafferpore. Dacosta sold the house to the Jaintpore

Mohunt, and he has given the house in *mokurrerie* lease to the members of the Muzafferpore Station Club. Pauling in about 1849 left Pupri and went to New Zealand, where he died.

WILLIAM FARLEY LETHBRIDGE

Came to India in the thirties. He had served in the English Navy and risen to the rank of Captain, I understand. He quarrelled with his people at home and left the navy to come to India to try a shake at the pagoda tree. He made a fortune, but lost it all at the failure of the Union Bank in 1847. He hailed from Newton Abbot, Devonshire. He left four sons, two of whom are dead, Thomas, Robert, and Rev. W. Lethbridge, Chaplain, leaving Alfred (now Sis Alfred Lethbridge) living, a man who has done good service in India. W. F. Lethbridge was a midshipman at the battle of Trafalgar.

GEORGE NEVILLE WYATT

Was managing Peepra Factory in 1847-48. The factory then belonged, I think, to Messrs. Noel and Co. In 1852-53 this factory was sold to Mr. Wyatt, who eventually made a fortune out of it and retired. The factory continued to do well It is now managed by his son, who is in England on leave. G. N. Wyatt was a great shikari and a good shot. There is a story told of him when he was at Bagwanpore, an outwork of Belsund. Some friends came to see him, and he had called up his servant to order a sheep to be killed for their entertainment. The flock of sheep, his private property, passing by at a distance, he said to one of his friends (he happened to have his gun in his hand loaded with ball), "Do you see that sheep ahead of the flock?" He fired, and the animal dropped. The little incident did not end there, for the bullet had travelled further and killed a boy who was working some distance beyond in some jungle. This was a grand opportunity for a native who was at feud with the factory. He immediately gave notice to the *thana* to the effect that Wyatt had had the man tied to a tree and had shot him. Luckily for Wyatt his friends were able to help him to prove the case utterly false. This, of course, happened many years ago. Wyatt on one of his jungle trips had picked up a tiger cub which he confined in a big cage is his garden. It grew to be a very fine tiger and one of the shows of the place. This tiger used to be fed on pigs which were thrust in beside him, when he killed and ate them, one daily. However, one day a pig was put in, and the tiger not being hungry let him live. Next day a rew pig was put in and was at once slain and eaten, the first pig taking a light meal off his brother when the tiger was done. The same performance went on for several weeks till the pig, favoured by the tiger, became familiar and tried to join the tiger when he fed. The consequence was that friend piggy got a smack on the side of the head that knocked out one eye, and sent him rolling to the side of the cage. Piggy lived for some time after with the tiger, but always kept his distance at feeding time. The pig used to lie down, and the tiger, making a pillow of him, would have a comfortable siesta. At last poor piggy from eating his own brethren got mangy and had to be destroyed. The tiger never made friends of any other pig. He too eventually got mange and had to be shot. This tiger, though very savage, was in mortal terror of a wheel used for measuring to which was attached a bell that sounded the number of poles. This, driven towards the cage, put the tiger into a terrible fright, and he would crouch into a corner and tremble all over. Wyatt retired many years ago and bought a very nice place in Cheltenham, where he lived for many years. He died not many years back, and is buried near some of his old Tirhoot friends who passed away before him. His second son is the manager of the Peepra Factory. He moves about between England and this country.

PHILIP CRUMP

Was manager of Munjoul and Sissowni Indigo Concern in 1847. I understand he owned it. I met him on my way through into the district in October, 1847. He seemed to me to live in breeches, boots, a black velvet hunting cap and a dressing gown, for the two days I passed at Munjoul this was his style of dress, and yet I never saw him mount a horse or even one brought to the door to be mounted. He had a queer idea about indigo, that is, disapproved of a thick crop, and when he had one he weeded out a good part of it. No wonder the factory came to grief.

CHARLES OMAN

Came up from Bengal, where he had been an indigo planter. He was noted as a good hand in improving colour. He went to Seeraha, where he did well both as to amount of indigo made and in improving colour. Joseph Hill came out and relieved him, paying him up his pay and commission to date when his engagement expired. This came to a good round sum, and Oman with cash in hand bought into Hotipore, where he did well, sold out of this, and eventually purchased Hatowrie. Falling into bad health, he sold out of indigo and retired to Cheltenham, where he died.

WILLIAM HAMILTON URQUHART

Before ending my communications anent Tirhoot and its past inhabitants, I must not forget one who, though not a planter, was a man who was much liked by all,—Mr. W.

Urquhart, who was Opium Agent in Tirhoot in 1847-48 (when I first came to this district), was a thorough gentleman of the old school; he and his wife were famed for their hospitality, and no planter who came into Muzafferpore were ever left in the cold. In those days the official element and the planter did not amalgamate, so Urquhart's open-handed hospitality to planters was all the more appreciated.—Urquhart was himself the personification of a fine old Scottish gentleman, tempered with Indian experience. What finer type can be found? Urquhart lived in a big house that stood in the large compound where now are the *teen kotiah*. The old house was knocked down and the three small houses built. Old Captain Becher and the old *Guru* David Brown, were great friends of the Urquhart's and were very often to be met there, and I can fancy I hear the old Captain's stentorian voice greeting some new arrival "Hullo! Cupid! Where are you from?"

He was born 6th August, 1800, died in London in March, 1881, and was buried at Kensal Green Cemetery. He came out to Calcutta in October, 1821, in the E. I. Co.'s ship "Marquis of Wellington," Captain Blanchard. He came out to a Mr. Hutton. From his arrival in India till 1836 he lived in Calcutta, Chunar, Bhagulpore, and Colgong. He married in Calcutta, and went to Gaya in 1836, where he got the appointment of Sub-Deputy Opium Agent under Mr. Archibald Trotter, who was then Agent of Behar. He remained in Gaya four years and then was transferred to Tirhoot in December, 1840, where he remained till 1862; he was then transferred to Shahabad and in 1867 to Tirhoot again, where he remained till he retired from the service in 1870. He lived there with his daughter at Arrah, and in 1871 left for England to live with his sisters, but his eldest daughter going home in 1872, he took a house and lived with her at Twickenham till 1873, when she returned to India. He then lived with a married sister, and died in her house. He had been in India fifty years without coming to England or having any sort of change.

He was most strict in all matters of etiquette, and there is a story of how he called out the Collector, old Wilkinson, because he considered his wife had been insulted as she was not taken into dinner at his house by the proper man. Old Mrs. Urquhart was even more particular in these matters, and it was said that she insisted upon Urquhart calling out Wilkinson, and so he did, and they turned out in the very early morning on the Secunderpore *maidan* and satisfied their honour by blazing into the air. This happened long before I came to the district. After many years in Tirhoot, where he had seen most of his daughters married, his wife died of cholera, and great was the mourning in the district over the death of this kind old lady. Shortly after Mrs. Urquhart's death Urquhart was transferred to Arrah. It was a black day for Tirhoot that saw our hospitable old friend leave. His daughters were all married in this district, and his sons became indigo planters. His eldest son died leaving a son who is now a planter in this district. His second son has retired and now lives in Cheltenham, and his eldest son, again, is an officer in the Bays, while his second son helps his father at home. In days gone by old Urquhart perched on a high coach-box with a tall white hat on his head was to be seen daily driving his family on the Secunderpore *maidan*. He always drove; and his horses were so well tended that they were as fat as butter, and were never allowed to travel beyond a slow trot. I have often driven one of these pampered horses with one of Urquhart's sons, whose great delight was to give the old animal a taste of the whip and make him travel a bit, remarking: "Fancy what the governor would say if he saw this!" Urquhart was a great sportsman, and was always one of the Stewards of the

Muzafferpore Races. He was a first-rate judge of a horse, and a good rider, and could sing a good song, one of his favourites being "Sing me an English song," which he sang with great pathos. Dear old Urquhart and his wife were as nice a couple as Tirhoot had ever seen or may hope to see.

DR. STOKES.

In finishing off Tirhoot and its inhabitants of the past I almost forgot our learned doctor, and though there are not many now present who remember him, my history would be incomplete without a short biography of Dr. Stokes. He succeeded Dr. David Begg, but whether Dr. Begg secured his services or not I do not know. There was no doubt that Stokes hailed from within the sound of Bow Bells, as he found himself at war with his H's now and then. In those days doctors were not bound to stick to the art of curing and bone-setting only, but dabbled in other little things that brought grist to the mill, and among these the sale of indigo seed (as agent) was one. Well, old Stokes, like Dr. Begg before him, added to his income in this way. One day our doctor waxed cheerful, for there had been a bad hailstorm, and he knew seed orders would come tumbling in. As he was promenading the T. P. Club verandah, up drove a trap, and out jumped Jemmy Cosserat. Stokes at once tackled him with the facetious query "'Ave a little 'ail, Cosserat?" Cosserat, who was warm and thirsty, replied, "All right, old chap, if you have a bottle of ale open I don't mind a glass." Esculapius at once saw the mistake he had made and ordered a bottle of Bass to be opened at once! The doctor, though not a bad chap, was a bit peppery in temper, and there were many little rows at the Club in his days over loo and other games of cards. As Secretary to the T. P. Club he often got into hot water, as he was very fond of giving little dinner parties to a few friends, and if one of these parties were on, and a member of the club turned up, he had a poor chance of being served. Donald H. Macfarlane —now Sir Donald H. Macfarlane—then a planter in Tirhoot, made him very wrath by publishing a jocative little piece in the *Englishman*. 'Tis said this made Stokes so angry that he got out his pistols, and swore vengeance; but it did not come out till some years after who the writer was, so the pistols had to be put up again.

Stokes did very well for himself; he had the whole of the practice of Tirhoot and Champarun, with Durbhanga. He was fond of horses, and kept a good stable, so that he could at an hour's notice drive out a long distance to see an urgent case. Our doctor eventually came to grief. He had bought a very handsome horse, a racer, as a riding horse —I forget the horse's name. He was a blood horse, and a bit *bobery*. Stokes went out for a ride, the horse started at something, reared, and came over on our doctor, breaking his leg near the hip. He was very carefully attended by our Civil Surgeon, Dr. Simpson, who after several months set him on his legs again, but Stokes could not move about with the ease he used to, and at last made up his mind to retire. In about 1850 he left for New Zealand, while there he purchased a good deal of what proved to be very valuable land. He came in for some money that had been in Chancery, and eventually died in New Zealand leaving large and valuable property. I don't think Stokes ever married, and no one knew if he left any heirs. He had not many personal friends in Tirhoot. Old Christopher Strachan was about the only one who was on very friendly terms with the doctor, and he did not know very much about him. Stokes was succeeded by Dr. Cooke, who remained in our district some years, but he was one who wished to be everything. He was clever, but flighty. He eventually died on board one of the river steamers, where he got a berth to look after coolies. Donald Macfarlane was very kind to him, and so were all the then members of Messrs. Begg, Dunlop and Co. Dr. Cook's son was the tea planter that showed such pluck when one of the Assam or Cachar tea gardens were raided by the Looshais, I think. After Cook came Booth, who is still living in Ireland; he was one of the best doctors we have had, very active, fond of shooting and pig-sticking and, therefore, very popular. He married in Tirhoot and soon after retired. He made a great hit in curing Nultoo Chowdry's son of cholera. Old Nultoo rewarded him handsomely, which allowed Booth to retire earlier then he might otherwise have done. Booth was followed by Sandiford, who retired after a few years, and is now in England. Our present sawbones is a very active young man, and seems to thrive equally in a railway carriage, or on horseback, or at his own hospitable home

---

OLD WAYS AND MANNERS.

The customs and manners of the past were rather of the rough and ready order except where a lady ruled the family circle. These were few and far between, and even where they were in those days the refinement to be found in Tirhoot homes nowadays did not exist. There was but one spinster in the district in 1847-48, and she was not over young though much run after.

In bachelor establishments things were managed in a very primitive way. For instance, suppose one young bachelor made up his mind to go over and pay a neighbour, say Bill Jones, a visit, he would write him a *chit:* "Coming over to see you for a spell; send a *dak* to the half-way house, and I'll be with you to dinner—we are going to give you a party!" Having despatched this his bearer is called up and told to arrange clothes for a week's outing. The bearer at once sends for a *banghy wallah* who is to carry two *petarahs*, which are filled with all requirements for the visit. On the top of one of the *petarahs* will be placed a *chilumchee* and on the other its stand, a *dhuri* and a vessel with a spout something like a tea pot, also your *razaie*, or quilt, for blankets were not used in those days.

In charge of these your bearer starts, and on arrival at your friend's house he is shown into the room you are to occupy. He at once sets to work to prepare for his master's arrival. The room holds nothing but a *charpoy* and a chair or two. On this *charpoy* there might be a mattress. Your bearer takes out of the *petarahs* sheets which he spreads on the bed and over this your *razaie*. He then adorns the pillows with pillow slips, and his master's bed is ready. Then proceeding to the verandah outside the bed room he prepares an *extempore* dressing room. Spreading the *dhuri* on the floor he places on it a teapoy (provided by your host). Then he sets up your *chilumchee* on its stand with the tea-pot-looking utensil beneath standing on the *dhuri*. Your comb, brush and tooth brush, with a small looking glass with a folding back as a stand, are placed on the teapoy. This with a piece of soap, with which you had also to provide yourself, completed your dressing arrangements. The bearer then hangs up in the bath-room a big bathing towel, and places at the bath-room door a pair of wooden clogs which you were supposed to seize between your toes so as to keep your feet dry. This operation I never mastered.

Having arrived at your host's house and refreshed yourself with a glass of gin and water (soda water was too much of a luxury in those days) you retire to your room to wash away some of the dust which you have acquired on your ride over. You find your clothes laid out on the bed all ready for use, and you proceed to the verandah to have a wash. The bearer stands by the *chilumchee* with the teapot in his hand, there being no water in the *chilumchee*. Into your hands he pours water with which you wash your face. In those days water that had been used to wash your face once was never taken up a second time, as it was supposed to have been defiled so that by using the spouted vessel you had always fresh pure water. These were the conditions under which you were allowed to make your ablutions. After this you proceeded to put on your clothing. Thus adorned you proceed to the front verandah, where easy and lounge chairs were to be found and there await your host, who at last comes and ushers you into dinner. Seated at the festive board the first performance was that of your *kitmutghar*, who with much importance produces a silver salt cellar and pepper pot out of his *kumerbund*, and places them on either side of your plate. These salt cellars, etc., were in great variety of designs, some representing a tower, others owls or egg-shaped according to fancy. The next proceeding is on the part of your host, who requests the pleasure of taking a glass of beer with you, which compliment you shortly return by asking him to do ditto. Should your host be a married man it was considered to be a most essential piece of attention on your part to start dinner by taking a glass of beer with your hostess. I have known a lady take great umbrage at this ceremony being deferred till a later period in the feast. An honoured guest was always treated to what was considered the best; this to the planters' taste was a good saddle of mutton. Fowls they had daily. I have heard men from Calcutta say they visited half-a-dozen indigo factories and the *pierr de resistance* was always a saddle of mutton. They would have preferred the *moorghee* of the period, which was a *rara avis* in Calcutta. In 1847-48 the custom of smoking a *hookah* was still in existence, and I remember Mr. Alfred Gouger, who lived in Tank Square, indulging in one of these luxuries. A very respectable old bearded *hookah-bardar* used to march in after each meal and unrolling a carpet place the *hookah* on it, and in a most majestic way pass the gold and amber mouthpiece under the master's arm and retire. While in Calcutta at that time I dined at several houses where I found many of the guests smoked their *hookahs*. These pipes were very neatly ornamented, some in a most costly way. The smoking of *hookahs* began as the desert came in, and *hookah* smokers had the pull over those who used cigars as it was not considered etiquette to smoke cigars till the ladies had left the dining-room. A thing that seemed strange to me was that drinking water was always served out of bottles. I afterwards heard that this was because the water had to be cooled by means of saltpetre and glauber salts, and that having water in bottles was most handy for this purpose. There was no ice in Calcutta in those days. Men of those days moved about in buggies, but only those who were pretty well off could do this. Assistants in the mofussil rode, and it was considered a great honour if your manager drove you out in his trap. *Syces* always ran by the side of the conveyance, and I have known these men run fifteen miles at a stretch, only stopping when a fresh horse was put to, which took place every five miles. Clerks in Calcutta moved about in palanquins. In many houses, especially in Calcutta, old servants, generally *bearers* in bachelors' houses, were much spoiled. They levied black-mail on any guest, especially if he was a new comer. I remember the old sinner who was head servant at Mr. A. Gouger's presenting me with a memo stating what I was to give to each servant as *backshish* when I was leaving Calcutta. I need not say his name headed the list. I as a griff, and a guest, did not like to say anything, so I just paid.

Christmas is always a great time in the mofussil, and that day was always celebrated by a picnic where shooting and hunting were the order of the day. I remember hearing of a queer occurrence at one of those picnics. Our host had busied himself in having an extra good plum pudding made, and he had talked a good deal about it. It was to be produced at the picnic. Dinner over we were all expectation, but there was no plum pudding. Our host waxed wrath but still it came not. At last he got up and made for the extempore kitchen. The cook seeing his master coming, and evidently on the war path, jumped up and bolted, and strange to relate the pudding jumped out of the pot and followed him. He had forgotten taking a cloth to boil the pudding, and so wrapped it up in the end of his *dhoti*, and when his master made for him he cleared, the pudding jumping after him. The story goes that neither the cook nor the plum pudding was ever seen again.

Before I end I must tell you the yarn about the adjutant and the crow, as I heard it at one of these jolly picnics. An officer from Dinapore was telling a party at home of how a crow in the barrack yard there had made itself objectionable to an adjutant by trying to get off with a bone the big bird was picking. The adjutant just turned round on the crow and swallowed him. Shortly after this story had been told the relator went on talking of his regiment and of what a plucky chap Captain So and So was, how he had done this and that during the Mutiny, finishing off his yarn by saying he was our adjutant. A young lady of the party remarked in a most innocent tone of voice—"And was it he who swallowed the crow!!!" Was this chaff or ignorance?

FRED. COLLINGRIDGE

Was born on 26th April 1815. He came out to India in 1829 and went to Shikarpore, one of Messrs. Watson and Co.'s Factories. After leaving this appointment he got employment, as an interpreter to a Native Infantry Regiment at Buxar. This billet he held for a short time. He was offered an appointment about the time he left in the Seryeah Indigo Concern and Tirhoot, which he joined in about 1833. In 1835 he built Coalpoorah an outwork of the Seryeah Concern. From Coalpoorah he went to Dholi as manager for a year about the time Charles Mackinnon bought Dholi Concern. Thence he went to Dynechuppra and managed Amooh Factory from there. In 1842-43 he went home to England and married in 1849 returning to India in 1858 when he took charge of the Poopri Indigo Concern and stayed there for a year. He was then promoted to Dooriah and was in charge for about a year when he bought Dowdpore Factory with Dr. C. N. Macnamara and J. S. Begg in 1861.

In 1867 he again went home and returning managed till 1876, when his son Herbert took charge. In the spring of 1880 he retired from India and died in September 1905 in his 91st year.

About a year before his death he met with an accident; he fell over a luggage truck at a railway station, which injured him and brought on blood poisoning from the effects of which he died. Up to the winter before his accident, the wonderful old gentleman hunted regularly with Garth's hounds and rode as straight as any of the hunt. F. Collingridge was always a keen horseman and his name will be found among those who rode at Hajeepore where Sonepore races were held in the early thirties. He loved a game of polo out here to the last and delighted in a game at racquets or lawn tennis and when there was a dance on old Collingridge did the light fantastic and was among the last to leave the Ball room.

The natives tell a story of him when at Dynechuppra he was attacked by some *budmashes*, who broke his arm. He rode into the Factory and got his tailor who was a bit of a bone settler to bind up the fractured limb and mounting his horse again with his Hog's spear in hand rode through the *budmash* village, but not a soul dared to face him.

SIMON NICOLSON

Was a son of Major Nicolson and grandson of Dr. Simon Nicolson, a man well known in Calcutta many years ago. Simon came to Tirhoot in 1861 as an assistant to Kontai Factory, he was sent out by Dr. D. Begg. He was posted to Ragai, an outwork of Kontai, in 1862. He unfortunately had very bad health and had to go to Naini Tal in 1864 for a change thence he returned to Tirhoot, but had to go home in 1887. After a time in England he returned with his brother Charles a retired Lieutenant in the navy.

His old friend, the late George Toomey, got him appointed Secretary to the Tirhoot Planters' Club, where he reigned for several years off and on as he had to go away on leave on several occasions either home or to the hills. At last he had to go to sea to Burma and died during his return voyage in 1901 of consumption. Poor old Simon was a kind hearted man, but his constant ill-health made him very cranky at times.

W CAMPBELL

Was a son of Dr. W. Campbell, of Ederline, Argyleshire. He came out to India in the end of 1857 and joined the Jeetwarpore Concern as an assistant. Some years after he took charge of Herni and thence bought a share in Parihar where he took up the management. About 1866, he left Parihar and took charge of Jeetwarpore and remained there till the early seventies when he bought a share in Kurharry and took up the management. Having made a profitable season he went home leaving John Morton in charge.

The Factory did not do so well after his return and he eventually fell into bad health, lost his sight and after lingering some time died in 1895.

JAMES BEGG

A brother of Dr. David Begg's came out to India to his brother in 1848. I think his brother's first intention was to keep him in the office at Bathgate and Co., Calcutta. But Jim preferred a country life and was at last sent up to Rajkund Factory to Andrew Crawford where he began life in Tirhoot. From Rajkund he went as manager to Bekonpore, some years after and thence got charge of Japaha in 1859 (then belonging to MacKillopp Stewart and Co.). In 1861 he got charge of Kontai. From Kontai James Begg retired home. He had purchased a share in Dowdpore, but this he sold shortly after as he was alarmed at the production of the alazarine dyes. *Badishe* had not come into existence then. On his return to India he managed Seeraha Factory for a year in about 1873. He retired home after and died in about 1896 or 1897. He left two sons one in Messrs. Begg Dunlop and Co.'s office, the other manager of a tea garden in Assam, and two daughters who married Calcutta merchants.

Behar Light Horse in Camp.

THE

SOUBAH BEHAR MOUNTED RIFLES.

An Epitomised History of the B. L. H.

In penning this short history of the Soubah Behar Mounted Rifles I do not pretend to give an officially detailed account of the Corps, but a short story that may interest those now alive who helped to set the movement afoot as well as those who are at present on the active list; some of these are sons and grandsons of those who garrisoned Fort Pillbox in 1857.

There are, to the best of my knowledge, only a few men left of the garrison, namely, L. Macdonald, J. F. Mackenzie, A. McD. MacRae, E. D. Urquhart, M. J. Wilson, H. Hudson, F. H. Hollway, and perhaps a few more whose names have escaped me.

I have to thank the present Adjutant, Captain McMullen, for his kind help in assisting me with information and records I have required where my memory failed me.

Mutiny, 1857.

In 1857, when the Native Army broke out into Mutiny, a body of some forty men, principally planters and officials belonging to the districts of Tirhoot and Darbhanga, assembled in Mozufferpur where they garrisoned the house at present occupied by our District Judge, but then by our Civil Surgeon. Thence the name Fort Pillbox. As might have been expected, the men, from want of a military man to drill them, were but a very undisciplined and unwieldy body, who had no idea of how to work together in case of an attack. They were armed with their double-barrelled muzzle-loading fowling pieces, no cartridges,

Fort Pillbox.

and had to trust to their powder flasks and loose bullets in case of an attack. Here is an account of what happened during those stirring times.

As it would not do for us to be scattered over the place, the Doctor (Simpson) and Mr. Weston, a Sub-Judge of Mozufferpur, offered us their houses and grounds, so we formed two camps and messes.

Mr. Weston's house was situated where what is now the Maharaja of Darbhanga's Joran Chuppra Palace, so the two houses stood about five hundred yards apart, but almost in the same grounds.

The houses were occupied by the ladies and children, numbering about eighty. The men slept in tents pitched in small camps one on each flank of the houses and one in front as an advance guard. Each camp supplied two sentries.

M. J. Wilson, Commandant.

At a meeting, one of their number, Mr. M. J. Wilson, was appointed Commandant, and he named his subordinates, placing a man in command of each small camp. Besides the camp there was a portico guard composed of old gentlemen who did duty till 11 P.M.

This "Vielle Guarde" was ordered to prevent any surprise attack, as the young men, would, encouraged I am sorry to say by the young ladies, go on dancing till past ten in the evening, and refused to do sentry go till eleven had struck, so the Commandant had to make a compromise and issue an order that all lights were to be extinguished at 11 P.M.

Thannadhar of Burooraj arrested.

During this time under instructions of the Magistrate the Commandant ordered out three men, F. H. Hollway Wm. Pratt and W. Baldwin, who, with the Assistant Magistrate, Robinson, started for Burooraj Thanna when they arrested the Thannadhar in the act of writing a letter to the Patna rebels inviting them over to loot the Treasury. This gentleman was even tually sent to Patna to Mr. W. Tayler, the Commissioner, and hung. Another case was where two of our men, W. C. Baddely and J. F. Mackenzie, were ordered to arrest a man near Dowlutpur Factory. They started in the very early morning, and by evening had returned with their prisoners, having travelled, going and coming, over one hundred miles.

During our stay in Fort Pillbox the Commandant organized a mounted patrol. These patrolled the town at night and gave the more peaceful natives confidence. One night just as our mounted patrol came in an alarm was given by our sentries at the front, Charles Oman and Archd. MacRae, at the west gate and L. Macdonald and J. F. Mackenzie at the east gate. It was found that a long line of men with lights were advancing on us and all stood to their guns, just then one of our men in handling his fowling piece accidentally pulled the trigger, when in a second all the approaching lights were extinguished, our mounted patrol, as I say, had just come in, and they, some five men, headed by a hotheaded Scotchman, put spurs to their horses, cleared the ditch opposite the present Judge's house and went for them, but alas! by the time they reached the spot where the enemy had been seen, they found nothing but smoking *masals* (torches), and though they circled about could fine no one. This was supposed to have been a feint by the Nujeebs (a provincial Battalion who acted as jail and treasury guard, who had an eye on the ten lakhs just then in the treasury) to see if we were prepared. We could never find out quite what was really the reason for this business. The natives passed it off by saying it was a wedding procession.

Night alarm.

Not long after we had occupied these houses we protected them in case of a sudden rush by loopholing and sandbags. We also stored on the top of the house rice, *dhal*, firewood and water, and were ready to resist a siege of some weeks. However, shortly after this a report came to us, which afterwards proved to be false, of the fall of Delhi, and we dispersed in groups to different factories. It was about then we heard of the mutiny of Holmes' regiment at Segowile and the murder of the gallant Colonel and his wife, and the doctor and his wife, and that a section of this regiment had taken possession of the Mozufferpur Post Office.

Mutiny of Holmes' Regiment, Segowlie.

Some half dozen of our men who had accompanied the Commandant were despatched from Jeetwarpore Factory, among them James Cox, Geo. Toomey, B. Anderson, A. MacRae, F. Wingrove to take possession and give confidence to the people in the town. These men sent on their horses to near Mozufferpur and drove to where they were, and rode in to find the enemy gone. Not long after this some of Jung Bahadoor's Gurkhas turned up at Mozufferpur and the Yeomanry Cavalry had reached Pusa; volunteers were called for to carry despatches to Colonel Richardson who was in command of the Yeomanry, and the writer and Mr. L. MacDonald, one of the survivors of the garrison now living at home in Scotland, took out the despatches and returned that evening. On entering Mozufferpur they were stopped by the Gurkha outlying sentries but all being well were allowed to proceed on their way. My readers will understand after perusing the above that we had good reason to wish to be properly drilled and armed in case of necessity arising at any future period. Therefore those who had formed the garrison and had appreciated the want of military training with others determined to petition Government to be allowed to form themselves into a mounted corps.

Gurkhas at Mozufferpur and Yeomanry Cavalry at Pusa.

In 1861 a meeting was called under the guidance of Mr. C. T. Metcalfe, then Magistrate of Mozufferpur, to ask Government

Soubah Behar Mounted Rifles formed.

to allow the formation of a Mounted Volunteers Corps to be called the Soubah Behar Mounted Rifles. In 1862 the Government having given their sanction, steps were taken to at once enrol those who were willing to join. The first parade took place about the end of that year on the piece of ground to the east of the Dâk Bungalow and west of where the Kacharie now stands. It had been arranged that the uniform was to be a grey tunic, breeches and boots with a helmet and red plume. No uniform had been received from the tailors, so the members present wore *mufti*. We were armed with muzzle-loading carbines, not breech loaders. The breech loaders came some years after. We also carried swords.

First Parade.

Metcalfe and Argles.

Mr. C. T. Metcalfe, who had, when a young man, been an officer in a Yeomanry Cavalry Regiment at home, assisted by Mr. C. V. Argles who had also served in a cavalry regiment, undertook the drilling of this, then, very irregular body of men mounted as they were on all sorts of animals from the steady studbred and waler to the roaring Kaboolie. Metcalfe was rather rusty in his drill, but Argles being last from his military training was better up in it.

Inspection at Sonepore by Sir S. Corbett.

In 1863 the regiment was inspected by Sir Stewart Corbett at Sonepore. There is no record of this inspection, but I give what happened from memory. I cannot remember the number of men on parade, but should say about one hundred, as there were men from all the Behar districts.

Colonel James Forlong, First Commandant.

Colonel James Forlong was in command, but as he had not much of a military training, Metcalfe, before the inspection, took him into an empty tent to show him what he should do on Sir S. Corbett's arrival on the parade ground and how he was to salute, etc.

When the time came the regiment was put through some simple manœuvres. Then came our grand flourish. The regiment was to advance at a gallop. The squadrons outward about wheel and form again where we had started from and then advance in line and general salute. I don't know if this evolution is to be found in the drill book of these days, or whether it was a movement evolved out of Metcalfe's brain. It seemed to puzzle Argles who had never seen such a movement in the 16th Lancers. However, the order was given march, trot, gallop, then at a certain point squadrons outwards about wheel. After that it seemed to me the regiment vanished, for the men in their anxiety to do the thing smartly had no hold on their horses. Some were carried off to their stables at the camp, while many of the Chupra troop disappeared altogether. However, after a time what remained of the regiment advanced in line and saluted.

Puzzling Manœuvres.

Colonel Forlong was mystified at the grand display. He sat his horse a proud man. He had quite forgotten Metcalfe's instructions to carry his sword, this lay across his horse's withers. Sir S. Corbett and his staff advanced and, addressing Colonel Forlong, made a very nice little speech to the regiment which, though not exactly true, was pleasantly flattering. When the General had finished Forlong thought it incumbent on him to reply and oh! Metcalfe's face when, with his sword still gracefully reclining over his horse's shoulder, he began, "General Sir Stewart Corbett! Hu! Hum!! On the part of the officers and men Hu! Hum!! of the Soubah Behar Mounted Rifles Hu! Hum!! I beg to thank you Hu! Hum!! for the few kind words you have spoken Hu! Hum!!" Here the old gentleman paused, when Metcalfe, taking advantage of this dismissed parade. Thus our first game at playing at soldiers ended. It must be remembered we were but very young and uninstructed at the work and not what we are now in the year of our Lord 1904. That evening Sir S. Corbett dined with the Regiment. Here our old Colonel was much more in his element for he was a genial host and a perfect gentleman of the old school. We were determined to receive the General and his staff strictly *a la Militaire*, so we had a sentry posted at the entrance to the mess tent to carry arms as they entered. It was late in the evening before this pleasant party broke up and I am sure the General enjoyed himself as much as any of the youngsters and old James Forlong entertained his guests with numbers of his Bengal yarns interlarded with many Hu! Hums!!

Sir S. Corbett dines with the Regiment.

In 1865 the district was visited by the Lieutenant-Governor, Sir Cecil Beadon, who came up to open an Agricultural Show. This was held to the east of the present racecourse. On that occasion the Soubah Behar Mounted Rifles escorted the Lieutenant-Governor and I must say made a very picturesque show, their red plumes dancing to the breeze. In this year Colonel Robarts brought down a squadron of his regiment from Segowlie to drill with us. The Colonel was a great favourite with us all and as a compliment to him we put his men to the right of the line. But, alas! Robarts' Horse were better mounted than drilled, for the mixed regiment in advancing by squadrons right in front were ordered to wheel into line. Robarts' squadron wheeled on the wrong pivot and found themselves formed up to the left of the line and as Sergeant Godby, then our Sergeant-Instructor, remarked "These niggers are all wrong." Robarts was furious, he being a spectator on foot. He rushed to the front of his men and called them unparliamentary names. He was very angry. On our way to our camp he

Visit of Sir C. Beadon in 1865.

Robarts' Cavalry.

drew up on the Secunderpur bund facing outwards and saluted Robarts' Horse as they passed on their way to their quarters. This put the old Colonel into great good humour again. He was a kindhearted, genial man, a great sportsman, and kept a pack of hounds and several race horses.

Death and Burial of W. Garstin.

On this day we buried my old friend W. Garstin. He was found dead on the road the evening before. He had been at a ball given at the house where our present Collector lives and driving home seems to have fallen dead out of his trap. Poor Garstin was a gallant chap. During the Mutiny he volunteered to go out with the troops at Dinapur to relieve Arrah. This was the occasion when Fraser Macdonald gained the V.C. The relieving party were caught in ambush and had to retire. Garstin was wounded in the spine, which was grazed, and it was found at the *post mortem* that the base of his skull was affected and this caused his sudden death. Garstin was a nephew of Colonel Garstin who built the Golghur at Patna. The Soubah Behar Mounted Rifles escorted the hearse to the burial ground in recognition of his gallant services during those troublous times.

Sir Cecil Beadon presents the cup.

Sir Cecil Beadon during his visit announced his intention of giving a cup to be shot for. The cup was a very handsome one, having on the top an effigy of Colonel James Forlong, mounted in the full uniform of that day. The terms were that the cup must be won two years consecutively by the same trooper. The first year it was won by M. Lloyd, the second year by Augustus Elliott, the next by W. Llewhellin. The next two years M. Lloyd came in winner and the cup became his. This cup has been presented to the Regiment by Mr. Trevor Lloyd, Mr. M. Lloyd's brother. It is a very handsome piece of plate and is used to ornament the dinner table on festive occasions

Winners of cup.

Since then many cups, purses, etc., have been presented for competition by successive Lieutenant-Governors, the different Maharajas of these districts and others, but I have no record of who competed or won these.

Inspection by Major Kaunts.

The regiment was next inspected by Major Kaunts of the 2nd Queen's Bays, but there is no record of how many men were on parade. In fact it was not for several years after that proper records were kept. About the time of Major Kaunts' inspection the regiment was just what might be called emerging out of its infancy. It had not so far had the benefit of an Adjutant, though Sergeant-Instructor Godby had just started bringing us out of our babyhood. In about 1886 the regiment was inspected by Lord Roberts. I can find no record of this or the number of men on parade, but I remember how this grand old soldier enjoyed himself taking the men out for sham fights. He seemed in his element, and as active as the youngest. His staff were all very nice fellows and very musical.

Lord Roberts' Inspection, 1886.

Our first Commandant, as I have already said, was Colonel James Forlong who died on his way home to England and was laid to rest in the Red Sea. After him came Colonel F. Collingridge, but there is no record of when he first became Colonel. He retired several years ago, and is at present living at home. Then came W. B. Hudson in 1884. He was made A.D C. in May 1891 and K.C.I.E. in January 1893. This decoration was considered a great compliment to the regiment. Colonel John Hodding succeeded in 1890. The regiment for a long time had no military man as Adjutant. First Cornet M. J. Wilson acted as Adjutant, then Lieutenant A Urquhart, but

Colonel F. Collingridge.

W. B. Hudson, 1884

Colonel J. Hodding, 1890.

neither of these gentlemen knew much more than what they could learn out of the drill book and were therefore not of much use.

Adjutants.

Our first Adjutant appointed by Government was Captain E. Money, then Heranc, followed by Higginson, Vousden, V.C, and O'Maley and Adÿe. Then H. Stewart, a member of the Corps, acted after him. Next came Carandini, Edwards, Carruthers and then our present Adjutant, Captain MacMullen. There is no record of when Money joined, but he was with the regiment when our present King, then the Prince of Wales, visited Bankipur. Up to Carandini's time there is no record. He joined in 1888. Baldwin, D.S.O., Disney and FitzHenry acted, but there is no record of when Major Maxwell was also Adjutant. I cannot find any trace of when Captain Edwards joined in 1891, Carruthers in 1897 and MacMullen in 1902. There have been many Sergeant-Instructors—Sergeant Godby was the first—all good men under whom the regiment has become what it is.

Sergeant-Instructors.

Annual Inspections.

General Kinloch inspected us in 1892, when there were only ninety-two men on parade; there are no records of 1893 and 1894. In 1895 Colonel Crawley inspected, when one hundred and fifty-four men were present Colonel Elliott was inspecting officer in 1896 and one hundred and seventy-six men appeared on parade. The Commander-in-Chief, Sir George White, and General Waterfield inspected the Corps in 1897, when one hundred and forty-seven men answered to their names. General Waterfield again inspected one hundred and fifty-seven men in 1898. In 1899 General Clifford was inspecting officer, when one hundred and seventy-nine men turned out. General Mitchell inspected in 1900 and one hundred and seventy-nine mustered. He again inspected one hundred and seventy-eight in 1901.

Colonel Clayton inspected in 1902 one hundred and seventy-one men, and in 1903 General Abbott one hundred and fifty-one. In 1904, our last inspection, there were one hundred and forty-one men inspected by General Spens.

Uniform changed 1896.

Towards the end of 1896 the uniform was changed to khaki and a helmet without plume.

In 1886 an offer of one hundred men was made to Government for service in the Soudan to assist in the relief of General Gordon, but this was not accepted. In 1890 men who were not young enough to stand the knocking about with the Behar Light Horse on Government calling for reservists enrolled themselves as such.

Hodding and six men help Police at Sewan.

In 1893 Colonel Hodding (then Major) was called on by the Magistrate of Sewan to go to the assistance of the Police who were attacked by a mob who were bent on rescuing cattle that were being driven to Dinapur. Major Hodding on receiving this call immediately sent word to those volunteers who resided near him, some six troopers in all ; these were afterwards joined by six more, and the Police were relieved, the cattle rescued and escorted a part of the way to their destination. For this act Major Hodding and his troopers received the thanks of the officiating Lieutenant-Governor and the Commander-in-Chief.

Camp-of-Exercise, 1895.

A camp-of-exercise before inspection was started in 1895, and these camps have been continued yearly ever since. The following will give an idea of the kind of work done. An enemy is reported advancing from Gorakhpur *viâ* Chupra towards Mozufferpur and has pushed on the cavalry of its advanced guard. The southern force to seize the boats and other means of crossing the Gunduk River and hold them between Sohasi and Rewa until reinforced by the main body of the advance guard, etc. On the occasion the regiment had a very pleasing outing and covered a great deal of ground. In this year Mr. L. Macdonald, of Skaebost, Isle of Skye, one of the few I mention as being alive who had been one of the Fort Pillbox garrison, presented the Behar Light Horse with one hundred saddles. This was a handsome gift and showed his appreciation of the usefulness of this regiment after his experiences of 1857.

L. Macdonald presents 100 saddles.

It was in 1883 that the Corps visited Calcutta for Proclamation Day. The Calcutta papers of this time speak in high terms of their efficiency on the occasion. It was about this time the old denomination was changed for that of Behar Light Horse.

Corps in Calcutta. Proclamation Day, 1883.

His Royal Highness the Prince of Wales, now our King-Emperor Edward VII, visited Bankipur in 1876, where he was entertained by Sir R. Temple. On this occasion the Behar Light Horse had the honor of escorting His Royal Highness from the railway station to Sir R. Temple's camp. After a *levée*, at which all those who had done good work during the famine of 1873-74 were presented, His Royal Highness was escorted back to the railway station. The Prince was rather puzzled as to who the B.L.H. were, and asked if they were Yeomanry, and when told they were all gentlemen,—indigo planters, who had some of them come over one hundred miles to escort His Royal Highness, he expressed himself much pleased at their loyalty.

Corps escorts Prince of Wales at Bankipur.

In January, 1900, Lumsden's Horse for service in South Africa was formed. Colonel J. Hodding applied for command, but was refused "with very great reluctance as Colonel D. M. Lumsden of the

Lumsden's Horse, 1900.

Assam Valley Light Horse had been entrusted with the formation and organisation of the proposed corps" But Colonel Hodding was asked to give his support and aid to Colonel Lumsden. On this, volunteers were called for Lumsden's Horse, and fifty-three men were duly enrolled. The B.L.H. became the left half of the "A" Co., and were commanded by their own officers. They left Mozufferpur on the 6th June 1900, and were given a hearty send-off after a successful entertainment at the Station Club the evening before. They spent a fortnight in camp at Calcutta. Lumsden's Horse sailed in two transports for the front, 'A" Co., going in the *Lindula*. They were about a month at sea and landed on 24th March. They were detained a week at Maitland Camp and were then pushed on by train to Bloemfontein, where they were attached to Colonel Ross' regiment of mounted infantry, and were in the front rank of the division moving on the right of the rail. They took a share in hard work and heavy fighting.

B.L.H. in South Africa.

Their actual baptism of fire occurred at Karee Siding, when they suffered considerable loss. They gained a high reputation for steadiness and courage. Here Troopers Daubeny and Lumsden were killed, and Firth and Macgillvray captured; Sergeant-Major C. M. Marsham, who commanded after Lieutenant Crane fell, was himself in turn severely wounded twice, but was carried out of fire. Sergeant Macnamara, on whom now devolved the command though himself wounded, completed the retirement. Two men told off to hold horses, L. Williams and R. MacDonald, were also captured in endeavouring to rescue wounded men; out of twenty-five men there were no less than ten casualties. For a full account of this little set-to see "The Great Boer War" by A. Conan Doyle, page 401. Captain J. B. Beresford wrote Colonel Hodding about the men from Behar—"They were the most cheerful and willing fellows I have ever had to serve with."

In 1899-1900 the B.L.H., won for the third year the Inter-Volunteer Challenge Cup for Tent-pegging.

In 1901 Sir John Woodburn presented medals to those who had won them in South Africa, when Captain Rutherford was decorated with the D.S.O., and Sergeant Percy Jones the P.C.M.

In 1901-2, Hooley as the best man-at-arms won the Cup presented by Mr. Newcomen of Cawnpore.

B.L.H. represented at the Coronation.

Colonel Hodding and Sergeant Percy Jones were selected to go home to England to represent the regiment at the Coronation, and some twenty-four rank-and-file under command of Captain J. Rutherford were sent to Delhi to be present at the Great Durbar of 1903. Here Colonel Hodding was decorated with the C.I.E.

Maxim gun purchased.

In 1896 Mr. F. Shaw got up a subscription among the proprietors of indigo factories at home to purchase a Maxim gun. Mr. L. MacDonald, H. Hudson and many others subscribed and Lieutenant G. Disney undertook the purchase and selection of the same, and in 1897, when General Sir George White, Commander-in-Chief, inspected the regiment, the Maxim was also inspected by him. That year Lieutenant Disney took out a detachment to a camp at Waini for practice, Captain Carruthers in his R.O. says: "The amount and excellence of work done in the few days at their disposal and the excellent condition of the horses on their return after the long and trying marches reflect great credit on all concerned."

The regiment is daily increasing in efficiency, and though from hard times the members of the corps find it as much as they can do to keep themselves going, they still meet the extra expense entailed by camps and parades as cheerfully as ever.

I have written all that my memory and the records I have been furnished with will supply. If my epitomised history does not follow dates *seriatim* I must ask my readers to consider I have jotted down these lines as they come to my memory.

As I say above these do not pretend to be an official record, but a short story that may interest members of the Corps present and past and show them the reason why the regiment of mounted volunteers was raised.

Under the auspices of our present Lieutenant-Governor, Sir Andrew Fraser, who knows the value of such a body of men as the Behar Light Horse, and with better times which we all hope for, let us trust that the Regiment will continue to increase in numbers and flourish, and that we will always be "Ready, aye Ready."

NESTOR.

YARNS OF TIRHOOT OF OLD.

How Tulsi Ojah had his revenge on Budmash Ojah.

Well back in 1830 there lived in North Tirhoot a young native lady named Sunder, the sister of one Tulsi Ojah. Whether she was beautiful as her name would indicate or not no one could say, as she was what an old gentleman in this district used to call a "Purda Machine" (his knowledge of Hindustani was limited)! Beautiful or not she had the repute of having many charms in the shape of rupees and jewellery. So one Budmash Ojah made up his mind to place his heart at the feet of the fair one with an eye to the needful at the same time. Arrangements were duly come to between Tulsi Ojah and Budmash Ojah and all preliminaries settled for the marriage.

From spite or jealousy a young native lady, a resident of the same village, gave out that Sunder was not the beauty she was reported to be, in fact her beauty consisted in her ugliness. This ill-natured report came to the ears of Budmash Ojah and he sent for the village barber, the great authority on matrimonial subjects, and asked him what he knew as to the reputed beautiful Sunder. Unfortunately for that young lady the barber's family and hers had had a difference and the *hajam* saw an opportunity of paying off old scores, so he reported that Sunder was anything but beautiful, she had two *goîtres* as big as pumpkins on her throat and was a little thick in her intellect. In fact, as he said, she was more like a she buffalo than a beautiful woman, and as to the cash charms, the barber had his doubts of that also. Budmash Ojah was terrified at this and made up his mind to break off all communications with the Tulsi family. There was, of course, great wrath in the family of Tulsi Ojah when Budmash's determination was made known to them especially when he heard that his sister was likened to a she buffalo. The lady Sunder beat her breast and fasted and swore vengeance against Budmash and sixty generations after him. Tulsi Ojah said little but thought a good deal and bided his time for revenge.

Things in the village seemed to have settled down. Sunder to pass her time away and rid herself of melancholy, took to spinning thread, which she sold, and thus earned a little pocket money. It so happened that one Hussiar Jolah came to her and purchased some of her thread and in course of business sold this cotton to Budmash for his family use.

As the quantity purchased was not all ready it was arranged that it should be delivered by instalments. The wily Tulsi now saw his chance of serving out Budmash, and this was how he managed it. He sent for Hussiar Jolah and told him his grievance and, having promised a little tip, arranged as follows. Hussiar was to take the last instalment of thread to Budmash's house and then disappear. His wife was to feign great distress and seek her husband everywhere, throwing out hints of foul play on the part of Budmash Ojah.

The first thing to be done was to call in the policeman, for it was in the days when Darogajee ruled the land. That honest gentleman having been made acquainted with proceedings one of Hussiar's family went to him and put her troubles before him. Her dear brother Hussiar had taken a supply of cotton to Budmash Ojah's house on a certain date and had never been heard of since. "Have pity Darogajee, have pity Company Bahadoor !! and bring me back my brother." Darogajee at once ordered his steed to be saddled and a few chaprassis to accompany him (there were no constables in those days) and off he set to the unsuspicious house of Budmash to search the premises. This they did from top to bottom but no signs of the missing one. The Daroga put on a look of baffled astonishment and was on the point of bringing his investigation to an end when a smothered voice was heard proceeding from a small hut where *boosah* or chaff was kept. Darogajee cocked his ears and made for the place and there found the lost one tied to a post looking the picture of misery and distress. His bonds having been cut, and after going through signs of great bodily pain and distress, put forth the following tale of woe. He had come to Budmash's house with cotton that had been bought through him, delivered it and demanded payment. On this Budmash and others set upon him, seized him and threw him down and then tied him to the post in the little hut, hiding him behind heaps of *boosah*. He did not know why this had been done, he was a poor man, the Daroga and Company Bahadoor were his father and mother, and if Budmash and Company were not punished how was he to live, he would have to run away from this country? The Daroga, who was in the swim and had been well fee'd by Tulsi Ojah, put on his sternest look and ordered the wretched Budmash to be at once seized and bound with raw cowhide ropes and to be taken off to the Thanna. The cries and shrieks of the Budmash family could be heard for miles as the unfortunate one was dragged away by the chaprassis. What became of the matter eventually I never heard, most likely the gay Budmash spent a few years in jail.

Tulsi was, however, heard to remark to a friend with a twinkle in his eye, "This will 'teach' friend Budmash not to call a 'respectable' lady a 'buffalo'."

The Story of Dookit and Sookit Bunniah.

In about the year 1835 there lived in the town of M—in this district two Bunniahs, Dookit, the elder, and Sookit, the younger. They worked in partnership and seemed very much attached to each other. However, one fine day, while settling their monthly accounts of profit and loss, Dookit and Sookit fell out over a cash balance of Rs. 2-4-9 and Dookit, losing his temper, called his younger brother names and threatened to box his ears. Sookit being, when tackled, of an irate disposition, at once went to the Magistrate and complained that his brother Dookit had used language to him likely to cause a breach of the peace. In these days Law was not so much considered as speedy Justice, a thing much wanted in the present day, when petty thefts are so common. The Magistrate at once sent for Dookit and asked him what he meant by using unparliamentry language to his brother and so doing an act likely to cause a breach of the peace. Dookit was a man of independent spirit, so he raised his voice, speaking in a way that the Hazoor considered cheeky. The Magistrate therefore acted summarily and ordered Dookit to pay a fine of Rs. 50. The culprit, however, was not to be browbeaten thus and at once *blurted* out "Trotter (for this was the Magistrate's name) laylon O Dookit daylon," which means Trotter has got it and Dookit has given it, or in short parlance, "Don't you wish you may get it?" On this the Magistrate arose in his wrath and ordered his chaprassi to administer twelve blows with a shoe on the tenderest part of Dookit's body if the fine was not at once paid. Sookit, on hearing this order, was at once moved to tears, his dear brother to be beaten with a shoe and disgraced! "Bap re Bap! Father oh Father!! What a disgrace to the family!" Dookit like a man held his ground and refused to pay and operations were about to be commenced when Sookit, with tears streaming down his face, plumped down the fifty rupees and the two brothers, after having disbursed certain tips to the nazir and chaprassi, marched home sadder if not wiser men, the crowd in Court exclaiming "Wah! Wah!" what splendid justice, while poor Sookit grieved over his fifty rupees and did not seem to be of the same opinion as the multitude.

The Biter Bit.

In years gone bye there lived in neighbouring villages two men. One, Zubberdust Sing, was the head cultivation servant or Jemadar of a flourishing indigo factory. The other, Neel Prosaud, the head native writer or moonshee at another equally prosperous concern. Somehow their interest clashed and there was great jealousy and rivalry between the Rajpoot and the Khaist.

Neel Prosaud was determined to try and take Zubberdust Sing down a peg and kept his eye on him till the opportunity arose. Zubberdust Sing's daughter being about to be married he got leave to visit his home and started to have a few weeks with his family. Meanwhile Neel Prosaud—or, shall we call him Moonsheejee?—arranged his plans to get his friend into trouble. As soon as he heard that the jemadar had left for his home he sent for a trusted servant and sent him off with some brass pots and pans and told him to go quietly to the house the jemadar occupied at the Factory and bury these in the floor of his residence and to be careful no one saw this done. Zubberdust Sing meanwhile living happily with his wife and children, never dreamed of what was being done to entrap him. At last time was up and he had to return to his work, some forty miles away, so bidding his family adieu, he mounted and was at his Factory home by next morning. What was his astonishment and dismay to find the thana daroga was on the spot and that he was accused of having stolen several brass pots and pans and that he had buried them under the flooring of his house to conceal the theft. Poor Zubberdust was seized with dismay. He at once knew who was at the bottom of his trouble, the complainant being a man from near his (Zubberdust's) village. What was he to do? Suddenly a thought struck him. An old master who he had served for many years was on his way home to England and was at a Factory near by and he would go to him for advice. Mounting his horse off he galloped, just in time to catch him. He at once told him his troubles. "That *budzat* Neel Prosaud has done for me. How am I to disprove this matter, the pots and pans have been found buried in my house and Jute Sing, the plaintiff, swears they are his own stolen from his house. How am I to get out of this trouble? Do help me all you can." His old master, who was a shrewed Irishman, replied: "Why you old stupid, don't you remember buying these pots and pans from Goolam Sonar just before you went home on leave and how you for safety buried them under the floor of your house? Many of the Factory servants must surely remember this circumstance." The light suddenly came into jemadarjee's eyes. He smiled a smile, made a low bow, and rode off. It was a victory for him. He got back to his Factory, proved he had bought the brass utensils and *buried* them for safety. The village sonar deposed that he had sold them to him and the Factory chowkidar gave evidence that he had helped Zubberdust Sing to bury them before he went away on leave. The whole thing ended in a triumph for Zubberdust. He got a set of brass pots and pans for nothing. The plaintiff got jail for a false case and Neel Prosaud, who had to pay all the expenses of this little game, including the Darogajee. thought it would be better to leave Zubburdust Sing alone for the future. They are both dead now, but lived for many years after the occurrence and it was a picture to see them meet—the Khaist the picture of virtue and the Rajpoot with a knowing smile of defiance on his face as they salaamed politely to each other.

How one took possession of a Factory in Bengal in 1830 or thereabouts.

This yarn I heard from an old Bengal Planter very many years ago.

An Indigo Concern in Bengal had got into bad hands and therefore into debt. The agents in Calcutta were the large creditors, so they sued and foreclosed, and after putting up the Concern for sale, bought it in. So far so good, but the thing was to get possession. The Bengal Planter was looked upon by Calcutta merchants as one of a band of wild Rob Roys. However, the head of the purchasing firm dashed off a rollicking letter to an Indigo Planter who lived near the new purchase. "Dear So and So,—I have just bought the *Bobbery* Concern, please just go and take possession for me. Hope to be up shortly and have some shooting," etc. The Planter read the letter and remarked that old Greens of Carrots & Co. thinks taking possession of an Indigo Concern as easy as eating one's breakfast. However, as the firm had done him a good turn he wrote back "All right, will do what I can" He then wrote to his two assistants to come in and bring as many good "lathials" as they could get together and meet him at the place where roads met on the way to *Bobbery* Factory.

"Here's a lark," says Bob Jackson to Bill Smith. "The Boss is going to take possession for Carrots & Co. If Pretty John only gets wind of this and a few tots of whisky into him there will be a jolly flare up and, perhaps, murder." "It will be a lark,' replied Bill Smith. They both ordered out their forces and started on the march. The two assistants armed with hog spears. They were not long before they met their Manager who stated plans of attack. It was to be a frontal one as a kind of *feint* to see if the attacked were on the alert. The Manager in command of the centre and each wing in that of an Assistant. All advancing carefully they were soon made aware that they were watched, for *bang, bang* went a right and left and two bullets flew over heads. "By jove," says the Boss, "I did not bargain for this. However, we can't well back out of it now." So calling up an old fighting native he held a council of war and it was arranged that the main body were to advance slowly while he—the fighting native—edged off to the flank to reconnoitre. After a short time the native came back and said "As far as I can see there is only one man firing through the jhilmill door and he I believe to be well on in liquor. If you be ready to make a rush when I call we will get possesion at once." The native again disappeared, well to the right flank and sneaked along till he got to the wall of the house. There, crouching down, he crawled along close to the wall and waited. The jhilmill window gently opened and out came the muzzle of a double-barrelled gun. The native with a shout to advance came down on the gun with his *lathi* or *bludgeon*, which knocked it out of the hands of the firer, and quick as lightning the native followed up. The man who was firing was very drunk, and on the blow falling on his gun he jumped back and fell, meanwhile the main body had made a rush to find Little John (who represented the attacked) on the floor. He began talking in a maudlin kind of way of one planter turning against another ; what a shame it was, and while he was doing this he was fumbling with his pocket,—all of a sudden the native gave him a smack over the fingers with his stick, which made him drop a pistol, which he was trying to get cocked to fire at one of the assailants This was looked upon as treachery on the part of the defence. So Master Little John was trussed up like a dead bullock (the poor man was nearly dead drunk) and carried off to another factory.

By that day's post a letter was sent to Calcutta: "To Greens, Messrs. Carrots & Co. Taken possession. Send up Manager Yours faithfully——"

The above was how Planters in Bengal took possession in the last century.

A story is told of the same fighting native. One of a big firm of merchants came from Calcutta to have a little shooting. Ducks and snipe were the principal game to be had. His host, the Manager of the Factory, was busy, or did not care for shooting, so he called up his servant and told him to take his friend round and show him where game was plentiful. The

Calcutta man was no shot, though very keen. The first right and left into a flock of ducks proved unsuccessful. The native to encourage said "Very near, very near indeed," but after a succession of misses the native, having expended all his soft words of encouragement, exclaimed in Bengali as the ducks flew away "They have gone home to die." The sportsman merchant after this sarcastic speech thought he would go home too, and he did.

How the Griff saw a Total Eclipse and tried to Shoot the Black Cat.

The arrival of a Griff from Home was looked forward to with great excitement by a certain few of the elder hands in this district, and if he was at all raw or one of the "know alls" or '*sub junta* type," he generally had a bad time of it.

There came to this district over forty years ago a young man who had evidently never been far from the Sound of the Bowbells. We will call him Mr. Green, he was consigned to a man who took the greatest delight in what is called "selling," and on the very day of Green's arrival a sell was all ready to be dished up. At dinner the subject of conversation was turned on to total eclipses, etc., and after a time all retired to bed. Not very long after Green had started a good sound sleep, his Manager appeared ready dressed, booted and spurred. He awoke the new arrival. "Do you always sleep so late as this, its past eleven in the morning and breakfast is on the table, but the total eclipse of the sun is on," Green got up feeling very exhausted, managed to swallow some breakfast and started the work he was put to. He wrote to friends in Calcutta to ask if they had noticed the total eclipse and was rather put out when he heard in reply that he had been made a fool of. Here is another trick played Green during his griffinage. He was walking in the garden with the Manager when a black cat ran across the path. Green at once seized a a bit of brick to throw at the animal. "Stop! for goodness sake stop!" cried the Manager "if you hurt that cat I do not know what terrible thing might not happen to the Factory, for it is not a real cat but the ghost of Mr. Morgan who died here in some suspicious way many years ago! Unless the cat can be killed outright, when a large reward will be given, any one who attempts to interfere or injure the animal always comes to grief or the Factory suffers." "What h'awful rot," replied the cockney; "I will shoot the brute any day." "If you do and care to take the consequences of failing I will be under great obligations to you," replied his Boss. Shortly after this they were just sitting down to dinner when one of the servants rushed in, looking very excited and crying out "The black cat is in one of the bathrooms." On this the Boss jumped up with a face of alarm and said "I told you Green how it would be our only chance is to shoot it and who is to do it?" Green, though rather alarmed could not well go back on his words, at once said "I will," A gun was produced ready loaded and all advanced to the bathroom on tip toe. The venetians opened quietly and there, sure enough, was the black cat sitting on the bathroom floor. "Now's your chance," whispered the Manager, and Green, with faltering hands, introduced the barrels of the gun between the jhilmills and, taking steady aim, fired. With an unearthly yell the black cat flew into the air and disappeared out of the bathroom door, which flew open at the some moment. "You've done it now," said the Boss in great alarm. Lights were called for and the place examined and where the cat had been the place was riddled with shot, but no dead cat. The Manager and Assistant retired to their dinner and had barely commenced when weird cries of *Kalla billee* were heard all about the compound. "Now you see the consequence," says the Manager; the black cat is *at* his *tricks* biting everyone and that is certain death." Still Green had doubts and after a time *went to bed*. The whole night through cries of *Kálla billee* in the same weird tones filled the air. Green rose in the morning, ordered his pony to go out for a ride and see if he could not find out what was up. To his despair the pony he had ridden every morning as if joining in the conspiracy refused to budge. "Get off at once," cried the Manager; "he has been bewitched by the black cat and will do for you." So our Griff got off, very down in the mouth. Shortly after this he was loafing about the factory when he saw some men carrying a *corpse* to the Ganges and he thought he would inquire as to the cause of the man's death and in very unintelligent Hindustani inquired if the man had been bitten by the black cat. The reply was *Ji han*, a reply generally given by ignorant natives when a question is not understood, but the reply made Green's heart sink within him. He wrote to his friends in Calcutta to have him transferred to another factory. But with what result I do not remember. I need not say that Friend Green in time became one of the most finished practical jokers in Tirhoot and had his revenge on other Greenhorns that came after him from the Old Country for education in Indigo.

These kinds of tricks have been dropped in the present day, with bad prices of Indigo men are not so light hearted as they used to be. I may explain how this sell was carried out. A black cat was caught and tied to the bathroom door and a man instructed to pull it suddenly open as the gun exploded, which he did, and the poor cat, who was tied by the neck to the door, flew out half strangled. As this took place men were instructed to give a yell in imitation of a cat in anger and distress. The door had been punctured with a fork to represent where the shot had struck, but the gun had been loaded with powder only. The amount of trouble taken to complete this joke was hardly worth it. This happened in the days of Long Ago when grown-up men were more childish in their amusements than they are nowadays.

The Fighting Fouzdhar Rout. How He Managed to Live. His Rise and Fall.

There lived in days of yore to the north of this district a very pugnacious old gentleman called Fouzdhar Rout. He was a little square built old man. He had some five sons. They were tall, well built young men. They and their near relations were the terror of the zemindars of this district. These men were in a constant state of feud with the surrounding villages and particularly with an Indigo Factory a few miles from their village. The Magistrate had his eye on these men, but they had no fear of jail. In fact, on one occasion the Magistrate had lost his way and found himself near this village rode up to a well, when one of the Rout family was drawing water and inquired the way to the Indigo Factory. No reply was given. "Don't you hear me," cried the official very angry; "reply at once, you pig." For reply Mr. Rout swung his *lotah* (brass pot) round his head and knocked the Hazoor of his horse—rather a rough way of answering a question. Of course after this one of the Rout Family had to spend several months in jail, but this was nothing new to them, they always left a set of brass pots and pans at the jail awaiting their return. The greatest punishment that could be meted out to old Fouzdhar Rout when he was under punishment was to be made to pull the magisterial punkah. Fouzdhar Rout loved not his neigh bour of the Indigo Concern. I remember meeting him on my way back from breakfasting with the Manager. I had to pass through the old Rout Village. Fouzdhar and I had somehow become pals. The old gentleman seeing me riding past advanced towards me with a net full of mangoes in his hand. "Where have you been, Saheb?" he asked. "I have been to see Mr. Snooks at the Factory." "Oh, did he give you anything to eat, because if you are hungry I have brought you these mangoes." This was said in the most cynical and sarcastic tone. Mr. Snooks had the name of being an awful screw.

The way old Fouzdhar made a livelihood was, first of all, he made a point never to pay his rents. He was all on to follow the example of the Irishman who, when asked to pay rents, called to his son to bring out the blunderbus. Secondly, if a free fight was on between any villages he and his sons hired themselves out to both sides for the fray. Their proceedings on these occasions were peculiar They fight on and the two armies arrayed against each other. Then a general rush when Fouzdhar or one of his sons tapped one of their own side,—but not one of the family,—on the head, dropped him bleeding and senseless on the ground. The next move was to bolt like men. The darogajee appeared on the scene and many witnesses testified as to how the opposite party had attacked a peaceful few and nearly killed the poor man who lay stretched out on the ground, etc., etc. This was always the ending of any fight where Fouzdhar and his sons were employed, they were a terror on both sides. The daroga of olden days found these fights too paying to put a stop to them, but eventually the Magistrate took steps to stop these disgraceful proceedings, and it was said that the minute he (the Magistrate) heard the name Fouzdhar he, without further inquiries, ordered the man to be run in, and a story is told of how an innocent Fouzdhar, who was accused of something very mild being ordered jail cried out : "*Huzoor*, *I am not that Fouzdhar*, I am quite another man." "Then the sooner you change your name the better," replied the Beak. The village where Fouzdhar Rout lived changed hands almost yearly ; proprietors could get no rent. At last by some mistake a shrewd old native bought the village ; no rent came in, and he had to pay Government revenue. This he did not like. However, one day a happy thought came into his head. He would present the village and its revenue to the Government School. This was done and the gift accepted, and eventually a *khilat* was presented to the donor as a mark of appreciation of the Government. This was a bad day for Fouzdhar and his family for the Government of Bengal ordered a Deputy Collector to attend to the collection and settlement, etc. Fouzdhar Rout and his family were turned out from their house, lands and the village. But alas! for the neighbouring zemindar for they went and squatted there. However, the loss of house, home and repute was too much for Fouzdhar Rout, he became a broken down old man and a few years after died, his sons one by one following. There are not many now in this district who ever heard of Fouzdhar Rout and his fighting sons. The village he lived in still bears its old name, but the inhabitants are perfect lambs, who pay their rents regularly. *Sic transit, etc.*